750

CANADA AND THE
UNITED STATES

CANADA AND THE UNITED STATES

Dependence and Divergence

THE ATLANTIC COUNCIL WORKING GROUP
ON THE UNITED STATES AND CANADA

WILLIS C. ARMSTRONG, *Chairman and Rapporteur*

LOUISE S. ARMSTRONG, *Co-Rapporteur*

FRANCIS O. WILCOX, *Project Director*

Foreword by
KENNETH RUSH

BALLINGER PUBLISHING COMPANY
Cambridge, Massachusetts
A Subsidiary of Harper & Row, Publishers, Inc.

International Standard Book Number: 0-88410-872-4

Library of Congress Catalog Card Number: 81-20607

Printed in the United States of America

Library of Congress Cataloging in Publication Data

Atlantic Council Working Group on the United States and Canada.
  Canada and the United States, dependence and divergence.

  Includes bibliographical references and index.
    1. United States — Regulations — Canada — Congresses.
  2. Canada — Relations — United States — Congresses.
  I. Armstrong, Willis C. II. Title.
  E183.8.C2A87 1982   327.71073   81-20607
  ISBN 0-88410-872-4   AACR2

CONTENTS

LIST OF TABLES

LIST OF THE MEMBERS OF THE ATLANTIC COUNCIL WORKING GROUP ON THE UNITED STATES

CHAIRMAN AND RAPPORTEUR

Willis C. Armstrong,* Consultant; former Assistant Secretary of State

CO-RAPPORTEUR

Louis S. Armstrong, Director of Research, the OMNI Group; retired Foreign Service Officer

PROJECT DIRECTOR

Francis O. Wilcox, Director General, Atlantic Council; former Assistant Secretary of State and Dean, School of Advanced International Studies, The Johns Hopkins University

MEMBERS

Theodore C. Achilles, Vice Chairman, Atlantic Council; former Counselor of the U.S. Department of State and Ambassador to Peru

Frank A. Bauman, Attorney; former Adjunct Professor of International Law, Lewis and Clark College

William H. Christensen, Consultant, American Natural Resources; retired Foreign Service Officer

Howard H. Cody, Professor of Political Science, St. Thomas University, Fredericton, New Brunswick

* Italics indicate members who are also directors of the Atlantic Council.

H. A. Sawyer, Jr., Senior Vice President, AMAX

Adolph W. Schmidt, former Ambassador to Canada

Henry P. Smith III, former Member of U.S. Congress; former Chairman, U.S. Section, International Joint Commission

Rufus Z. Smith, Executive Director, International Visitors Center; former Deputy Assistant Secretary of State for Canadian Affairs

Roger F. Swanson, Executive Secretary, Committee on Canada–U.S. Relations, U.S. Chamber of Commerce; former Director, Canadian Center, SAIS, the Johns Hopkins University

John M. Volpe, Director, International Research and Special Projects Section, U.S. Chamber of Commerce

Richard Wiley, Executive Vice President, First National Bank of Boston; former General Counsel, U.S. Department of Defense

Robin W. Winks, Professor of History, Master of Berkeley College, Yale University

Curt Winsor, Associate Director, Alliance for Free Enterprise; former Vice President and Manager for International Relations, Chase Manhattan Bank

Edward F. Wonder, Senior Consultant, International Energy Associates

Charles G. Wootton, Senior Director, Foreign and Domestic Policy Analysis and Planning, Gulf Oil Corporation

T. S. Wylie, Consultant, Aerospace Industry

PROJECT ASSISTANTS

Kathryn Coulter, Staff Assistant to the Director General, Atlantic Council

Eliane Lomax, Staff Assistant to the Deputy Director General, Atlantic Council

FOREWORD

Americans interested in Canada are frequently concerned that the U.S. government at senior levels—preoccupied with the eastern hemisphere—may not pay enough attention to our neighbor to the north. Although Canada and the United States have much in common, there are competing as well as parallel interests in the economic, military, political, and cultural fields. There are also politicoeconomic developments on the Canadian side that could have a marked impact on the bilateral relationship. It is therefore important that the United States take account of the likely future trend of Canadian events and consider where U.S. interests lie and what the United States can do to safeguard these interests.

In 1979 the Atlantic Council of the United States decided to undertake a foreign policy study of the implications for the United States of trends that may be anticipated in Canadian affairs during the next ten or fifteen years. We believed that such a study could lay the groundwork for U.S. policy by identifying the bilateral and multilateral issues where friction is most likely and where cooperation is most essential. We invited a working group of forty-five members to undertake this important task, which began in March 1980.

The group is composed of Americans who have had considerable experience in Canadian affairs or who are identified with organizations with strong interests in the relationship. Represented are government, business, and academe. The group is responsible as a whole for the approval of the attached policy statement, although it should not be inferred that every member supports every statement therein. Individual members are responsible for statements of dissent or qualification.

The group has benefited from work done by the participants who wrote the background papers presented as Chapters 2–8, following the Atlantic Council's policy paper on Canada and the United States. These chapters treat federal–provincial relations in Canada, the Quebec issue, trade issues, mutual investment matters, energy, the environment, and defense. Their authors are responsible for the views they express, which may or may not be shared by the group.

It is the hope of the working group and of the Atlantic Council that the study will be of value in clarifying issues and identifying U.S. interests, so that American policy and what Americans can do to advance it will be better understood by both Americans and Canadians. Ignorance and lack of precision can be the enemies of mutual understanding. Considerate candor and respect for national sovereignty and individual differences are in the best tradition of Canadian–U.S. relations, which are bound to be highly pluralist, enmeshed in myriad detail, and occasionally contentious.

I want to express my deep appreciation to the members of the working group, whose collective wisdom made this book possible. Special thanks go to Willis Armstrong, who served ably as chairman of the group, and to Louise Armstrong, who gave valuable help as co-rapporteur. Finally I would like to thank the Donner Foundation, the Johnson Garret Foundation, the Atlantic Council board members, and the corporations whose contributions enabled us to move the project to its completion.

I commend the working group for the excellent job they have done. Those on both sides of the border who are interested in improving U.S.–Canadian relations should find this book both stimulating and helpful.

Kenneth Rush
Chairman
The Atlantic Council
of the United States

1 THE POLICY PAPER.
U.S. POLICY TOWARD CANADA
The Neighbor We Cannot Take
for Granted

The Atlantic Council Working Group
on the United States and Canada

There is a comfortable informal quality about the Canadian–American relationship. Officials of the two countries are frequently on a
first-name basis and communicate easily. Differences of opinion or
tough negotiating problems are usually put plainly on the table.
Efforts to resolve issues tend to be characterized by fairness and
mutual consideration. To most Americans, Canada is not really a
"foreign" country. Most Canadians feel themselves at home in the
U.S.A. The freedom of movement of people across the border lends a
singular aspect to the relationship. Canadian–American business
transactions are little different from domestic ones in either country.
Professional contacts are endless and easy, among bankers, doctors,
lawyers, scholars, and in countless other occupations.

In these circumstances, one might question the need for still another study of bilateral relations that have been relatively unevent-
ful for more than a century. Yet for all that may seem commonplace,
the U.S.–Canadian relationship is and always will be of unique importance for both countries. The durability of the relationship has
to some extent been a virtue of necessity. But its abiding strength
derives from mutual confidence and respect, mutual prosperity, and
from a fundamental political stability that is not at present characteristic of today's Canadian scene. (By the same token, there have been
times in the recent past when to Canadians the United States ap-

1

peared to be in the grip of a crisis of confidence. Each country tends to keep a finger on the other's national pulse.)

Canada today confronts the prospect of some years of internal political controversy and constitutional change that could conceivably alter the nation-state we have known and affect U.S.–Canadian relations profoundly. Speaking to a Yale University audience, a distinguished visiting professor had this to say: "Canadians like myself will do all we can to preserve our 'union.' American citizens should at least be aware that there is a potential for very upsetting changes to their north." Alarmist perhaps, but to some extent reflected in comments made publicly by both the external affairs minister and the Canadian ambassador in Washington, who speak of their country today as economically and politically less in control of its national destiny than the United States and who urge America, as the stronger partner, to be conscious of the risk of mismanaging the relationship.

Unhappily, the onset of this period of internal stress for Canada coincided with a declining coordination in policy and authority at the federal level of government in the United States. Issues in U.S.–Canadian relations that once received prompt attention from the executive and legislative branches have from time to time become hostage to differences between them. In both countries, regional pressures (reflected in the United States in Congress) threaten to prevail in a way that could adversely affect the bilateral relationship.

Americans, who in the past have been accused by Canadians of taking them for granted, can no longer proceed on the basis of their earlier assumptions about Canada. U.S. officials and business and professional people must give more careful attention to the trend of events to the north and their potential impact upon the United States, and they must increase their understanding of the basic forces at work in Canada. Prudence requires that we look to U.S. interests in this period of significant change. It also requires that we view our interests in the broadest possible context to enable us to be supportive of the integrity and viability of our most important long-term economic partner and ally.

The fact is that some American policies concerning Canada result less from planning and deliberation than from the need to respond on short notice to given situations. U.S. global or domestic policies will not necessarily be designed to serve the Canadian relationship and may give rise to unexpected bilateral problems. Canadians, on the other hand, usually make a more sustained and deliberate effort to identify their interests and define their policies toward the United States and put them into effect after considerable domestic discussion. The process is usually a highly articulate one, at times reflecting fairly wide swings across a spectrum between extreme nationalism and professions of close and friendly association with the United States. In contrast, the American reaction, often an ad hoc effort to ascertain the problem and do something about it so that it will go away, is to wonder why the Canadians get so excited on occasion. Americans are frequently astonished to hear from Canadians a long litany of complaints on topics not even within the U.S. consciousness. Except for those who live close to the border, Americans have few if any complaints about Canada. When disputes reach the media, the average American tends to be pro-Canadian and critical of the U.S. government.

There are fundamental disparities between the two countries that have a major determining effect on national perceptions and on the bilateral relationship itself. There are disparities in size and distribution of population, in aggregate national wealth (though not much on a per capita basis), and in respective roles in world affairs; and there are differences in focus and perspective. The United States is ten times the size of Canada in population and a bit more in gross national product. Normally, the burden of adjustment falls on the smaller partner; and frequently the larger is unaware that this is so. United States' foreign policy, and the American media, focus on Europe, the Middle East, the USSR, Asia, and Latin America (sometimes Africa). There is relative inattention to Canada even at the level of persons interested in foreign affairs. On the other hand, a much larger proportion of Canadians are quite well informed about the United States and are highly conscious of the impact of American affairs on their well-being and on Canada's status in the world. Most Canadians live close to the United States and think a lot about it. Only a small percentage of Americans live next door to Canada and pay it attention. U.S. history and economics have had a major impact on Canada. The reverse has been less true.

In the economic field there is a competition for certain sectors of world markets, a vigorous struggle by Canada somehow to reduce its dependence as a branch-plant economy for American capital, a Canadian determination to maintain control over its natural resources, to build its own industrial base to a level of major sophistication, and to keep Canadian cultural life Canadian. (Producers of Canadian culture are more determined than consumers.) At the same time, Canadians exhibit a keen interest in everything that happens in the United States and a strong desire to participate, not always vicariously.

More can and will be said in this policy paper, and in the collection of background papers that constitute the remaining chapters of this book, on the nature of the relationship and the factors affecting it. The purpose of this effort is to identify the chief issues for the United States in the relationship, to examine American policy options, and to suggest lines of policy, and their operational consequences, which the United States government and society might adopt with respect to Canada in the years ahead.

POLICY TOWARD WHAT?

Canada presents an unusual problem in U.S. external relations. One may fairly ask at the moment: What is Canada? After more than a century of confederation by consensus under an effective central government, that nation is now racked with federal–provincial jurisdictional disputes and threatened with plans for secession by the ruling party in at least one province. It is the scene of a bitter battle between the central and provincial governments over initiating a bill of rights and the amendment process of patriating a constitution that, at this writing, is still lodged in Westminster, London, as part of the British North America Act of 1867.

The federal–provincial struggle is made more complex by the geography of contemporary political party distribution. The federal government is controlled by the Liberals, who have almost no representation in Parliament from the western provinces and whose support in Quebec is partially negated by the fact that most Quebeckers prefer a less centralized federal system or outright independence. The Progressive Conservative party opposition has no strength in Quebec but is strong in the West and the Atlantic provinces. The New Democratic Party (NDP), with socialist and anti–NATO leanings, is strong enough in Ontario so that its views are heeded by the Liberals, but it has little genuine national base. Its status in western Canada is that of a provincial party. Thus all three political parties are essentially regional in their power base and unrepresentative of the nation as a whole.

The Quebec autonomy issue has been on the Canadian agenda for generations, becoming more acute since the electoral victory of the Parti Québécois in 1976. Other federal–provincial disputes have sharpened because of the surge in the world price of oil and other forms of energy, which has thrust Alberta and other energy-producing areas of Canada into the forefront of an argument over who should control natural resources, the federal or the provincial authority.

Meanwhile, a host of local provincial regulations have emerged affecting industry, agriculture, trade, investment, employment, and immigration, suggesting that Canada has, in effect, lost a measure of the benefit of what was supposed to be its equivalent of the interstate commerce clause of the U.S. Constitution. Thus, in economic affairs, a variety of provincial regulations affect the value of an investment in Canada that, if carried to extremes, could threaten the economic viability of the country as a whole.

Efforts by Prime Minister Pierre Elliott Trudeau to patriate the constitution and add to it a federally adopted bill of rights may well succeed, since his government has the necessary votes in the Parliament. Canadian votes may not be enough, however. The British House of Commons appears disinclined to be a rubber stamp, thus adding a new and interesting dimension to the problem. But the cost of Ottawa's constitutional success will be continuing political warfare between Trudeau and most of the provincial premiers. One would think that Canadian voters could instill some coherence into the system. On the contrary, Canadians vote on two planes, federal and provincial, which seem to have relatively little relationship to each other. A heavy majority for a strong federalist like Trudeau has no visible effect on the attitudes of the Quebec and some other provincial governments elected within the same general time-span by the same voters.

The federal–provincial argument is in large part about money, although cultural–linguistic and political issues dominate the case of Quebec. The federal government has for some years been accumulating a huge deficit. Provincial governments of resource-rich provinces, notably Alberta, and to a lesser extent Saskatchewan and British Columbia, have their own sources of wealth. Alberta has generated substantial surpluses. Hitherto impoverished Newfoundland is optimistic about its oil potential and determined to control it. Quebec also has resources such as hydroelectric power, forest products, and minerals. It shares with Ontario the location of most of Canada's manufacturing industry, which has historically been in need of tariff protection, to the distress of the rest of Canada. The regional argument between the industrial and the resource provinces is an old one, now exacerbated by the Trudeau constitutional program and opposition to it by individual provincial leaders.

There is a revenue-sharing scheme in Canada that automatically arranges for the transfer of a portion of federal tax funds from the richer to the poorer provinces. Oil prices are maintained at an artificially low level to aid the consumer through federal government price controls on domestic oil and through a subsidy program on imports, which is funded from taxes on exports to the United States, from general revenue, and from a gasoline tax. The energy program proposed by Prime Minister Trudeau and Energy Minister Lalonde in October 1980 would continue this pricing policy while introducing discriminatory measures to "Canadianize" the ownership of the energy industry and expand the role of the government in the energy sector.

The Quebec nationalist movement, although apparently concerned primarily with cultural–linguistic matters, is no less reluctant than other provinces to assert provincial jurisdiction over the internal disposition of federal transfers. Obviously, federalists like Prime Minister Trudeau wish to continue being the arbiters of the distribution of monies within Canada, and obviously the leaders of the wealthier provinces want to retain as much control as possible over provincial surpluses.

The press, the business community, and the intellectual elite of Canada are seized with the federal–provincial controversy, and the land reverberates with vigorous expressions of opinion. The Quebec separatist movement appeared to be coming to a head in the referendum of May 20, 1980. For a short period after the results of the vote were known it was thought outside Quebec that the defeat of the Lévesque sovereignty-association initiative might mean the quiescense of separatism, at least for the time being. But the Trudeau government, which many Quebeckers felt had implied significant concessions in the direction of provincial autonomy in exchange for a "no" vote on sovereignty-association, has only added fuel to the fire. Despite opposition by most provincial governments, including Quebec, Ottawa is currently proceeding with legislation to adopt a new constitution and bill of rights widely perceived as an expansion of federal authority at the expense of the provinces. Quebec's most recent response was a resounding victory for the Parti Québécois over the Liberals in the provincial elections of April 1981.

The fathers of confederation in 1867 were not entirely clear in their compromises over the delineation of provincial versus federal jurisdiction. Political and judicial action in the ensuing years has not improved the situation. The forces of economic change, domestic and global, have highlighted the issue of jurisdiction over natural resources. The action of the Organization of Petroleum Exporting Countries (OPEC) in dramatically raising oil prices has encouraged political leaders in oil-producing provinces to assert authority over production, prices, and revenues, while stimulating Ottawa to introduce countermeasures to implement a national energy policy.

Undoubtedly a different Canada will emerge from the present contest, one that may well afford more provincial autonomy in certain areas while confirming federal authority in others. But the transition will be uneasy and troubled. Meanwhile a great variety of American interests is at stake—from national security to private investment—in a situation that U.S. officials and individuals can do relatively little to affect.

One can certainly suggest to Canadians that Canada does not exist in a vacuum and that its internal political crisis could well have repercussions for the outside world and certainly for the United States. It is not out of order to point out that certain proposals are injurious to a sound economic relationship between important segments of the U.S. and Canadian private sectors (including even consumers). Nevertheless, what appears to be in prospect is that the Trudeau government will pursue federalism side by side with economic assertiveness, with such highly nationalist measures as the new energy policy described in the budget message of late 1980. The resulting dilemma for the United States is obvious. Indeed, Americans—or some American interests—may find themselves paying part of the price for a united Canada.

The following are some specific recommendations of the Atlantic Council working group with respect to U.S. policy in its relations with a politically divided Canada.

1. The public posture of the United States with regard to the complex of Quebec issues should continue to be one of concerned

noninvolvement. The U.S. government has made it clear on a number of occasions that it prefers a united Canada but has never specified a preference for any particular constitutional formula. Spokesmen representing diverse viewpoints in Canada may look to a U.S. audience for support for their opinions, seeking access to public forums, the media, and government and private groups in the United States. A reasonable posture for Americans would be to express hope for democratically arranged solutions that will make possible a constructive relationship with the United States.

2. The same hands-off attitude should apply to other potential breakaway provinces. Clearly our defense interests in NATO and the North American Aerospace Defense Command (NORAD) are best served by a united Canada. American business has enjoyed certain advantages in being able to deal in one market to the north, with one government, even when that government is protectionist or occasionally strongly nationalist. Whether U.S. business would be better served—or as well served—by dealing in multiple markets is an open question closely related to the type of business involved and to the kind of provincial regulation to which it would then be exposed.

3. A significant change in the political structure of Canada would leave the United States with enormous problems on its doorstep with which it is now ill-equipped to cope. Such a prospect is far less likely, however, than that of a limited devolution of federal authority to the provinces, affecting cultural–linguistic and certain economic relationships, with the federal government retaining full authority in such domains as monetary policy, diplomacy, international economic relations, and defense. From the standpoint of U.S. interests, public and private, an alteration of this kind in the pattern of government north of the border need not pose serious difficulties. But it must be emphasized that such a negotiated compromise of the current political contests is not in sight at present. Prime Minister Trudeau appears to be firmly dug into his position, and so are the provincial leaders. Intransigence seems the order of the day, and it is not possible to predict how or when the crisis will be resolved.

Whatever the outcome of present federal–provincial tensions, relevant agencies of the U.S. government, as well as business and professional circles, should expand their Canadian contacts and their awareness and understanding of the Canadian .scene. They should know more about Canadian institutions, public and private, and about political, intellectual and emotional forces at work. More American universities should undertake programs in Canadian studies, and more scholars should be encouraged to engage in them. A start has been made in this direction, but it is still only a modest one. Support for such programs should be forthcoming from private foundations and business as well as from state and federal governments.

ECONOMIC RELATIONS

Two basic facts influencing economic relations are that the United States is ten times the size of Canada in population and more in GNP. Thus economic relations are perceived very differently by the two countries, depending on the vantage point. A further major difference has been the historical struggle by Canada, often through government programs, to maintain economic unity and national identity along east–west lines, against the magnetic forces pulling toward the south.

The two countries are immensely important to each other in economic terms. The United States customarily buys large quantities of raw materials in Canada—forest products and minerals—and in certain areas counts on Canada for electricity. In manufactured goods Canada is a major market for the United States. At the same time Canadian sales of industrial goods to the United States are increasing. In agriculture the two countries compete for overseas markets, notably in feed grains and wheat. There is reciprocal across-the-border marketing of fruits and vegetables, often of a seasonal nature, and a competitive struggle over fishing. Canada is the locus of the largest proportion of American foreign direct investment. Canada's investments in the United States, which already outstrip all its other foreign investment ventures combined, are growing rapidly.

The asymmetry in size of the two economies, however, means that Canadian investment in the United States has scattered local impact. On the other hand, the American economic presence in Canada is a major factor in Canadian politics. It is also a major factor in any Canadian view of the relationship with the United States, the totality of which is very extensive, complex, diverse, difficult to define, and not well understood by the general American public.

Tariff and nontariff barriers affecting bilateral trade are still substantial for certain manufactured goods and agricultural products. In farm equipment there has for all practical purposes been a single market. The Automotive Agreement provides a historic first in something close to a negotiated common market in a major industrial sector. Canada now screens new direct investment, whereas on the U.S. side foreign investment is regulated primarily in certain strategic sectors, like banking, transportation, and communications, where Canada also imposes restrictions. At the same time, there is a condition of easy transferability of funds from one country to the other and what amounts to a single market in portfolio securities.

Understandably, frictions arise in such a highly interdependent and intimate economic environment. There are always continuing discussions of major issues involving national authorities, or state/provincial authorities, or local jurisdictions. Inevitably, there is a competitive scramble for markets, profits, money, resources, oil, gas, and water. The Canadian economy has grown rapidly with the postwar inflow of American capital. Canadians have become self-conscious about the direction and impact of this growth. They have made a major effort for some years to define a national economic policy, to establish rules and guidelines for investors and traders, and to employ government assistance to direct the economy in this way or that; for example, to stimulate regional development or to "stand up to" its larger economic partner. In international trade they have spurred efforts at trade diversification, out of concern for what they consider to be Canada's economic dependence on the United States and vulnerability to unilateral U.S. economic actions.

On the other hand, the much larger U.S. economy has operated with relatively more openness and less deliberate federal government direction. Market forces have generally determined the flow of money and trade in industrial goods, within existing tariff and other regulatory limits. Agriculture tends to be shaped by government programs in both countries. Government export restrictions or disincentives are more characteristic of the United States. Canada offers important incentives to exports of manufactured goods but maintains few disincentives beyond those limiting exports of energy.

Canada's economy is now more subject to governmental direction and control than has been the case in the relatively laissez-faire past. Prime Minister Trudeau has expressed himself publicly as to what he considers to be the shortcomings of the "capitalist" system. His present minister of industry, trade, and commerce is an avowed economic nationalist, and there is a new discriminatory federal policy to Canadianize foreign owned investments in the energy industry. Similar policies in other sectors are not unlikely.

Previous nationalist programs in Canada have been less extreme in their final form than in original concept. But the 1980 program came at the peak of the constitutional crisis, and it is hard to escape the conclusion that the two developments are closely linked, and that the Liberal government is making a distinct appeal for NDP support on both constitutional and economic nationalist grounds. This identification of Ottawa's economic assertiveness with the constitutional issues tends to make any U.S. effort to defend its own economic interests appear to be interference in Canadian domestic matters.

The mandate of the Foreign Investment Review Agency (FIRA) is to screen prospective foreign investments on the basis of "what is good for Canada." Initially the FIRA simply reviewed proposals for foreign takeovers and new investment projects, approving or rejecting them. Most were approved, sometimes with limits or modifications. FIRA then began to impose certain conditions upon approval, such as commitment to export their products and the performance of minimum levels of processing or of research and development in Canada. Now it is proposed that FIRA review all *existing* foreign investment. Obviously, much will depend on the subjective judgment of individual FIRA commissioners as they apply the administrative criteria, and upon the political judgment of the cabinet, which has the ultimate word.

The complexion of the 1980 Trudeau cabinet, the "new look" at FIRA, and the new energy policy all lead to the conclusion that economic nationalism, or "industrial policy," or dirigisme, is the order of the day in a much more explicit and positive form than has been the case in the past. Furthermore, individual provinces are practicing their own forms of economic nationalism. Perhaps Ottawa's national economic policy is intended to be the mortar to be applied to the outer walls of Canada, now threatened by cracks and fissures.

Under these circumstances it behooves the United States to take careful note of what is happening. For a very long time American government and industry, although occasionally apprehensive, have tended to take trade with Canada for granted, to bask in the relative protection afforded U.S. investment by Canadian tariff barriers and local encouragement and to react only as necessary when some major economic event occurred. The United States needs Canadian resources, Canadian markets, and opportunities for investment in Canada. Canada has reciprocal needs. For a variety of reasons, there is no treaty of friendship, commerce, and navigation between the United States and Canada that would establish a definitive legal basis for action regarding national treatment of foreign investment. The absence of such a treaty and the current Canadian reluctance to recognize its Organization for Economic Cooperation and Development (OECD) commitments to the principle of national treatment are complicating and disturbing factors.

In trade, the guidelines are more indicative, since both countries are contracting parties to the General Agreement on Tariffs and Trade (GATT). Current trends in Canada, however, suggest a diminished interdependence and complementarity in bilateral trade with the United States, a development that could have unfavorable consequences for defense production sharing and other bilateral national security interests.

If a government of Canada determines to use its very considerable powers to control and direct the relationship in a manner it deems helpful to Canada, the U.S. private sector and the U.S. government must analyze Canadian actions and policies, determine whether or not the effect is detrimental to their interests, and decide, if necessary, on an appropriate course of remedial action. What the United States does and how it does it can have a decisive impact on what Canada does. Interaction is endemic in such a situation. The best hope of those who believe in a market economy and in healthy Canadian–U.S. relations is that the interaction will not escalate to a contest of economic power in order for each country to receive what would be described as fair treatment from its good neighbor and long-term economic partner. All current indications are, however, that the present Canadian government intends to discriminate in favor of Canadian owned enterprise. It has the votes to do it, at least for the life of the Trudeau government, and it could seek to use the occasion of an economic contest with the United States as a unifying force in its domestic politics.

Under these circumstances the Atlantic Council working group proposed that the United States government should:

1. Maintain a close watch with respect to Canadian government actions in the economic field, analyzing with care all evidence of

government economic plans and intentions that could have an impact on U.S. interests. Information, impressions, and interpretations acquired by either the U.S. government or the business community should be freely exchanged and made the subject of close consultation.

2. Continue to press bilaterally and within the OECD framework for the fullest possible recognition by Canada of the principle of national treatment of investment, which was a key factor in the OECD declaration to which Canada subscribed in 1976. Such U.S. action is specifically called for in the case of Canada's National Energy Program.

3. Review all agreements negotiated in the Tokyo round of multilateral trade negotiations to be sure that Canada and the United States are complying with their obligations. In addition, the United States should actively encourage full attention to bilateral trade problems. Most Canadians have a philosophical bias in favor of nondiscrimination in trade and economic matters. Despite pressures for nationalist economics, classic precepts still have value for both Canadians and Americans.

4. Seek to expand the coverage of these multilateral trade negotiations (MTN) agreements by urging wider Canadian acceptance, for example, of the government procurement code, at least to the extent of reciprocity with the United States.

5. Study the use of subsidies by Canada and of countervailing actions by the United States, so that the United States is adequately prepared for what may well become a negotiation of the problem of subsidies and countermeasures.

6. Examine with care the economic actions and regulations of the Canadian provinces. Significant in themselves, such actions can signal important developments in Canadian internal politics.

7. With respect to energy—obviously an area to which both governments have directed a great deal of their legislative and regulatory efforts—seek to assure that energy projects affecting both countries are handled with genuine reciprocity and in the spirit of promoting production and efficient conservation for the benefit of both peoples. Canada and the United States can both contribute to meeting the world's need for additional sources of energy. Pragmatic cooperation can be significant in helping to meet energy needs of certain areas of the United States while being financially rewarding to Canada. Further, the lower forty-eight states need Alaskan gas, which

cannot reach them overland without Canadian cooperation and a readiness to act on the part of the U.S. government. The 1980 energy program of the Trudeau government (presented in the 1980 budget message) casts considerable doubt over future general energy cooperation and seems likely to impede gas and oil production in Canada for some time to come.

8. In multilateral economic forums—the seven-power summit, the General Agreement on Tarrifs and Trade, the Organization for Economic Cooperation and Development, the United Nations, United Nations Commission on Trade and Development, United Nations Industrial Development Organization, the Organization of American States, the International Monetary Fund–International Bank for Reconstruction and Development, etc.—seek to work closely with Canadian representatives in a rational approach to the world's increasingly difficult economic problems.

9. Undertake a dialogue with the Canadian government to clarify the ground rules of FIRA and seek government-to-government consultations with respect to procedures affecting American companies. We should examine in this context what, if anything, the U.S. government could do, if necessary, with respect to reciprocal treatment of Canadian investments in the United States. The absence of a treaty of friendship, commerce, and navigation and Canada's vagueness about its 1976 OECD commitment to the principle of national treatment, make firm consultative undertakings essential.[1]

10. Work with the U.S. Senate to resolve the impasse over the East Coast fisheries and boundary treaties negotiated with Canada and sent to the Senate some time ago for consideration. This issue is a thorn in the side of informed Canadians, whereas few Americans outside the fishing industry will have heard of the matter. If necessary, we should also examine what could be done to change our approach to the treaties, perhaps by separating the boundary and fisheries aspects. Fishing disputes have been a recurring feature of Canadian–U.S. relations since at least 1790. It is time to develop a modus vivendi in this area once and for all.

---

1. Comment by Elliot Feldman: FIRA is a domestic Canadian institution. The United States is entitled to defend its economic interests, and if the government of Canada does not choose to work cooperatively in FIRA it would be appropriate for the United States to consider seriously measured responses. The United States should welcome an invitation from Canada to discuss policies in FIRA, but it is not for the United States to press for "government-to-government consultations" with a domestic Canadian government agency.

11. Avoid, where possible, extraterritorial U.S. actions affecting Canadian entities or individuals. Nothing has a more infuriating impact than U.S. antitrust foreign assets control or other actions taken by the Department of Justice, Treasury, or other U.S. agencies in areas Canadians properly regard as their sovereign domain. As an important first step we should complete the pending antitrust cooperation agreement, which would provide for advance notice and consultation. Perhaps such an agreement could include FIRA rulings that place requirements on U.S. entities.

12. Assuming the new U.S.-Canadian double tax treaty is acceptable to American business interests, proceed promptly toward approval, seeking Canadian consultation on policies that might suggest delay or caution.[2]

13. Resume the consultations on the world grain trade that have been sporadic in the past. As the two greatest grain exporters, the United States and Canada can do much to promote stability in world food supply. The nature of world food demand assures highly profitable export prospects for both countries. They should not become estranged by competitive squabbles, and they should bear in mind their broader responsibilities for assuring freedom from hunger in various parts of the world. They should also seek agreement on how to handle grain sales to the USSR and the People's Republic of China.

14. Review intensively the Automotive Agreement and its impact on U.S. relations with Canada. It must be remembered that the agreement was concluded as a result of a Canadian effort, through subsidies and rebates, to expand domestic automobile production in Canada, thereby provoking a U.S. counterreaction. The agreement is a marriage of convenience, not well-defined in its objectives. Rough reciprocity is called for over time, but there are no agreed standards of measurement or compliance. Further, the history of the pact shows that each government at one time or another has complained that it works unfairly. The United States is committed to free entry for Canadian cars. Canada extends reciprocity in principle, with certain limitations. The attitude of the United Auto Workers (UAW) is important in this matter. With the industry in trouble because of

---

2. Comment by Elliot Feldman: There is no reason for the United States government to depend on the approval of "American business interests" for the negotiation of treaties. Business interests are not always the same as the public interest for which the government of the United States bears responsibility.

competition, this is an area that calls for clarity and cooperation, instead of the mumbled complaints one hears. Trade balance on a bilateral basis is less important than productivity, competitiveness, and the general economic health of the industry.

15. In connection with environmental regulations, seek to achieve reciprocity and cooperation. Obviously this is easier said than done. Plurality of jurisdictions in both countries makes this problem very difficult indeed, and the disparity of size and number of industrial establishments guarantees contention. More effective use should be made of the International Joint Commission mechanism, and both governments should be positive in their approach to negotiations on environment. The United States should be aware that the Canadian public and government, as well as the provinces, are extremely concerned about the acid rain issue and view it as a major bilateral problem.

16. Seek a solution to the border TV and radio broadcasting issue, which arises from a Canadian measure that makes nondeductible for tax purposes expenditures by Canadian firms on American programs targeted for Canadian listeners. Allegedly necessary as a defense of Canadian culture, this measure has aroused vigorous resentment in a small and localized segment of American business. For some time there was thought of linking the issues to the U.S. tax treatment of Americans attending conventions in Canada, but recent legislation has provided an exemption for such conventions, and the leverage is gone. Perhaps some new linkage could be found.

A word on linkage is in order. There are countless issues in Canadian–U.S. economic relations, and the temptation to link a solution of one issue to that of another is always present. Linkage will work when it is mutually evident that a basis for reciprocity exists. It will not work if an attempt is made to pair obviously extraneous and unrelated issues or grievances or if one side is determined to bargain very hard and to extract every small advantage. The United States must be prepared for hard bargaining if the partner is of this mind or be ready to be generous and constructive if negotiations are more genial. In general no major national interest should be held hostage to a case that is important to only a few people in one country. A sense of decency and proportion must prevail in our relations with Canada and a sense of humor as well.

Periodically suggestions are made for the creation of a free trade area or common market for the United States and Canada; also for a trilateral U.S.–Canada–Mexico relationship. In fact President Reagan, in his 1979 candidacy speech, called for a trilateral "accord," one that would multiply the potential of each country without in any way infringing on its sovereignty. With sagacity he observed that such an accord might take 100 years to work out. As president he may have in mind a more general concept of closer consultation and cooperation among the three countries that can be readily endorsed.

The idea of a closer economic relationship has attraction for certain members of the U.S. Congress as well. There is a reference in the Trade Agreements Act of 1979 to closer economic ties within the northern half of the western hemisphere. A congressional study of the subject was undertaken as well as a report to the Congress by the executive branch. Other public and private groups are making their own studies.

What is seldom clear is exactly what the proponents of closer economic ties have in mind. A free trade area, which would eliminate trade barriers between the two countries but retain them in trade with third countries, would almost certainly arouse opposition from Canadian economic nationalists of various hues, including the NDP, as well as from Canadian secondary industry, fearful of being overwhelmed by American competition. A customs union or common market, eliminating trade barriers between Canada and the United States and establishing a harmonized common external tariff, seems even less practicable and less likely of Canadian acceptance.

Special sectoral free trade arrangements between the two countries have also been discussed. The only one in existence, the Automotive Agreement, does not seem very popular in either country. There may be other sector candidates, but it would be prudent to wait until the Automotive Agreement is on a sounder and better accepted basis before moving on to other fields. In contrast to the Canadian FIRA, the United States offers a relatively free market for direct and portfolio investment, and Canadians are investing in this country at an increasing rate.

Any proposal for a free trade area in one or more sectors is more likely to be successful if it does not come from the larger economic entity, especially if that entity is larger in GNP by a factor of ten. The history of past discussions between the United States and Canada is instructive. There were negotiations in 1910 for something called "reciprocity," with the nationalists in Canada demolishing the idea. There have been official talks between U.S. and Canadian diplomats over the possibility of a closer economic relationship. They were held in secret, their existence later denied but eventually confirmed. Undersecretary of State George Ball once unveiled a suggestion for a common market in a speech in Toronto and was quickly rebuffed by Canadian opposition. Any suggestion of this kind from an official American source is likely to be suspect, received with hostility by a large segment of the Canadian community, and might even set back the cause of closer relations by years.

MONETARY RELATIONS

Because of the closeness of U.S.–Canadian financial links and the asymmetry in the size of the two economies, Canadian monetary policy has alternated historically between a relatively free and floating exchange rate and a managed float with a fixed target relation to the U.S. dollar at any given time. Consultation between Canadian and U.S. monetary and financial officials goes on constantly. Except for occasional strains and pressures, the relationship has been harmonious. Canada's interest is in a stable currency, with a relation to the U.S. dollar that is not disadvantageous to Canadian exports. The United States is interested in being able to count on a steady dollar relation free of the problems attending the U.S. dollar relation to such major international currencies as the pound, the yen, the franc, and the deutschemark.

Interest rates are an extremely important aspect of financial relations. Any significant differential can result in flows of money to the more attractive rate. Consequently Canadian rates tend to follow U.S. trends, often to the distress of Canadians, particularly in times of interest rate volatility such as the present. Fiscal policy in both countries can also have a major impact on money flows, and again the much larger U.S. influence tends to play a governing role. If the economic program of the Reagan administration succeeds, it will inevitably have an important impact on the Canadian economy and government policy.

NORTH AMERICAN DEFENSE POLICY

"Under the irresistible dictates of geography, the defense of North America has become a joint enterprise of both Canada and the

United States." So said John Diefenbaker when he was prime minister of Canada. The problem with the U.S.-Canadian defense relationship today is that this joint enterprise has been downgraded in recent years. Both countries have allowed their defense establishments to decline in effectiveness and basic strength, for a variety of reasons.

The task of the present decade, as seen by military experts, is to redefine the defense relationship in terms of changing political and technological conditions and to seek more efficient means of achieving agreed ends.

Although Trudeau's leadership has not been lacking in terms of commitment to the defense of the North Atlantic Community, his earlier policies were in part responsible for the underequipped state of the Canadian forces. Canadian public opinion and both major parties remain supportive of both the North Atlantic Treaty Organization (NATO) and NORAD.

The chief psychological problem for Canadians is sometimes a sense that they are not in a position to have an effective input into global military and security decisions. Nevertheless Canadians are aware that Canada's geographic position makes it an essential part of any North Atlantic defense system, both in the air and on the sea, and that in the missile age Canada's location between the United States and the USSR is clearly a key one.

Canada's continued commitment to the defense of North America was reemphasized by the renewal of the NORAD agreement in March 1981. For the first time Canada greed to a change in the name of the organization from Air Defense Command to Aerospace Defense Command, recognized the space surveillance mission, and did not require a caveat in the document excluding Canada from participation in space defense. These changes reflect a mellowing of former Canadian attitudes opposing any Canadian involvement in space defense, while opening the door for greater Canadian contributions in this area.

It is to be hoped that the NORAD renewal will provide the basis for a new definition of the Canadian-U.S. air defense relationship and a clarification of other aspects of defense relations as well. The prospect for such an improved and strengthened defense relationship rests in great part upon the domestic political environment in Canada, the sensitivities of the Canadian public, and the support of the Trudeau government.

A key element in any Canadian defense effort is business for Canadian industry, whether from domestic orders from the Canadian armed forces, or from foreign orders. World War II induced in effect a shared defense production effort among Britain, Canada, and the United States, Subsequently, when arming for NATO and NORAD requirements, Canada and the United States formulated the defense production sharing program, which gives Canadian firms an opportunity to obtain defense orders from U.S. forces. The goal was a rough balance between the cost of weapons systems sold by the United States to Canada and the value of defense orders placed in Canada by the United States. The system has worked reasonably well, and the balance has been generally maintained. Recent purchases of patrol aircraft and fighter plans by Canada have made significant changes in the figures, although in each case there has been a substantial offset arrangement whereby subassemblies are manufactured in Canada. The offset system in effect defies the principle of comparative economic advantage and probably results in higher costs for taxpayers, but it seems necessary for employment and hence political reasons.

There are numerous specific measures in U.S. law and procurement regulations that adversely affect the operation of the defense production sharing program. These measures derive from successful legislative efforts by individual companies or industries in the United States designed to make it impossible for the Defense Department to buy certain articles from other countries. Such measures are altogether contrary to the basic trade policy of the United States as well as to U.S. policy toward Canada in the area of defense procurement. In a generic sense they compare with "Buy Canadian" commitments extracted by FIRA from potential foreign investors in Canada.

The Canadian armed forces continue their warm and friendly relationship with the military in the United States. Many military operations are well interwoven between the armed forces of the two countires, and the respective services offer reciprocal sympathy when their governments are inattentive or unsupportive.

Specific policy recommendations advanced by the working group include the following:

1. The United States should demonstrate continued interest in the reequipment of Canadian armed forces in a fashion consistent with the mission of these forces, in NATO, NORAD, or elsewhere. Primary emphasis is best placed on the NATO and NORAD areas where the need is greatest. Air defense and antisubmarine warfare require-

ments are important priority needs. An equitable cost-sharing arrangement must be developed.

2. The United States should encourage the Canadians to maintain their airlift capacity at a high level of efficiency. The Canadians run an excellent military air service that has proved extremely effective in a number of crises, notably in UN peacekeeping activities. The commitment of Canada to the NATO civil augmentation program is also significant.

3. Canadian defense efforts in the Pacific should be supported. Although the Pacific is outside the NATO area, ample precedent exists for naval cooperation between the two countries, notably in submarine detection.

4. The United States must continue to review with Canada the numerous existing bilateral military arrangements (such as those dealing with overflight rights and the use of Goose Bay in Labrador), and specific basic defense plans, recognizing the sensitivity of the Canadian public to such matters.

5. The armed forces of Canada, which include significant and proportionate numbers of Canadians from all provinces, are a manifestation of Canadian unity. In view of the U.S. security interest in a united Canada, the United States should continue to nurture its Canadian military ties.

6. Close coordination should be sought with Canada on arms control, particularly of strategic weapons, and on matters affecting the development of antiballistic weapons systems. Canadian cities could be as much Soviet targets as are U.S. cities, and Canadian defense authorities need to be privy to U.S. strategic thinking and planning.

7. The United States should recognize that Canadian defense of Arctic territories and waters is strategically important for the United States, as is the protection of Canada's natural resources.

8. The defense production sharing arrangement between Canada and the United States should be clarified so that there is a full public understanding of the relationship and of the reasons for it. Barriers on both sides should be removed (examples in the United States are the "Buy American" Berry, Burns–Tollefson, and Bayh amendments to defense procurement acts and small-business and minority setasides). Moreover, foreign military sales regulations should be made fair and comprehensible, and many of the restrictions on access to security information should be removed insofar as Canadian military professionals are concerned. On the Canadian side, there should be

elimination of the "Buy Canada" and duty differentials, and Canada should be encouraged to buy U.S. equipment where the price and specifications are right. Simplified and equitable offset understandings should be sought.

WORLD POLITICS

The extent of Canada's involvement and influence in world affairs is necessarily less than that of some other powers. Nevertheless Canada plays a wide and constructive role for which it is much respected in the international community. Its perceptions are sufficiently similar to those of the United States as to provide reenforcement for the U.S. position abroad on many issues. At the same time Canada is at pains to maintain an independent identity and to pursue an independent course. It has ties of its own overseas, particularly with the Commonwealth countries, the Third World and the European Community.

Canada has an excellent diplomatic service, a knowledgeable intelligence element, competent security forces, a superior communications system, and efficient foreign aid and commercial promotion services. Professionally, Canada ranks with the best. When its political leaders have sought to play major roles in world affairs they have performed with distinction as they did with outstanding success at the San Francisco conference on the United Nations in 1945.

Canada has employed its competent armed forces and superior logistics in vital peacekeeping roles. It is an active partner in NATO, constructive and broad-minded in counsel. Its diplomacy in the UN and other multilateral forums is intelligent, practical, and morally motivated. It has on countless occasions been helpful to the United States, often because it shared American perceptions of the problem at hand; sometimes because it sought to come naturally to the aid of an ally. At such times as it has been critical of American policies and actions, it has spoken its mind quietly and confidentially as befits a friend. Rarely does it appear vigorously opposed to the United States in multilateral forums. When it does, the reason may well be that the issue impinges on the bilateral relationship.

Canada appears on the world scene as moral, virtuous, constructive, and friendly to all—an image it seeks. There are, of course, the stern realities of its NATO and NORAD military alliances. But Canada manages to conduct itself so as to emphasize simultaneously its separateness from the United States, its loyalty to its alliances, its attitude of détente toward the Communist countries, and its wide friendship with the Third World. All this takes skill, but the Canadians have it.

Frequent high-level intergovernment contacts could do much to enhance the bilateral relationship with a greater awareness by each country of how the other assesses foreign developments and identifies its own national interests. For all its global-mindedness and its constructive role in multilateral diplomacy and peacekeeping, Canada is primarily concerned with international economic-commercial matters, whereas the United States tends to be preoccupied with politico-military security matters. Individual cabinet-level contacts are fairly common for the discussion of purely bilateral issues. They could be extremely valuable on a group basis for the discussion of a wide range of matters relating to the world outside North America. Perhaps the U.S.-Canadian Joint Cabinet Committee should be revived.

U.S. GOVERNMENTAL STRUCTURES
FOR DEALING WITH CANADA

Canadian constitutional dissensions finds a counterpart on the American side in a lack of consensus and policy coordination in Washington, which has made it more difficult in recent years for the United States to identify its foreign policy objectives and to deal effectively with other governments. Canadian diplomats and officials are baffled by the lack of coordination between the Congress and the executive branch of the U.S. government, for example, and oftimes by the consequent inability of executive departments to be as responsive as their counterparts in the Canadian system.

Party discipline in the Congress has declined in the past decade along with cooperative relations with the executive branch. Members of Congress sometimes evidence little sense of obligation to their party leadership. Votes are often cast not on party lines but by regions or for ideological, idiosyncratic, or other reasons, in a manner contrary to the Canadian parliamentary system of government, which implies responsibility to party.

Fortunately Canada itself is not a political issue for Americans, although certain items in bilateral relations do arouse congressional interest, as have fishing, border broadcasting, environmental issues, and Canada's assistance to American hostages in Teheran in 1980. There are enough congressmen with a favorable attitude toward Canada, although perhaps somewhat limited knowledge of it, to warrant legislative branch support for good bilateral relations.

The Canadian embassy has observed that increasingly Congress looms as even more important than the executive branch in terms of what it might do, directly or indirectly, to affect Canada. In seeking to bring some influence to bear on the U.S. legislative branch, the embassy is staggered by the enormity of the task before it—how to inform and influence 535 members of the Congress of the United States, a problem that has confounded the U.S. executive branch for generations.

Obviously, similar difficulties confront other foreign embassies in Washington in an era in which there have been contests of strength between the executive branch and the legislature. But Canadians have a ringside seat from which they find themselves inadvertently affected by congressional actions intended to be limited to the domestic arena. They are better informed, by and large, about the U.S. Congress and its activities than are people in Europe, Latin America, Africa, or Asia. This greater awareness tends to increase their apprehensions, although they at least can speak to members of Congress in familiar and friendly accents.

Fortunately there is no lack of bilateral mechanisms available for the two countries through which to communicate or negotiate if they wish. The regular use of these channels can do much to educate those concerned and can often serve to dissipate problems before they reach substantial proportions. There is of course the primary official channel, the diplomatic one of the State Department, the Canadian Department of External Affairs, and the respective embassies in Ottawa and Washington. This diplomatic channel is in good working order but is subject to a certain amount of bureaucratic bypassing, as has always been true of neighboring countries whose officials across the spectrum of departments and ministries find it convenient to telephone their opposite numbers directly. Given two active, pluralist, closely interrelated, talkative societies, keeping track of intergovernmental communications and informal understandings can be quite a challenge.

In the United States, the Departments of Defense, Commerce, Treasury Interior Agriculture and Energy, and the Office of the Trade Representative, to name a few, all have channels of communication with their opposite numbers in Canada and all like to handle directly what they regard as their own business. A comparable situation exists in Ottawa. Frequently intergovernmental groups divide on other than purely national lines. Such cross-references can sometimes introduce a note of pragmatic rationalism to the bilateral relationship. On the other hand, they can make bilateral relations infinitely more complex, especially given the U.S. executive–legislative branch coordination problems, and thus can lead to stalemates.

A word might be said about the way Canada is handled in the State Department. The Office of Canadian Affairs is in the European Bureau. From time to time deputy assistant secretaries have been designated to deal with Canadian affairs. When their duties have been confined to Canada the system has worked well but when combined with responsibilities for other specific countries the result is often that Canada does not get as much attention at the assistant secretary level as might well be merited. There may be some temptation to group Canada and Mexico in a new bureau of North American affairs. This should be resisted because Canadian and Mexican relations with the United States have little in common and the cultures are quite dissimilar.

In an era of increased congressional activity in foreign affairs, it is worth noting that the two legislatures have their own channel, the U.S.-Canadian Interparliamentary Group, useful in concept, active on occasion, but limited in its impact on policy. Then there are various private Canadian–American committees, one cosponsored by the National Planning Association and the C.D. Howe Institute; another identified with the respective national chambers of commerce. The AFL–CIO and the UAW have close institutional relations with Canadian labor organizations, as do many professional organizations with their Canadian counterparts. The Permanent Joint Board on Defense and the International Joint Commission are both useful bilateral structures for handling specialized matters in their respective fields. Many other such mechanisms exist, often formed on an ad hoc basis to deal with particular issues.

There is no lack of available technical machinery. In many cases it will succeed in resolving the issue at hand or in reducing the number of issues that rise to the top of the agenda. Thus summit talks between president and prime minister often include only a limited agenda of bilateral issues, tending to concentrate on the world view—north–south problems, international money and trade, economic growth, and the price of oil—which is as it should be. The existing Canadian and American governmental mechanisms provide a system that makes it possible for most bilateral problems to be resolved on reasonable and equitable terms, assuming a political will to do so.

Canadians who deal with the U.S. government often complain about American ignorance, indifference, or inattention with respect to Canada or to U.S. domestic actions that affect Canada. In recent years the complaint is less sharp, for good reason. Somewhat more information about Canada is now available in the American media. More Americans with an interest in foreign affairs have begun to pay attention to Canada and have learned how intrinsically important and interesting its politics can be. Finally, more Americans have begun to generalize their specific experience so that there is a body of informed opinion, in business, academe, and the public at large. The U.S. government is therefore in a position to find some kind of constituency of a general nature with which it can interact regarding U.S. relations with Canada.

There is nothing wrong with the structure of bilateral relations. The fundamental difficulty is that Canada's preoccupation with its federal–provincial controversy began at a time when there was a lack of the coherence and consensus in Washington essential to a strong and definitive policy toward Canada. Whether in the U.S. case this weakness will be corrected remains to be seen. Even a well-articulated executive branch and a constructive, well-disciplined, and informed Congress could have a hard time coping with the consequences for the United States of a long-drawn-out reshaping of the Canadian confederation. With the best will in the world the United States could easily become involved in a situation in which numerous Canadians blamed us for their troubles or sought to enlist us in the solution. Clearly, for us it is a time for prudence, full information, painstaking analysis, and the avoidance of public rhetoric.

The ability of the United States or of Americans deliberately to influence events in Canada is very limited. It consists in large measure in pointing out to Canadians, in government and outside, the results that might flow from Canadian actions or proposals likely to disturb an otherwise open and constructive relationship with the United States. It is a task for the U.S. government, of course, but also for private business and others with a stake in good U.S.–Canadian relations.

Official representations or responses must take account of the fact that the disparity in the size of the two countries requires that the larger and more powerful act with an unusual degree of adroitness and sensitivity. Some Canadian officials will never forget or forgive the occasional insensitive treatment received from senior American officials who have acted inconsiderately toward Canada. Such tactics, however just the U.S. cause, are invariably unproductive in the advancement of U.S. interests.

In the last analysis each country must resolve its constitutional and jurisdictional problems in its own way, doing the best it can with issues as they arise and striving to achieve an ever stronger and more mutually reenforcing bilateral relationship. Meanwhile a look at what is happening in Canada may persuade Americans to try to think through U.S. policy with respect to Canada and to insist upon better coordination within the U.S. federal government to permit a ready and flexible response to the demands of an uncertain and rapidly changing situation.

U.S.–Canadian relations have survived protracted arguments and negotiations over a number of sizable, complicated, joint commitments and undertakings, like the St. Lawrence Seaway, the Columbia River treaty, the decisions about weapons systems, and a range of contentious economic issues. Some matters have been on the agenda for years; others have been put aside and may never be resolved. From a historical perspective, the current state of affairs need not warrant pessimism, provided there is a disposition on both sides to pursue policies of neighborly cooperation and fairness. The fundamental differences in the two governmental systems will persist, and by their very nature will tend to make the transaction of intergovernmental business difficult.

Today's situation differs from the past in one important respect, however. The United States will have seen five presidents in office since 1968 when Trudeau began his nearly unbroken period as prime minister of Canada. The fact that the Liberal party, of which he is the leader, is rooted primarily in Ontario and Quebec, with no constituency west of Winnipeg and little in the Atlantic provinces, means that his government is quintessentially the expression of one man's philosophy and personality. Mr. Trudeau is an authentic, if extraordinary, Canadian, part French, part Scottish, a leader of considerable intellect and rare political skills who is unswerving in his dedication to Canadian federalism. He is said to wish to retire from politics but not until he has given Canada his particular stamp: patriated constitution, a federal bill of rights, and Canadianization and government direction of the economy.

Such is the nature of the Canadian constitutional structure that it is possible for a prime minister to expect Parliament to enact his program without the hindrance of the American check and balance system and with the assurance of party discipline among his cohorts in the legislature. Earlier Canadian governments have functioned with the same basic authority but have been less ideological, less subject to control by a single personality. Thus the Trudeau regime appears qualitatively different as a partner for transactions with the United States.

The phenomenon of a strong, tightly focused leadership pattern, coupled with a somewhat ideological approach to policy, is a new experience for Canadians as well. One wonders about the future. Will the Trudeau program be enacted? Will it endure after his departure and transform Canada? Or will provincial and popular opposition transform Canada in a different way? Who will lead Canada when Trudeau retires, and in which direction? The answers to these questions may be more important for Americans than they think.

DISSENT TO THE POLICY PAPER
—Elliot J. Feldman

The responsible role of the professional policy analyst is to array choices from many different perspectives and to suggest their consequences. I have tried to assure, in the deliberations of the working group on the United States and Canada, that due consideration would be given to perspectives from the Canadian provinces as well as from Ottawa. I have tried, also, to assure that all sides of controversies, in the public and private sectors, between Canada and the United States, and between Ottawa and the provinces, would be appreciated. The conclusions of this policy paper, however, advocate policies for the government of the United States. Although I endorse most of the paper as a private citizen, as a scholar I can recommend policies only to the extent that I think they will serve particular interests. I might recommend wholly different policies for the governments of Canada or for the governments of the Canadian provinces. As an American citizen I might hope that policies will be pursued to American advantage, but as a scholar I express no preference for outcomes. I have made this distinction during the many discussions of this paper, and I want to reaffirm it here. What is good for the United States is not necessarily good for Canada, and a scholar cannot take sides.

It is also important to dissent from the paper in two respects. First, it rests on certain unexamined assumptions that I think require more study. The first assumption that concerns me is that a free economic market in North America is good for the United States and, by implication, for Canada and the rest of the world. Any impediments to this market imposed by governments are considered bad. The second assumption is that the United States must bolster its defense capability with Canadian cooperation. These views are assumptions because they seemed obvious to the majority of members of the working group. They are less obvious to me.

My second dissent involves the final tenor of the paper and the distribution of its emphases. We have struggled as a group to achieve neutrality in the federal–provincial dispute. The paper has come a long way in this direction. Nevertheless, it is not entirely successful.

In the end we have given too little consideration to the aspirations of the majority of Quebecois, and we have neglected the real policy implications for the United States of strengthened Canadian provinces. Perhaps the implications of the federal–provincial struggle for Canadian–United States relations will be the heart of future studies.

2 CANADA IN 1990
What Kind of Federation?

Howard H. Cody

The distinctive characteristic of Canada's first century has been the undramatic gesture, the incremental adjustment, the compromise nonsolution. So it has been with the relationship between the central government at Ottawa and the ten provinces. Slowly yet relentlessly the provinces, some more than others, have asserted for themselves a wide range of political powers in economic, cultural, and social service domains. Their advances have been impressive, but they have been more substantial in some respects than in others, and several provinces consider their destiny to be still unrealized.

A spirited debate is underway on the fundamental question of the kind of country Canadians wish to have in the future. Many observers agree that there are precisely two choices, but they disagree on what these choices are. As the Liberal federal government and a few provincial governments conceive it, the alternatives consist of a country with a smoothly functioning, centrally directed economy and a country with ten parochial and destructively competitive economies. As the Progressive Conservative (PC) federal opposition and most of the larger provinces see it, the alternatives are a "community of communities," where each province pursues its destiny without outside interference, and a highly centralized state, in which an alien and insensitive power dictates policy to the provinces. These contrasting perspectives represent two conflicting philosophies of what federalism should involve in the Canadian context.

31

This chapter elaborates on the positions and the stakes in the ongoing debate and speculates on its possible resolution in the 1980s. Aspects of federal–provincial relations and distribution of political power that have the greatest bearing upon the relationship between Canada and the United States, and on United States business interests in Canada, receive the closest attention. Implications of predicted trends for Canada and the United States separately and for their relationship are explored.

BACKGROUND

The trend of federal government withdrawal from some jurisdictions under provincial constitutional authority, the provincial assertion of economic powers that to some extent infringe on federal jurisdiction, and Ottawa's current initiative to reassert economic supremacy are clearly grounded in the conflictual quarter-century of federal–provincial negotiations that followed the Second World War. In this period Ottawa's attempts to perpetuate a dominant federal position, which it established in the Depression and war, were resisted by the provinces with increasing success. Ultimately, in the 1960s, the most crucial decade in federal–provincial relations to date, the provinces gained much ground largely because the federal government could devise no alternative strategy to counter Quebec's claims to autonomy in a wide array of "cultural" jurisdictions.

Canada's intergovernmental difficulties are inherent in the preamble to the British North America Act of 1867, which is the core of the country's written constitution. The preamble declares that the dominion, loyal to the mother country's example, is to enjoy a constitution "similar in principle" to the British model. Ever since, Canadians have wrestled with the questions of how a written and federal constitution can operate similarly in principle to an unwritten and unitary constitution and how "supreme" Parliament can be in a federal structure.

The fathers of confederation were not naive in drafting Canada's constitutional document. They expressly desired a country that was to be federal in name only but in other respects faithful to centralized British practice. A federation with provincial powers in a few "local" jurisdictions was in fact created only because Maritimers and, more important, Quebeckers insisted that they retain control over their own educational and cultural institutions. At the time there was no conception of the future significance of provincial jurisdiction over health, education, welfare, property, and civil rights and ownership of natural resources or the royalties derived from their sale.

In no sense did the requirements of the situation shake John A. Macdonald (Canada's first prime minister and the most important father of confederation) and his associates from their conviction and confident expectation that Ottawa should and would monopolize political power in the dominion. As a precaution against provincial efforts to undermine federal leadership, the constitution confers upon the prime minister and cabinet (in formal language the governor in council) the power to disallow provincial legislation of which they disapprove. In addition, Ottawa may "declare" a "work" (aspect of provincial jurisdiction) affecting more than one province to be a "work for the general advantage of Canada" and take over that activity (the "declaratory power"). The federal Parliament is also empowered to spend money in fields of provincial jurisdiction (the "spending power"). Federal emergency powers are vast, though not unlimited. Section 91 of the British North America Act authorizes Ottawa to enact laws for "Peace, Order, and Good Government" encroaching on provincial jurisdiction in an emergency. Such an initiative can be overruled by the courts, but the recent Supreme Court decision authorizing Prime Minister Pierre Elliott Trudeau's anti-inflation program of 1975 indicates that the emergency power can be applied in times of economic difficulty. In respect to extraordinary powers, the centralist tone of the British North America Act retains its force more than a century after its inception.

It might seem to Americans inculcated with a division of powers principle that such a federation is a sham, relegating the provinces to perpetual inferiority. In fact, there *was* a largely implicit federal principle at Confederation. Provincial powers, or at least influence, would be manifested inside the federal government at Ottawa rather than in provincial capitals. The fathers of confederation anticipated that representatives of all provinces in the federal Senate and cabinet would effectively advance provincial interests. Unfortunately, the Senate is appointed by the federal cabinet and lacks legitimacy, while recent elections have produced a succession of cabinets of both parties lacking respected members from crucial provinces. Moreover, because the House of Commons is elected on a population basis, more than 60 percent of its members represent Ontario and Quebec constituencies. Westerners and Maritimers understandably feel powerless to influence national policymakers. All told, Canada's federal principle has failed utterly and conclusively to operate as expected.

Emboldened by its panoply of extraordinary powers, the federal government used Parliament's spending power to become heavily involved in provincial jurisdictions early in this century, through a mushrooming network of conditional grants. It had become clear that the once trivial "local" social service responsibilities assigned to the provinces in 1867 were becoming important. Provinces were offered assistance in vocational and technical education, health, pensions, highways, and other fields in which Ottawa desired a national program with federally imposed guidelines and standards. With a few exceptions (largely in Quebec) before the 1960s, provinces reluctantly accepted these grants as the only means to provide services that their residents increasingly expected.[1] Even before the Depression, provincial revenues from direct taxation (the only form of taxation permitted the provinces in the constitution) were wholly inadequate to permit provincial funding of social services. In the 1930s provinces became virtual wards of Ottawa, a condition the federal government perpetuated during the Second World War "emergency" and afterward in what Ottawa called a "reconstruction" period.

The most ominous development for this centralized intergovernmental relationship occurred in 1960 with the election of a semi-autonomist government in Quebec on the platform *maîtres chez nous* ('masters of our own house'). Premier Jean Lesage's "Quiet Revolution" committed his government to securing all powers necessary for the political, social, and economic "affirmation" of the Quebec people. Lesage had Quebeckers' support as he addressed the awakening self-assertiveness of the province's French-speaking majority. It became clear that active federal resistance to Quebec's demands for autonomy would endanger Quebeckers' continued endorsement of confederation.[2] Meanwhile, an assortment of separatist movements was springing up in Quebec. All in all, Ottawa saw no alternative to granting Quebec greater jurisdictional autonomy. The two options available to the federal government in the 1960s were a major transfer of power to Quebec alone—in effect an acknowledgment of Quebec's "special status" as the homeland and protector of a distinct people—and alternatively a similar shift of authority to all ten provinces. In the face of this dilemma, a period of indecision was followed by a decisive choice for the latter alternative around 1966. By no coincidence Pierre Trudeau was gaining ascendancy in Ottawa at this time.

Trudeau, a onetime journal editor (*Cité Libre*) and social democrat, entered the Liberal government in 1965 as a heartfelt Quebec supporter of confederation whose conception of national politics was dominated by the issue of Quebec's place in Canada. It still is.[3] Trudeau's prime political objective is defeat of the separatist forces inside Quebec, which he considers the only possible secessionist province. At the same time, the prime minister may possess less appreciation of or concern about the alienation and the distinct perspectives of western Canadians—a perception to which Westerners have become increasingly sensitive in recent years.

For Trudeau "national unity" essentially means keeping Quebec in Canada. The major instrument for accomplishing this goal has been the bilingualism and biculturalism program. Its objective is to permit all Canadians, francophones especially, to move freely throughout the country, to obtain services in their own language wherever they may be, and to "feel at home" everywhere. Inevitably, such a scheme has sometimes required the provision of French language services in anglophone areas, a practice that has engendered more English resentment than French appreciation and Canadian allegiance. Although the program's overall effect may be negative, it probably is not politically possible to discontinue it.

The most significant aspect of Prime Minister Trudeau's "national unity" policy is his recognition that Quebeckers' "national" consciousness now requires that the provincial government exercise substantial economic and cultural autonomy inside its borders. So that all Canadians may move freely throughout the country and so that no Canadians (especially Quebeckers) perceive that any part of Canada enjoys a status significantly different from any other, the concessions necessary to facilitate Quebec's cultural autonomy and to keep Quebec in Canada must be offered to all provinces. Trudeau's antipathy toward special status for any province apparently stems from the belief that special status would be counterproductive and unworkable and would constitute an open invitation to national disintegration. He fears Quebeckers would interpret a unique status for their province as a symbol of Quebec's apartness, that Quebeckers would progressively consider themselves alienated from other Canadians and thereby lose their commitment to Canada. In other words, special status for Quebec actually would encourage separatism. Trudeau also opposes special status in the belief that if it were offered to one province, other provinces would demand equivalent concessions in jurisdictions (such as energy resources) that they consider important to their own affirmation.

Accordingly, as much as possible the federal government has maintained much the same relationship with all ten provinces throughout the lengthy Trudeau era. The fiscal and jurisdictional price for such a federal policy has been high. In fiscal terms provinces have been securing income tax revenues that help provide services without federally supervised conditional grants. Provincial income tax revenues were minimal (or nil) before 1957. Since that date the provincial share of income tax revenues has slowly approached one-third of the total tax collected. Provinces also receive sizable unconditional cash payments from Ottawa. Provinces poorer than the national average are beneficiaries of equalization payments that now amount to more than C$500 per capita in the Atlantic provinces. All told, the federal government annually transfers more than C$11 billion in totally unconditional cash to the provinces. Provinces have always owned their natural resources and have earned royalties from their sale. The three westernmost provinces have become or are in the process of becoming wealthy from this revenue source alone.

As provincial fiscal resources improve, so does their jurisdictional autonomy. Conditional grants often were replaced in the 1960s with negotiated shared-cost schemes (in which Ottawa reimbursed one-half of the cost of such provincial services as medical care and post-secondary education). Some shared-cost programs were replaced in the 1970s by fully unconditional income tax and cash transfers. Provinces have now negotiated for themselves a virtually free hand in health, welfare, and education, broadly defined. Federal involvement in social services is only with provincial approval and is now largely confined to frequently unsuccessful private persuasion. A statistical indicator of the shift of power to the provinces is the fact that, whereas Ottawa spent 60 percent of all public expenditures in the late 1940s, provincial and municipal governments now account for 60 percent. Moreover, several provinces now impose an assortment of restrictions on labor and capital movement, which collectively undermine Canada's economic union and Ottawa's capacity to manage the national economy.

Even so, Canada's federal government still draws upon formidable resources when it deals with the provinces. The declaratory, emergency, and spending powers in the British North America Act continue to stand (although the disallowance power probably has lapsed). Some of the income tax transfers and cash transfers to the provinces could conceivably be withdrawn (or more likely renegotiated) to the provinces' intense economic discomfort. Moreover, Ottawa has retained paramount power in key economic sectors, specifically including sale and pricing of energy resources. This practice is strongly contested by energy-producing provinces, and has been under negotiation nearly continuously since 1973. Several other jurisdictions largely under federal control have also been the subject of inconclusive negotiations in recent years, including communications, transportation, offshore resources, and interprovincial and international trade.

On balance, the provinces have scored a remarkable success in "turning the tables" on Ottawa in the years since the onset of the "quiet revolution." A generation ago, the federal position was "What's mine is mine, what's yours is negotiable," as discussions centered on the nature and extent of federal involvement in provincial jurisdictions. Today the refrain is the same, but it is the provinces that sing it, and negotiations increasingly concern the degree of provincial power in jurisdictions heretofore the preserve of the federal government. "Executive federalism" now is well established, as major national policies are hammered out in bargaining among the prime minister and provincial premiers.

CANADIAN FEDERALISM IN THE 1980s

Prime Minister Trudeau is not a committed Canadian nationalist determined to wrest control of the Canadian economy from foreign investors. On the contrary, the record indicates that he has sustained an irrevocable position on precisely one major issue, the issue that propelled him into politics and that dominates his political thought and career to this day. This is the need to preserve Quebec's membership in the confederation on equal terms with the other provinces. On most other issues, including economic nationalism, Trudeau's convictions are not easily determined. Although the prime minister has occasionally mused aloud about Canadian nationalism and the alleged deficiencies of capitalism, his writings have extolled rationalism and condemned nationalism. His contradictory performance in office gives no evidence of a firm philosophical structure. Trudeau's policies have undergone periodic changes over the years. He seems to be heavily influenced by his closest personal and cabinet advisors and by short-term political considerations. It is instructive to note that the prime minister established a Foreign Investment Review Agency (FIRA), and a flaccid one at that, only after he had been in office for six years and then only to fulfill a commitment he had made to the New Democratic party (NDP) in return for the latter's necessary support in a minority Parliament.

If this interpretation is correct, the majority Liberal government's present nationalist course requires explanation. The explanation probably lies in contemporary federal–provincial relations. The real target is the provinces, not foreign investors. The presence of foreign involvement in Canada's economy offers a convenient pretext for federal reassertion of economic powers at a time when provincial economic activity has reached a level that Ottawa deplores.

In recent years observers of Canadian federal–provincial relations have noted that Ottawa has lost much ground to the provinces since World War II partly because successive prime ministers have been unable to articulate compelling reasons for dominant federal power. Federal attempts to exercise influence over the scope and development of provincial social services (notably health, welfare, and education) have met with unanimous provincial resistance. On these matters Ottawa now appears to be conceding full autonomy to the provinces. There is strong opposition from some provinces to federal economic assertiveness as well, but the federal government has nonetheless embarked upon a concerted initiative to enforce an "economic union" and to "patriate" at least part of Canada's economy from foreign control. American investment in Canada, particularly in energy resources, may be hostage to the competitive maneuvering for power now underway between federal and provincial governments. It appears that Ottawa's energy policies, at least as they involve the diminution of foreign ownership in the petroleum industry, enjoy substantial public support in all regions of the country. Thus the federal government at last may have discovered its "compelling reason" for reasserting powers that it wishes to exercise in any case.

Foreign owned business interests in Canada may be victims of domestic intergovernmental competition. In this situation some American companies, notably those in energy-related enterprises, may hope for a resolution in the provinces' favor. Others, inconvenienced by provincial mobility restrictions, may wish for a clear victory for Ottawa. Both groups should bear in mind, however, that compromise and the avoidance of definitive resolution of conflict are the Canadian practice. By 1990 there may be no decision for either side, and intergovernmental jockeying for advantage may endure indefinitely.

In the sections that follow, the prospects for change in distribution of power in the following matters of intergovernmental contention are considered: energy resources, economic union and foreign investment, fiscal relations, tariffs and industrial strategy, provincial foreign policies, communications, transportation, the environment, electoral reform, Senate reform, and interdelegation.

Material for this section was obtained from a variety of sources. Senior civil servants and cabinet ministers were interviewed in Ottawa and three provinces. The most useful information was obtained in these interviews, but sources cannot be identified. Governments of all provinces, and representatives of the business community and appropriate private associations were approached by mail for information. Nearly all responded with letters and useful documents.

ENERGY RESOURCES

The most visible and contentious intergovernmental dispute of our time involves the price, sale, and control of energy resources. At stake in the 1980s are significant political power and twelve-digit revenues. Provinces own their resources (except offshore) and obtain royalties from their sale. They control production, which permits them to increase and decrease supplies unilaterally. The federal government regulates domestic and international trade and commerce and has nearly unlimited taxation powers. Because energy is a divided jurisdiction, negotiations between Ottawa and energy-producing provinces have been carried out annually since 1973 in advance of the setting of prices. The federal government effectively has the last word on prices and sales and on the allocation of revenues among industry, the producing provinces, and the federal government. The nature of this distribution of responsibilities provokes confrontations, punitive recriminations, and alienation.

Federal–provincial bargaining on this issue largely pits Ottawa against Alberta, which possesses about 85 percent of the oil and natural gas in the ten provinces. The two governments are engaged in a multimillion dollar dispute over price. The federal government, supported by energy-consuming Ontario, wants domestic oil and gas prices to increase gradually through the 1980s and, in effect, to remain well below the world price. (Natural gas prices are pegged at 85 percent of oil price on a BTU equivalency basis.) Ottawa also intends to increase its share of revenues from 9 percent in 1979 to 24 percent in 1981, largely at the expense of corporate revenues. Alberta wants the domestic oil price to rise to 75 percent of world price (what Peter Lougheed, premier of Alberta, calls "fair market value") by 1985. Note that Alberta favors a close relationship between domestic and world price, while Ottawa does not. Most provinces and business interests, including the Canadian Manufacturers' Association (CMA), support Alberta on this issue. (The CMA is Canada's chief spokesman for large business and roughly the Canadian counterpart of the National Association of Manufacturers in the United States.)

Beyond the disagreement over price is a more fundamental conflict over the responsibilities of the parties to a federal country. Alberta subscribes to the "community of communities" concept, which associates each province's own welfare and interests with those of the nation as a whole by holding, in effect, that what is good for Alberta is good for Canada. (It may be argued that Ontario was in a similar position when it was the wealthiest province.) Premier Lougheed invokes Alberta's perceived heritage of oppression (discriminatory tariffs and freight rates, inter alia) to justify placing Alberta's desire for a secure and prosperous future, once the oil runs out, ahead of an amorphous "national interest." Royalties are being put into the Alberta Heritage Trust Fund, an C$8.5 billion bank account as of May 1981, which will grow to at least C$10 billion in 1981 alone. Alberta's revenues from energy sales in the 1980s are projected at C$100 billion or more.

The federal position is that "fiscal equity" among the provinces is essential for the survival of the "spirit of confederation" and "spirit of equalization." None of these terms is clearly defined, but Ottawa firmly believes that no province should be permitted to amass wealth totally out of proportion to the national average. Ottawa is asking Alberta to forego billions of dollars in royalties so that Canadian consumers and industry can benefit from prices below world level and so that the federal government can afford to cushion the effects of Alberta's fiscal capacity on other provinces through equalization and other federal transfers.

Revenue is an important element in this dispute, but it is secondary. Power is the real prize. Money may be power, but power is much more than money. It is the capacity to determine the future course of a society. Premier Lougheed openly proclaims that he and the prime minister are fundamentally engaged in a struggle for power. The question is this: Who will shape Alberta's—and Canada's— energy future and, more broadly, its economic future?

In addition to a rapid price increase to near world levels, energy-producing provinces desire Ottawa's guarantees that extraordinary powers will not be invoked in this field. Alberta is deeply apprehensive about possible application of the emergency or declaratory power to take over oil production. Producing provinces also want jurisdiction over at least some interprovincial and international trade (discussed below). The federal government would like to retain all of these powers but is willing to share or surrender some of them and to agree to more rapid price increases as part of a constitutional reform package in which Ottawa might win guarantees of a strengthened economic union.

The excess fiscal capacity of Alberta has prompted concern about long-range implications of the province's wealth. Gratuitous suggestions of how its revenues might be spent have been offered. Ontario has recommended that Alberta respect the "spirit of equalization" by contributing half of Ottawa's equalization costs each year (nearly C$2 billion in 1981). Alberta has declined, but the province is now lending substantial sums of money to other provinces at attractive interest rates. Several "have not" provinces have taken out loans, and this practice may mushroom in the near future. There is concern about the leverage Alberta may enjoy in future intergovernmental bargaining when other provinces have become (or wish to become) heavily in debt to the richest province.

The offshore resource issue has become contentious now that an apparently large oil field has been discovered off long-impoverished Newfoundland. Offshore resources are under federal jurisdiction in

Canada's constitution. Newfoundland demands the same ownership rights over "its" oil that Alberta possesses. Most other provinces support Newfoundland and want the same offshore ownership rights. (Eight of the ten provinces have coastlines.) The federal government, fearing another Alberta, rejects such claims and insteads offers Newfoundland royalties equivalent to Alberta's until (and only until) Newfoundland ceases to be a "have not" province. Friction between Ottawa and Newfoundland over this matter will continue to sour the atmosphere of federal–provincial relations unless (or until) Ottawa capitulates or a compromise can be worked out.

ECONOMIC UNION AND FOREIGN INVESTMENT

Like other federations Canada always has taken for granted its status as an economic union. However, a widening network of provincial impediments to the unhindered flow of capital, labor, and goods is calling the economic union into question. Several provinces insist upon advancing their own economic interests, at the expense of their neighbors if necessary. Ottawa deplores this trend and is attempting to reassert federal economic supremacy. After the energy resource issue, this is the most contentious federal–provincial question in Canada today.

Federal officials and Canadian businessmen object to a variety of restrictive provincial laws. Ottawa especially dislikes Newfoundland's condition that its residents be hired first for offshore oil drilling, Prince Edward Island's limitations on land ownership by nonresidents, Quebec's preferential hiring requirements for construction firms and its 15 percent premiums to provincially based government suppliers, and Alberta's legislation permitting the government to forbid the sale of oil and gas outside the province. J. E. Newall, president of the Canadian Manufacturers' Association, regrets the limitations on labor mobility in Newfoundland and Quebec, as well as differences in certification and licensing of crafts and skilled trades, ten separate and often conflicting sets of rules for the trucking industry, and natural resource incentives that encourage processing inside the producing provinces. Newall recommends that provinces surrender some economic powers in the interest of mobility, standardization, and efficiency.[4]

In an effort to remedy these problems, the federal government has proposed the strengthening of Section 121 of the British North America Act. This section now assures free mobility of goods alone. Ottawa suggests that services, capital, and persons be included. Federal officials regard existing provincial restrictions as objectionable but tolerable. They fear, however, that their sudden appearance and diffusion may portend a blizzard of protective and (in time) retaliatory measures. Ottawa's threshold of tolerance has not been specified, but the Ontario government considers the European Community's level of integration to be a benchmark below which Canada's economic union must not fall.

Provincial response to the federal proposal is mixed. Alberta and Quebec (under the Parti Québécois) oppose any strengthening of economic union on principle. Saskatchewan objects to the proposal because it would place in the hands of judges the power to determine the limits of provincial efforts to protect economic interests. Saskatchewan believes that these issues involve economic and social objectives that should be handled by elected leaders. Its recommendation, supported by Newfoundland, is a (possibly annual) federal–provincial review of economic union in a cooperative spirit. Ontario sides with the federal government on this and most economic issues in the present period.

Bargaining on economic union is inextricably linked to the issue of regulation of interprovincial trade. Ottawa does not wish to lose this power, but it is now willing to let provinces legislate in this area provided that federal paramountcy is maintained. That is, federal laws would supersede provincial legislation. Provinces welcome this increase in their powers, but Ottawa wants it to be part of a package that includes strengthening of Section 121. Several provinces will not accept the package. The 1980s likely will bring provinces concurrent powers over interprovincial trade, whether or not Ottawa realizes its objective of a stronger economic union.

The question of foreign investment in Canada is bound up in this controversy. The FIRA, established in 1974, must approve all new foreign investment and takeovers of Canadian enterprises. Ottawa is now increasing its scope by authorizing FIRA to scrutinize existing foreign investment as well. Most provinces, especially in the West, oppose federal efforts to impede investment from any source, or to interfere in provincial economies in any way. J.E. Newall, an opponent of FIRA like most Canadian businessmen, believes that the agency has retarded investment in the West, Quebec, and the Maritimes. He suggests that Ottawa at least consult with leaders of affected provinces before the agency rules on investment applications.[5] Most provinces support this proposal.

An opposing school in the academic community condemns FIRA on the grounds that it undermines Canadian independence by facilitating foreign investment. After all, FIRA approves over 90 percent of takeover applications. Political sociologist Wallace Clement, an expert on Canada's corporate elite, charges that the agency encourages takeovers by legitimizing them and by making it easier to push applications through by integrating into one place all possible barriers to investment.[6] Although these arguments enjoy some credibility in the academic world, they are rejected by both supporters and opponents of FIRA in the federal and provincial governments and by the business community.

The review agency will continue to exist. Even with its seemingly increased powers, it will not seriously impede investment or takeovers. In its seven years FIRA appears not to have restricted foreign investment unduly, if at all. The federal government, which is not firmly committed to economic nationalism in any case, is well aware of the opposition of the provinces, the business community, and much of its own senior bureaucracy to major limitations on investment. Besides, the financial resources that would be required to "patriate" the Canadian economy are not at Ottawa's disposal.

FISCAL RELATIONS AND ARRANGEMENTS

Unfortunately for national unity, the federal government's fiscal policies have a highly differential impact on different parts of Canada. Ontario and Quebec accommodate most of the labor-intensive, recession-prone manufacturing industry; the Atlantic and western regions are more oriented to primary industries. Accordingly, when Ottawa pursues a tight-money, inflation-fighting fiscal policy, the results are negative for Central Canada but are generally favorable elsewhere, especially on the Prairies. However, as might be expected, this is not the policy approach of most Canadian governments.

In the Canadian tradition, a middle-of-the-road policy that satisfies no one has been the general rule. Still, under Trudeau there has been some preference for an expansionary and free-spending approach intended to minimize unemployment and maximize votes in populous Ontario. (The Economic Council of Canada's finding that variations in federal fiscal policy affect Ontario most profoundly, in both directions, may influence Ottawa's policymaking.[7]) The inflationary consequences of such a policy are deeply resented on the Prairies, where unemployment is minimal even in recessionary periods.

At times, particularly during periods of minority governments, Prime Minister Trudeau has deferred to labor-union-backed New Democrats in policymaking on fiscal and other issues. There does exist a comparatively right-wing, business-oriented element in the Liberal party epitomized by former Finance Minister John Turner. But unless Turner becomes prime minister (which is possible), the Liberals are likely to perpetuate western alienation from themselves and from Ottawa over federal fiscal policy. The federal Progressive Conservatives take more of a tight-money approach, but how often are they in power?

National unity is not the only victim of recent fiscal policies and intergovernmental disputes over them. Overall economic performance also has suffered. The Economic Council of Canada has suggested that economic performance might improve if fiscal policies were applied regionally, expansionary in the East and contractionary in the West.[8] So far this has not been attempted by Ottawa, where such an approach is thought to be nearly impossible to implement. It remains a conceivable future strategy, if only because of its potential to mitigate regional resentments against the federal government and against confederation itself. Even so, the further problem of a lack of federal–provincial coordination of economic policy and strategy remains. Not once have federal and provincial ministers of finance made a serious effort to harmonize their policies, presumably because they are only too aware of their intractable differences in interests and priorities. Coordination of eleven annual budgets is not a realistic prospect. Such a development, however desirable, would appear to be another victim of Canada's exasperatingly unequal distribution of industry and natural resources.

For several decades the federal government pursued a policy of constructive leadership (or, if you prefer, of blatant interference) in provincial social service jurisdictions. A succession of conditional grants permitted Ottawa to exercise influence over most health, welfare, and educational services. By the 1960s these grants were no longer acceptable to many provinces, notably Quebec. At present a program called Established Programs Financing offers provinces fully unconditional cash and income tax transfers to assist them to provide medical care, hospital insurance, and post-secondary education. Established Programs Financing expires in 1982. Difficult negotiations over its replacement or extension are underway, and the character of federal–provincial fiscal agreements in the coming decade is at stake.

Ottawa is under pressure to reassert itself in these jurisdictions. Canada's university community is deeply apprehensive that federal assistance will be reduced or ended altogether. The Association of Universities and Colleges of Canada (AUCC) has long preferred a major federal financial commitment and a direct federal influence over development of university programs to the not-so-tender mercies of provincial frugality and domination. However, the battle for federal funding may be over; for the provinces appear to have won definitive control of universities in the 1976 negotiations.

Provincial medical care schemes are also controversial. Their most objectionable feature for many Canadians is that in certain provinces (notably Ontario) doctors may "opt out" of the program and charge more than the prescribed fee. In this way universality of access, which the provinces assured Ottawa they would preserve, is undermined. There is pressure on Ottawa from the public and certain interests to make provinces restore universality.

All eleven governments seem to agree that, segments of the public notwithstanding, the federal surrender of influence over social services is irreversible. There is a feeling in Ottawa that since influence is lost in any case, why continue the huge (and rapidly escalating) cash and tax contributions, which reached C$8.7 billion in 1980? The likeliest prospect is a gradual federal retreat from these financial commitments, especially the cash payments. Provinces will object but cannot force federal participation. Federal withdrawal will compel provinces to search for new sources of revenue, although provinces soon will enjoy the power to levy indirect taxes. In this and other matters, some sort of deal is possible, however: for example, continued unconditional federal contributions in return for provincial agreement to guarantees of national economic union.

TARIFFS AND THE SEARCH FOR
AN INDUSTRIAL STRATEGY

Nowhere is Canada's tradition of making policy one step at a time, of compromise and of avoiding decisive choices, more evident—some would say more harmful to the national interest—than in the field of industrial policymaking. Decades of discussion have yet to result in an explicit industrial strategy for Canada.

Tariffs have always been controversial in Canada. Prime Minister Macdonald's national policy of 1879, which erected a "tariff wall" and encouraged the construction of branch plants of (foreign owned) manufacturing industries in Ontario and Quebec remains largely in force. It is still deeply resented in the Maritimes and the West. The tariff compels Canadians both east and west to pay higher prices for both imported and domestic goods than they would pay without the tariff, yet they realize little compensating benefit from employment in manufacturing. Today the province of Ontario alone accommodates 60 percent of Canada's manufacturing activity. Most of the remainder is located in Quebec. An interprovincial trade balance (or deficit) was computed recently for each province, assessing the tariff's annual impact on each provincial economy. Ontario's benefit approached $300,000,000, with Quebec's near $160,000,000. Every other province contributed to the $460,000,000 deficit, with British Columbia and Alberta leading the way.[9]

Federal officials are fully aware that the tariff still contributes mightily to Western alienation, but they find it difficult to devise an alternative. They know that any industrial policy will be highly controversial and will be strenuously opposed by powerful segments of the population. Yet deteriorating economic conditions in Canada and elsewhere, and the existence of three giant and potentially exclusionary trading blocs in the non–Communist world (the European Community, the United States, and the East Asian zone under Japanese economic influence), each of which has many times Canada's population, may force Ottawa to develop a more integrated economic policy in spite of its incrementalist tendencies.

Richard French, until recently a high official in the privy council office in Ottawa (the senior civil servants closest to cabinet ministers), contends that Canada has only two workable options as industrial strategies. The options are technological sovereignty and free trade. Technological sovereignty involves a massive federally funded and coordinated effort to improve the international competitiveness of Canadian owned industry in enterprises with a future. These include urban transit, electronics, aerospace industries, nuclear generation, and all aspects of oil and natural gas extraction and equipment. The objective is to make Canada competitive in a few specialized branches of high-technology industry, the goods and services of which will be in future world demand, while at the same time assuring that these companies are free of foreign control. Hopelessly uncompetitive industries, like much of the clothing and textile sectors, will have to fend for themselves. Technological sovereignty is nationalistic, somewhat statist, and centralistic in that it would require a great increase in federal expenditures and federal involvement in the national economy and in the provinces.[10]

The free trade position is deceptively simple. Free trade with at least the United States would be gradually introduced, bringing down consumer prices and forcing Canada's presently uncompetitive industry to become cost efficient. Much industry would undergo major transformation, although there is evidence that rationalization of Canadian industry, in respect to both export orientation and import penetration, has been proceeding steadily under the existing system.[11] Moreover, Canada is presently moving slowly toward free trade in GATT negotiations. Agreements at the Tokyo round provide that 65 percent of American imports will be duty free in 1988. Free trade advocates argue that since there is already a clear trend, why not follow it through to its logical conclusion?

The present cabinet is leaning slightly toward technological sovereignty. Herb Gray, minister of industry, trade, and commerce, has presented the cabinet with a blueprint for technological sovereignty in at least some of the sectors listed previously. The prime minister is now pursuing this general objective in the petroleum sector through "Petrocan" (Petro–Canada), the government's public oil company. The cabinet as a whole is lukewarm to Gray's proposal, but Liberal cabinets may be more receptive to technological sovereignty than to free trade. (The Conservatives have the opposite tendency.) The prime minister's personal views on this subject are unfathomable. Most senior civil servants, particularly in the Department of Finance, are incrementalists who resist all serious departures from established practice, including both technological sovereignty and free trade.

They could prove decisive in the long run. The Mandarins, as they are called, are thought to exercise great influence over divided cabinets.

Most provinces support free or at least freer trade, as might be expected. They have little manufacturing industry to lose. Ontario remains strongly opposed. A recent study by the Canadian Manufacturers' Association tends to support Ontario's concern that many Canadian industries, especially branch plants of American corporations, would not survive free trade. The same report indicates, however, that the overall balance sheet on the results of free trade is less clear and that as many Canadian businesses might emerge winners as losers. Its conclusion is that movement toward full free trade would be premature at this time. Unfortunately for advocates of free trade, the report also concedes that Canada would surrender a measure of political independence to the United States with free trade, as the Canadian socioeconomic policy environment would have to be brought into and kept in rough accord with that of the much larger neighbor. Among other things, Canada would be required to make wage and tax rates and welfare policies conform to American practices of the day and to follow all important changes in the United States with virtually identical changes in Canada.[12] Such a prospect might so offend the national pride of Canadians that free trade may be impracticable on that account alone.

If the Liberal party retains office for most of the coming decade, some movement (possibly halfhearted) toward technological sovereignty may be expected. A truly ambitious program will be implemented only if a prime minister committed to such a policy assumes office, if then. This is not likely to happen. Free trade is a still weaker prospect, even if the conservatives reassume office. Some tariff barriers will continue to be lowered in GATT negotiations. However, there is little enthusiasm in the civil service or the business community for the far-reaching changes in the manufacturing sector that free trade would require or for the uncertain future it would bring.

PROVINCIAL FOREIGN POLICIES

In recent years several provinces have expressed an interest in developing bilateral economic and cultural relationships with business clients and others outside Canada. The federal government is uneasy about such associations. Some of the most serious intergovernmental conflict in the 1980s may concern this subject.

Provinces that endorse the community-of-communities conception of Canada—above all, Quebec and the West—are determined to pursue their own destinies free from federal interference. These provincial destinies increasingly include the development of distinct economic interests, both inside and outside Canada and the realization of these interests through fully autonomous policymaking. For example, Alberta would like to sell its oil and natural gas to customers in the United States in return for commitments to build a petrochemical industry in the province. Alberta wishes to diversify its economy in accordance with its own priorities, through "clean" industries with good future prospects. The province complains that as long as Ottawa monopolizes international trade Alberta cannot realize its objective of diversification and the achievement of a "mature" economy. Other provincial governments advance similar views. Quebec has been seeking membership for itself, rather than for Canada, in *la Francophonie*, France's multinational association for cultural relations.

The federal response to provincial foreign policies is not the same as it is to provincial assertions of control over interprovincial trade. One major element of Ottawa's ongoing initiative in the economic sector is a firm discouragement of unilateral provincial foreign policies of any kind. The Quebec claims to members in Francophonie have always been denied, and it is the government of Canada and not Quebec that is represented at its meetings. Provinces may trade with foreign clients only with Ottawa's approval. For example, energy deals (such as hydroelectric sales) must be endorsed by the National Energy Board. Ottawa is unhappy enough with Alberta's aggressive American sales campaigns and does not wish to see provincial leverage in foreign dealings increase beyond present levels. However, some federal flexibility on this matter is possible as part of a constitutional reform package in which there are equivalent provincial concessions on matters important to Ottawa.

A promising relationship has arisen in recent years among governors of New England states and premiers of the five easternmost provinces. These executives have convened each summer since 1973. The meetings serve as a useful forum for exchanges of information on subjects of mutual interest, especially oil and hydroelectricity.

Governors in the market for Canadian energy exports may sound out the appropriate premier(s), but most export agreements are negotiated elsewhere. At least one participant in these meetings for several years considers them important and believes that it is only a matter of time before major deals are struck between states and provinces. Such arrangements will still require federal approval in the foreseeable future.

Some observers of Canadian federal–provincial relations believe that present trends toward increased provincial autonomy will eventuate in a new form of regionalism in North America. Political economist Garth Stevenson and others who favor an increase in federal economic powers predict that a continued shift of economic control to the provinces will result in provinces turning their backs on the rest of Canada and making arrangements with their American neighbors. This is already beginning in the West, where provinces are attracted to the booming western states. British Columbia will abandon Canada for the Pacific states and for American corporations, and so on across the continent, once provincial power renders the federal government superfluous.[13] Ottawa may share this view. Indeed, this may be one reason for the present reassertion of federal economic power. Stevenson and others of his nationalistic and centralistic tendency also assert that a weak and divided Canada suits the interests of American multinational corporations. They do not charge that American business interests, including those who covet Canadian natural resources, are actively interfering in federal–provincial relations to the provinces' benefit. Rather, they seem to perceive the Americans as vultures circling overhead, observing with satisfaction the increasing fragmentation of the country and thinking that their time will soon come.[14] The federal government may adopt this argument and use it to advance its public case for maintaining or, still better, increasing federal economic powers over interprovincial and international trade.

COMMUNICATIONS

Communications has traditionally been a federal prerogative. The Canadian Broadcasting Corporation (CBC) and its French language section, Radio–Canada, are federal crown corporations. Provinces are not involved in CBC activities or in licensing or interprovincial broad-

casting. In general, provinces are no longer willing to see this arrangement continue.

The separatist government of Quebec would like to exercise some influence over Radio-Canada. No federal government can accede to this. However, all provinces express an interest in regulation of the burgeoning cable systems and in playing some role in programming. Provincial governments in English-speaking Canada as well as Quebec are now assuming the role of protector and champion of community development programs and of each province's allegedly distinctive character and culture. Control over cable, they contend, is needed for them to carry out their cultural responsibilities.

Ottawa is likely to yield some ground on communications as on other noneconomic, broadly cultural matters. Federal officials concede that some decentralization in this field is inevitable. Provincial regulation of interprovincial cable systems through an interprovincial agency has already been offered by Ottawa and probably will be realized soon. Programming remains a point of contention. Provinces may or may not win concessions here, beyond a federal promise to consult annually on programming and related matters. Certain provinces—Quebec, Ontario, and Saskatchewan perhaps most of all—accord this matter great importance. Pressure for Ottawa to authorize a federal-provincial or interprovincial programming agency will continue until the provinces achieve satisfaction.

TRANSPORTATION

Transportation controversy has poisoned the atmosphere of federal-provincial relations since the nineteenth century. Westerners have long believed that national transportation policy, especially the rail freight rate structure, was deliberately designed (and has been perpetuated) to retard industrial development in their region. This policy has never been reversed, although some federal cabinets in recent decades (notably Prime Ministers John Diefenbaker's and Joe Clark's) have been headed by Westerners supposedly sensitive to western concerns. A standing joke in the West is that reform of railroad policy is ritualistically promised by each party in every election campaign but is never delivered.

Transportation issues are not usually a major topic of discussion at federal-provincial or constitutional conferences. Provinces do not

advocate any change in Ottawa's ability to regulate interprovincial freight or passenger transportation or in federal jurisdiction over airports and harbors. Yet it is well understood in the federal government that transportation has served and still serves as a major factor in Westerners' alienation.

There may soon be a comprehensive new federal initiative in the West. Federal officials are putting together a multibillion dollar package that may include transportation reforms; reversal of deteriorating soil conditions; increased water supply at a time of depleting availability; manpower programs to accommodate the flood of new arrivals (and new jobs) underway, particularly in Alberta.

Federal officials hope that these programs will demonstrate federal capacity to respond to regional economic conditions and will help to restore Western support for Ottawa. In this spirit provinces may be granted substantial powers over the implementation of these programs. Certainly these problems do exist: Ottawa anticipates that by 1986 Alberta alone will require over 300,000 new employees in the public and private sectors. When (and if) this massive federal initiative is eventually announced, we may expect much publicity for public relations reasons. Reaction from provincial governments is not easy to predict. It will depend on whether there is sufficient advance consultation (a chronic problem with past federal initiatives) on the extent of provincial implementation powers and on the cost of provincial participation. Still more difficult to foresee is public response, although it is hard to believe that Westerners will soon become advocates of federal power in transportation and related fields.

ENVIRONMENT

Environmental concerns so far have been generally free of intergovernmental contention. The sometimes bitter controversy in the United States over the relative merits of industrial development and a pristine environment has largely been absent in Canada, because Canada still lacks powerful, publicly supported environmentalist lobbies. Existing disagreements tend not to divide Ottawa and one or more provinces. Western provinces strongly desire the manufacturing and other industry they have traditionally lacked, and they do not always support the National Energy Board's environmental safeguards. Provinces seeking industrial development believe in lenient federal standards for themselves. Ottawa will modify some regulations if there is no other way to bring industry to an area that wants and needs it. There remains some possibility of serious disagreement in the future, especially if a particularly obnoxious polluter or pollution across provincial borders is involved.

For both the federal government and most provinces from Ontario eastward, the most crucial environmental problem at this time is acid rain, most of which is a byproduct of industry in the Ohio Valley, the Great Lakes, and Northeastern states. Thousands of Ontario lakes are already "dead." Worst affected is "cottage country," where wealthy Torontonians traditionally spend their summers. The Maritime provinces and northern New England are also seriously affected. It is true that acid rain in smaller quantities is inflicted on Americans by Canadian industry, but Canadians consider Canada to be the aggrieved party. Acid rain overshadows fisheries treaties in the consciousness of the Canadian public and is a major contemporary problem between Canada and the United States. Canadians want a cleanup, and soon. A provocative move in the opposite direction would feed anti-American sentiment in Canada. A calculated increase in the industrial use of coal upwind from susceptible Canadian lakes and forests through conversion of oil-fired plants would constitute such a provocation (although such conversions are under consideration in Canada as well). The two countries must reach an accord on this matter, the sooner the better.

REFORM OF THE ELECTORAL SYSTEM

Canada's electoral system and the uneven distribution of electoral support for the three parties have created two distinct yet closely related problems that are all the more serious because they have defied solution for so long. The first problem, which is universally recognized and lamented, concerns the single-member-district plurality electoral system imported from Britain for the House of Commons. In Canada this arrangement creates a pattern of legislative representation often highly disproportionate to the support of each party in the population.

Recent federal elections have left the Liberal party virtually unrepresented from the four western provinces. The conservatives have faced a similar predicament in Quebec through most of this century.

The House of Commons is the sole elective body in Ottawa; the prime minister and his cabinet colleagues are drawn from it. When a party assumes power with neither numbers nor quality from an important region of the country—an outcome that nowadays is a virtual certainty—it inevitably incurs resentment from that region. It is unfortunate enough when this resentment is directed against the ruling party ("They don't represent *us*"). In recent years this alienation has increasingly been directed against confederation itself, especially in the West. Because the Liberal party is nearly always in power, the West has suffered most from underrepresentation in the federal cabinet. When the numerical domination of Ontario and Quebec in the House of Commons because of their larger population is also noted, the basis for a severe problem of Westerners' alienation becomes clear.

A second result of the electoral system, less often discussed in Canada but striking to an American observer, is the prolonged period during which a particular "government" party remains in office in Ottawa and in some provinces. Federally, Liberals have formed the government for all but twenty-two years in this century and for all but nine months in the past eighteen years. Although some Canadians cannot agree whether the country enjoys a two-party or three-party system in federal elections, John Meisel, Canada's most respected psephologist, accurately labels it a "one party plus" system. The Ontario Progressive Conservative party has ruled the province for thirty-eight years without a break. In Alberta there has been one change of government in the past forty-five years. Seemingly permanent minority status for a federal or provincial party is highly undesirable. Its supporters become demoralized and bitter, and its leaders encounter serious problems in recruiting able candidates for hopeless electoral contests. Electoral failure quickly becomes self-perpetuating. The consequences for the "government" party are also regrettable. Governments too long in power characteristically display complacency, insensitivity, and arrogance. Westerners consider the attitude of the current Liberal government in Ottawa to be a case in point.

There are essentially two proposals for changing these circumstances: revision of the electoral system and Senate reform. Electoral reform probably would involve full or modified proportional representation. The Canada West Foundation, a private lobby that advances western interests, endorses modified proportional representation for the House of Commons, as do some other prominent individuals and groups.[15] With any sort of proportional system, several Liberals and Conservatives would be returned from each province that now elects monolithic one-party slates. If proportional representation were introduced in the provinces, the present extreme legislative overrepresentation (and underrepresentation) of some provincial parties would end. Unfortunately for this scheme, however, most proportional representation (although not the Canada West Foundation's proposal) would bring a nearly unbroken succession of comparatively unstable minority governments to Ottawa, to Ontario, and to some other provinces. Liberal and Conservative leaders in both Ottawa and the provinces firmly agree that minority government (which involves sharing power with a third party, usually the New Democrats) is an evil to be avoided. (Who can blame them?) Besides, proportional representation violates the ingrained single-member-district tradition. Strong opposition from all eleven governments assures that there is little hope for proportional representation in the foreseeable future.

SENATE REFORM

The second alternative to the existing system is reform or replacement of the Canadian Senate. The present Senate, which was originally intended to champion provincial and regional interests, evidently cannot serve this purpose in its present form. Senate reform had occasionally been discussed inconclusively when in 1978 British Columbia presented a thoroughly researched proposal for a revised Senate modeled on the German Bundesrat. British Columbians are impressed by the Bundesrat's "power to veto," which encourages Bonn to consult leaders of the Laender in advance of major policy initiatives. Subsequent discussions of Senate reform have largely centered on the merits of the British Columbia proposal.

The essence of British Columbia's argument is this: Canadians in several provinces feel unrepresented in Ottawa. The federal government can and does ignore their interests in policymaking. Under the existing electoral system the sense of alienation in several provinces will continue indefinitely. What is required is a second chamber (possibly to be called "House of the Provinces") comprising appointed representatives of provincial governments who must ratify certain federal actions before they can become effective. The most commonly proposed powers for a new Senate include ratification of the cabinet's appointments to federal regulatory boards, commissions, agencies, and the Supreme Court; of federal laws to be administered by the provinces; and of invocation of federal declaratory, spending, and emergency powers. The regulatory appointments are especially important, as Senate reform would give the provinces an opportunity to influence federal policy on energy, communications, transportation, fiscal and monetary policy, and other matters. Only such a new institution, it is claimed, will convince "hinterland" Canadians that someone in Ottawa speaks for them and can exercise real power on their behalf.

An excellent possibility exists that a reformed upper house will be established in the near future. Before that is done, however, several problems will have to be resolved. First, larger provinces want more representation for themselves than for smaller provinces, while smaller provinces favor equal representation for all. Second, some but not all provinces wish the new chamber to have the additional power to review all (or certain) federal legislation. Ottawa strongly opposes review powers for a provincially appointed body. Third, some provinces (Alberta, Quebec, New Brunswick, and possibly others) and the federal government are reluctant supporters of any kind of Senate reform. Ottawa's public price for accepting a new Senate is the power to appoint half of its members, or to have senators elected, possibly through proportional representation. Neither option is acceptable to most provinces. Premier Lougheed of Alberta also dislikes Senate reform. He prefers exercising power personally at first ministers' conferences, not indirectly through appointed representatives. Fourth, there is some question whether the present senators will accept their own political extinction.

These problems may somehow be resolved fairly soon. The premiers reached a "best efforts" consensus on a reformed Senate in 1980. Each province would appoint three representatives, and powers would be limited to the ratification function. Some provinces and Ottawa still harbor serious reservations and are not committed to the best efforts draft. Everyone finally seems to recognize, however, that no better proposal to compensate for the deficiencies of the electoral system may be available. The federal government is now willing to accept the best efforts proposal as an element in a larger package. Ottawa could then present its acquiescence as a concession that would require equivalent provincial concessions on other parts of the package (as on economic union). Agreement is not imminent, but by 1990 Canada finally may have a working upper house that will help to reduce feelings of alienation, resentment, and powerlessness in peripheral regions of the country.

To date, no major upper house reform proposal has recommended that the new body exercise treaty ratification or other powers infringing on the cabinet's freedom to maneuver in foreign policy. However, provincial veto power over appointments to the National Energy Board might favorably influence the province's ability to gain approval for energy sales to American customers.

INTERDELEGATION

One other potential reform theoretically could lessen regional alienation. It is interdelegation, or "special status for all," which is the delegation of one level of government's power over some matter to a government at a different level. Delegation could go in either direction and would be for a specified period. Interdelegation is not permitted in the existing constitution. If it were authorized the probable result would be a unique status for each province and a different relationship between Ottawa and each province. If certain provinces desire jurisdiction over, say, unemployment insurance, while others do not, all can be accommodated (with federal approval). The major argument for interdelegation is that large and wealthy provinces aspire to (and can afford to pay for) more responsibilities than the small, poorer provinces. Why not make everyone happy? At present most of the larger provinces think interdelegation is a good idea. The poorer provinces are not so sure, but the provinces reached a best efforts consensus in favor of interdelegation in 1980.

As we are aware, Prime Minister Trudeau strongly opposes special status in any form. This includes interdelegation. Trudeau feels that interdelegation would produce a chaotic checkerboard or patchwork pattern of federal and provincial responsibilities. Another objection is that if each province has different powers, how could votes and other activities of backbenchers and cabinet ministers in the House of Commons be distributed equitably? Federal tax legislation in particular would be a knotty responsibility to sort out in Ottawa if federal tax rates were different in each province.

If interdelegation ever comes, it will not be in the Trudeau era or anytime soon. Interdelegation in practice could have major implications for relations between Canada and the United States, as individual provinces conceivably could enjoy foreign trade and cultural powers now reserved for Ottawa. This is sheer and possibly idle speculation, however. The logistical and other drawbacks of special status for all make it an unlikely prospect at least in the foreseeable future. If interdelegation is seriously considered at all, it might be so narrowly circumscribed that it would have little impact on the distribution of powers or on the conduct of foreign relations.

SUMMARY AND CONCLUSIONS

Provincial governments have gained substantial ground at Ottawa's expense in the past two decades, largely because of irresistible "national" feeling in Quebec. In the competitive maneuvering and compromising that characterize the eleven-cornered negotiations of executive federalism, Prime Minister Trudeau has made only those concessions to provincial demands that he considers necessary to keep Quebec in confederation. Although these concessions have been offered to all provinces, they are often not responsive to the demands of the western provinces. Many English-speaking Canadians, Westerners especially, resent what they think is Trudeau's preoccupation with Quebec at the expense of their own distinctive interests. This resentment, exacerbated by Westerners' basically accurate perception that they are unrepresented in the federal government, has contributed to the popularity of the highly decentralized community-of-communities interpretation of the Canadian federation.

Canadian political leaders recognize that Ontario contains about one-third the House of Commons constituencies and about one-half the closely contested "swing" ridings that determine the outcome of every election. Federal policies to minimize domestic energy prices, to monitor foreign investment, to enforce an economic union, to maintain a tariff that protects domestic manufacturing, and to perpetuate transportation policy, largely serve Ontario's interests and antagonize Westerners. Yet Ottawa knows that major changes in these federal policies would endanger the support in Ontario that all governments must maintain to survive. Accordingly, prime ministers face a dilemma: the flexibility needed to accommodate western grievances may be politically dangerous.

Prime Minister Trudeau would like to arrest the trend toward increased provincial power. Recent federal initiatives, notably those in respect to enforcement of Canada's economic union and to the partial nationalization of the energy sector, suggest an effort to reassert federal primacy in economic (but not necessarily other) fields. Only the energy policy may succeed in the long run. Trudeau's reputation with future generations may rest on his (at least temporary) suppression of Quebec separatism, his assertion of Canadian nationalism in energy matters, and his achievement of constitutional reforms like the charter of rights, rather than on the protection or advancement of federal authority generally. Overall, the well-established centrifugal evolution of the exercise of political power—at least in respect to domestic and international trade, energy resources, fiscal relations, communications, and possibly Senate reform—should continue throughout the 1980s, whoever heads the federal government.

As Prime Minister Trudeau approaches the close of his remarkable and prolonged career at the center of Canadian affairs, it is instructive to ponder the changes that will and will not follow his departure. The first matter to consider is the future course of intergovernmental relations and distribution of power. The shift of power to the provinces will continue in "cultural" areas and, despite federal resistance, in economical areas as well. Notwithstanding the personality-oriented media's focus on Trudeau as the personification of federal initiatives, his policies generally have been what might be expected of any Liberal government. His successors of both parties are unlikely to change course dramatically. Such a move would be incompatible with Canada's incrementalist tradition. The likeliest major change in the near future may be a reexamination of language policies or some form of special status for one or more provinces. Language and special status are the subjects where firm conviction has kept Trudeau from a traditionally Canadian compromise. Everything considered, the Canada of 1990 may conform to the community-of-communities model than to the one of a strong central government.

The first ministers' conferences (executive federalism) will continue, whatever institutional change is effected. To the extent that Prime Minister Trudeau's temperament and conduct of intergovernmental diplomacy have fostered deadlocks at these sessions, future meetings may prove more harmonious. However, there are enduring differences in economic interests among the eleven governments, and between the community-of-communities philosophy of several provinces and the perspective of a federal government under any conceivable leader. We must note the natural inclination of political leaders not to negotiate away more of their own personal power or their base of electoral support than they deem necessary.

Prime Minister Trudeau inherited western alienation already firmly entrenched in history (or mythology). The conflicting priorities of energy-producing provinces on the one hand, and of Ottawa and Ontario on the other, have assured the exacerbation of regional tension in the 1970s and beyond. Although the media portray the prime minister as the chief cause of western nationalism, he might just as accurately be described as its major target. Some people may be western nationalists because they dislike Trudeau and his policies, but many dislike Trudeau and his policies because they are western nationalists. Trudeau's departure may be necessary, but is not sufficient, to reduce regional tension. Incompatibility of interests between Ottawa and western provinces (and between Ontario and western provinces) will long survive Trudeau and will continue to bedevil intergovernmental policymaking in future years. In short, the prime minister himself is not the essential problem. His retirement may improve the climate for negotiations, but there is no basis for optimism that it will fundamentally affect their substance.

Some change in Canada's political institutions is likely in the 1980s. Although many Canadians recognize that the British electoral system hinders the resolution of regional grievances, electoral reform is unlikely. The economic importance of relatively sparsely populated provinces due to their energy riches, in addition to obstacles to other reforms, make a revised (or replaced) Senate the best possibility. This new body may exercise little more than ratification powers over some federal appointments and actions. It will in no way supersede the first ministers' meetings where much intergovernmental policy is made or lessen provincial demands for legislative power. Provincial premiers have "seen Paree" and will accept neither a loss of their hard-won power to participate personally in the making of national policy nor limitation of their ability to exercise autonomous authority in a multitude of economic and cultural jurisdictions. Senate reform does offer an opportunity to improve the policy environment by increasing Ottawa's sensitivity to regional opinion and by convincing people outside Central Canada that their interests are being advanced inside the federal government. If we perceive Canada's policy environment as a dynamic interaction between an inappropriate institutional structure and the conflicting interests of eleven governments, change of the former may facilitate accommodation of the latter. Even so, Senate reform is no panacea for Canada's problems. Closest attention must still be focused on first ministers' conferences, where the crucial policy decisions will continue to be made.

Canada's foreign policies and domestic policies with implications for the United States and American business interests are no more likely to change dramatically in the post–Trudeau era than are other aspects of policy. Provinces will continue to press for power to regulate international trade and for other concessions. Because of the conviction in Ottawa that foreign affairs is a federal preserve, provinces may advance in this field only as part of a package that includes something for Ottawa. Compelling forces opposed to major policy changes, not to mention economic and fiscal concerns, make free trade, comprehensive technological sovereignty, and serious limitations on foreign investment most unlikely. Partial patriation of the petroleum industry is already underway, but it probably will not be accompanied by comparable policies outside the energy sector.[16] All in all, Canada should remain an attractive home for investment. This assumes, of course, that foreign governments and businesses can accept the unsettled character of intergovernmental relations and of the federation itself. American business also will have to be forbearing when caught in crossfire during Ottawa's "nationalistic" initiatives directed at the provinces.

Canadians retain a favorable impression of the United States as a country and as the leader of the non–Communist bloc, and of Americans as individuals. Many Canadians feel emotionally closer to Americans in nearby states than to Canadians in other parts of the country. Efforts to unleash latent anti–American sentiment probably will not succeed (but see below). We may anticipate a friendly political and business climate in 1990.

Robert Thompson, a one-time leader of the Social Credit party noted for his malapropisms, once observed that the Americans are our best friends and our closest allies whether we like it or not. This much ridiculed statement is inadvertently insightful: the intimate political, economic, and military relationship between the two countries is not wholly a matter of choice for Canadians. Any relationship between a self-perceived mouse and an elephant has its awkward aspects, one of which is the acute sensitivity of the smaller and more vulnerable party. United States' government and business policymakers should keep Canadian realities in mind. Canadians want progress toward an acid rain cleanup. Canadian nationalism in the energy sector will endure, as will the related Canadian apprehension about a "North American accord" that would give the United States ready access to Canadian resources. It would be counterproductive for United States business or government to apply pressure that could be interpreted as bullying or intimidation. There are political groups in Canada, including an element of the Liberal party, that would eagerly exploit the ensuing anti–American sentiment. In the long run the best interests of both countries will be served if Canadians perceive nonexploitative goodwill to be the hallmark of United States government and business policy.

NOTES TO CHAPTER 2

1. The best discussion of the evolution of federal–provincial fiscal relations is D.V. Smiley, *Canada in Question: Federalism in the Eighties*, 3rd ed. (Toronto: McGraw–Hill Ryerson, 1980).

2. For Quebec's recent evolution, see Kenneth McRoberts and Dale Posgate, *Quebec: Social Change and Political Crisis*, rev. ed. (Toronto: McClelland and Stewart, 1980).

3. Trudeau's best known writings of the 1960s are contained in his *Federalism and the French Canadians* (Toronto: Macmillan of Canada, 1968).

4. J.E. Newall, "Industry's Stake in Constitutional Reform," mimeograph, Canadian Manufacturers' Association, Toronto, August 19, 1980.

5. Ibid.

6. Clement's most appropriate study is *Continental Corporate Power: Economic Elite Linkages between Canada and the United States* (Toronto: McClelland and Stewart, 1977).

7. Economic Council of Canada, *Living Together: A Study of Regional Disparities* (Ottawa: Supply and Services Canada, 1977).

8. Ibid.

9. Ironically, it was Ontario that publicized these figures, in an effort to convince Quebec that confederation has been in Quebec's interests. E.W. Darcy McKeough, *Interprovincial Trade Flows, Employment, and the Tariff in Canada* (Toronto: The Queen's Printer for Ontario, April 19, 1977).

10. Richard D. French, *How Ottawa Decides: Planning and Industrial Policy Making, 1968–1980* (Toronto: Canadian Institute of Economic Affairs, 1980).

11. The findings of a study by the Canadian Manufacturers' Association are reported to the Canadian Senate in Senate of Canada, *Proceedings of the Standing Senate Committee on Foreign Affairs*, Tuesday, December 9, 1980 (Ottawa: Queen's Printer, 1980).

12. Ibid.

13. Garth Stevenson, "Canadian Regionalism in Continental Perspective," *Journal of Canadian Studies*, 15 (no. 2, Summer 1980).

14. Provinces with weak bargaining power would like to see such fragmentation averted. The premier of a small eastern province believes that large provinces are outmaneuvering the federal government in their negotiations with business and government in the United States. He proposes that Ottawa triple its staff in Washington and exercise greater initiative and aggressiveness in its relations with Americans.

15. David Elton and Roger Gibbins, *Electoral Reform: The Need is Pressing, The Time Is Now* (Calgary: Canada West Foundation, 1980).

16. A serious blow to the nationalist and centralist forces, which will become evident in the 1980s, is the gradual transformation of the federal New Democrats from an Ottawa and Ontario-based party to a western based champion of provincial rights.

3 U.S.-CANADA ENERGY RELATIONS

Edward F. Wonder

Over the past decade both the United States and Canada have become increasingly preoccupied with energy self-sufficiency and vulnerability to disruption of oil supplies. Both countries contemplate substantial investments in very expensive and technologically challenging energy projects, and in both countries government policies, especially in the areas of pricing and regulation of industry activity, have been controversial. In Canada, however, the energy policy debate has gone a major step further, becoming a central element in the definition of federal–provincial relations and of overall U.S.-Canadian relations. The Trudeau government's National Energy Program stands at the center of this debate. In the process, a profound and long-standing transformation of U.S.-Canadian energy relations has occurred.

U.S. perspectives on U.S.-Canadian energy relations have tended to focus on the size of Canada's energy resources and have frequently assumed that a considerable portion of those resources would eventually find their way to American customers. Indeed, the premise that there is a "continental logic" at work, rationalizing energy flows along north-south lines, has been a tempting one. Upon closer examination, however, several points become clearer. First, an unqualified view of Canada's energy resources, without regard to the technical, economic, and political factors affecting their development, can be very misleading. Second, the politics of energy policy in Canada have

left the basic economic and political ground rules of energy development in Canada very unsettled, posing a substantial impediment to
major new energy projects. Finally, rather than a major expansion
of oil and gas exports or "continentalist" cooperation, let alone
integration of energy markets, the most likely prospect for U.S.-
Canadian energy relations, unless governments in both countries act
to avoid it, is conflict over energy and energy-related issues.

The supply relationship between the two countries has changed
considerably over the past decade. U.S.-Canadian oil and gas relations prior to the 1970s were based on a mutual desire to assure
access to markets in order to encourage domestic production. For
Canada this meant a policy of exporting to the United States, while
in the United States this need justified a quota system to limit imports, which was not applied to Canada until 1970. In 1973, the
peak year of Canadian oil exports to the United States, Canada supplied 17 percent of U.S. gross oil imports. By mid–1979 the Canadian share of U.S. oil imports had fallen to 5 percent and has continued to fall as oil exports are phased out. It is worth noting that as
the Canadian and Venezuelan shares of a burgeoning U.S. oil import
market declined in the early 1970s, the position of Middle Eastern
and African suppliers increased.

The primary concern of both countries in the 1970s, however, has
been access not to markets, but to supply. For Canada this has meant
a strategy of displacing foreign with domestic supply and reducing
exports where they interfere with that goal. The reduction in exports
has been the most dramatic in the oil sector, where only heavy oil
that could not find a Canadian market was unaffected. Gas exports
have held steady, and while exports of new volumes have recently
been authorized, Canadian needs may grow if domestic use of natural
gas expands in order to displace imported oil or if there is a decline
in the domestic supply of oil.

Change has not been confined to supply relationships. The linkages between energy and other bilateral issues are becoming more
sensitive. This is especially true of trade and investment relations,
where Canadian desires for access to U.S. markets for processed raw
materials, such as petrochemicals, and for a reduction of U.S. ownership of the Canadian oil and gas industries are potential sources of
conflict. Environmental relations, where the long-range transport of
air pollutants from mid–American coal-fired generating plants is
attracting increasing Canadian attention, may also be becoming
touchier.

Canada clearly does not have the ability to "solve" the problem of U.S. dependence on insecure oil imports. Nevertheless it is likely that energy and energy-related issues, especially investment, will occupy a prominent place in the bilateral agenda. Regional dependence in the United States on Canadian gas, the construction of the Alaskan gas pipeline across Canadian territory, the treatment accorded U.S. energy investment in Canada, and the importance of energy to the political structure of Canada necessarily mean that the United States must be vigilant with respect to the energy policies and problems of its northern neighbor.

Several questions guide the discussion of U.S.–Canadian energy relations presented here:

- How significant are Canadian energy resources, and what are the potential constraints on their development?

- How does the Canadian policy process affect domestic energy and export policies?

- To what extent will exports to the United States occupy an important position within the federal–provincial bargaining process and in the national energy policy that process might produce?

- What are the energy development and marketing options facing Canada, and what are their implications for the United States?

- What are the factors and interests affecting Canadian energy pricing policies, and what are the potential consequences of these policies for the pace of energy development and demand growth?

- What will be the nature of the Canadian contribution to U.S. energy supply in the future?

- To what extent will other bilateral issues, such as trade, investment, and environment, develop a more explicit energy content?

- Finally, what are the prospects for future energy cooperation?

THE CONTEXT OF CANADIAN ENERGY POLICY: RESOURCES AND POLITICS

Resources

Two points are particularly important in considering the Canadian energy resource position. The first is the range of uncertainty in resource data, especially for frontier regions, and a tendency toward conservatism on the part of the federal government in appraising these resources. The second is that major exploration and production activity in the future will tend to concentrate on the so-called frontier areas of the Beaufort Sea, High Arctic, and offshore East Coast, as well as the Alberta tar sands, where significant climatic, technical, and transportation problems, to say nothing of the cost and investment requirements, must be overcome. In any event, substantial lead times on a number of fronts will be dominant factors in determining the level and timing of production in frontier areas.

Crude Oil. Canadian conventional oil fields can be classified in two categories: the established producing areas south of the sixtieth parallel; and the frontier areas north of the sixtieth parallel and the offshore areas east of Newfoundland. The established producing areas are located in Alberta, Saskatchewan, British Columbia, and to a much lesser extent in western Manitoba.

The last official estimate of Canadian oil supply and requirements was issued by the National Energy Board (NEB) in September 1978. (The NEB is currently revising these estimates.) The NEB in 1978 placed recoverable conventional light and heavy oil reserves at 5.7 billion barrels, with another 5.4 billion (2.3 billion light, 3.12 billion heavy) in reserve additions, bringing the total recoverable conventional crude to over 11 billion barrels.[1] These reserves are in the established producing areas. Far more important are the resources located in frontier, offshore, and tar sands areas. Industry and government officials agree that frontier, offshore, and tar sands resources are the key to anything resembling energy self-sufficiency for Canada. Briefly, the prospects for these areas are as follows:

- Canadian Beaufort Sea. Geologic estimates of the Beaufort Sea basin reach 30–40 billion barrels. Dome Petroleum has set a production target of 200,000 barrels per day (b/d) by 1985 and 750 b/d by 1990, delivered by tanker and later by pipeline. Estimated development costs to reach 1990 target are in the area of $25 billion.[2]

- East Coast offshore. Estimates of the potential range from 7.4 billion barrels (Department of Energy, Mines, and Resources) to 10 billion off Newfoundland and another 10 billion off Labrador (Acquitaine Oil estimate). Costs per barrel in the Hibernia field are twice that of North Sea oil. Gulf Canada estimates that 300,000 b/d could be available from Hibernia by 1990 if priced at the world level.

- Alberta tar sands. Discovered resources of 931 billion barrels, but due to low recovery rate may yield only 80–190 billion barrels of upgraded crude. Production capacity could exceed 750,000 b/d by 1995, surpassing production of conventional light crude in established areas. Significant constraints include price levels, investment required (possibly $40 billion to achieve a 1 million b/d capacity) and labor and equipment availability.[3]

The foregoing data represent corporate estimates. Speaking before the natural resources and public works committee of the Canadian House of Commons on February 10, 1981, D.F. Sherwin, director of resource geology at the Department of Energy, Mines, and Resources, estimated potential recoverable oil in the Beaufort Sea–Mackenzie Delta area to be 9.4 billion barrels, in East Coast offshore areas to be 7.4 billion barrels, and in the Arctic Islands area to be 4.3 billion barrels.

Natural Gas.   Canadian gas fields are located in the same general region as the oil fields. Moreover, gas appears to be more abundant than oil in the frontier regions. The NEB's gas reserve estimates, as of February 1979, are presented in Table 3–1. The NEB in December 1979 revised its estimate of discovered conventional reserves in Western Canada, raising that figure to 72 trillion cubic feet (Tcf). The other estimates remained unchanged.[4]

As was the case with oil, there are new or potential producing areas that could force revision of NEB forecasts but that are not now producing because of a lack of transportation or because they are not yet developed. In the conventional producing areas, the potentially most significant such area is Deep Basin in Alberta. The National Energy Board so far has been very cautious in treating Deep Basin and in 1979 credited it with only 1 Tcf of established reserves.[5] Canadian Hunter, by far the most bullish source of data on this field, claims on the other hand that 440 Tcf can be recovered at various levels of price and technology, with 50 Tcf at today's levels.[6] This estimate is regarded as highly speculative by other companies, whose own estimates are significantly lower. A figure of 7 Tcf for proved reserves in Deep Basin is now accepted by many. The important fact

Table 3-1. Canada's Discovered Gas Resources and Estimated
Additions, 1978, Trillion Cubic Feet.

	Discovered by End 1977	Additions, 1978–2000	Ultimate Potential
Conventional producing areas			
Western Canada	65.8	38.0	146
Ontario and other eastern Canada	0.3		1
Total	66.1	38.0	147
Frontier areas			
Arctic Islands, Mackenzie– Beaufort	14.5	34.0[a]	63[c]
East Coast offshore	–	18.0[b]	27
Other	–	–	6
Total	14.5	52.0	96

Source: National Energy Board, Canadian Natural Gas – Supply and Requirements, Ottawa, February 1979, pp. 8–10, 32–34.

a. Industry figures.
b. Newfoundland forecast, 90 percent probability.
c. Geological Survey of Canada, 90 percent probability.

is that the higher Deep Basin estimates do not yet rest on a solid foundation of drill data.

Production in the frontier areas could compensate for decline in conventional areas. Dome Petroleum's estimate of 320 Tcf for the ultimate potential in the Beaufort Sea overshadows estimates made by other sources.[7] In the Arctic Islands, Panarctic expects to identify reserves of 30 Tcf by 1981, with 20 Tcf needed to justify a pipeline. Established Arctic Island reserves are currently 16 Tcf. Panarctic believes 60 Tcf can be proved in the Arctic Islands in the next fifteen years, or nearly the same level currently proven in conventional areas.[8]

None of this will make much difference if there is no means of bringing the gas to market. Several projects to transport this gas by pipeline or LNG tanker are currently under study. In all cases the availability of a market is of key importance to the timing and magnitude of production in these areas. This raises the issue of whether some exports at the beginning stage of production could accelerate the pace at which these fields could be developed. Companies developing oil and gas on the frontier foresee the use of tankers to move these resources to market as early as possible in order to generate the cash flow necessary to expand production to the point where pipelines become economical.

The NEB has refused to include supply estimates from frontier areas in its forecasts, since this gas is not yet deliverable to market. Although there is no official NEB estimate of frontier supply capability, corporate estimates for this area range from Dome's high estimate of 3,364 million cubic feet per day (MMcf/d) from the Mackenzie Delta–Beaufort Sea area delivered in 1995, and another 2,700 MMcf/d from the Arctic Islands, to Imperial's more representative estimate of 1,972 MMcf/d from the Mackenzie–Beaufort region in 1995 and 2,800 MMcf/d from the Arctic Islands.[9]

Coal.   In contrast to other resources, coal is more widely distributed throughout Canada, although actual production is concentrated in Alberta (over 40 percent), British Columbia (30 percent), and Saskatchewan (16 percent). Canadian coal resources are on the order of 260 billion tons, but only 2 percent of this (5 billion tons) is economically recoverable. Steam coal accounts for about 88 percent of economically recoverable resources.

Canadian coal production more than doubled between 1970 and 1978, when the total reached 37 million tons. Utility demand for steam coal may now be the greatest incentive for increased production. Metallurgical coal, nearly all of which is exported, mainly to Japan, was more important in the early 1970s. In 1978 coal production was nearly evenly divided between the two types, with steam coal accounting for 55 percent. A very ambitious fourfold increase in coal production is projected for 1990, with the steam proportion growing to 70 percent.

Potential constraints on this expansion include rising production and transportation costs, environmental regulation for both mining and air quality, and higher provincial royalty rates. Major factors governing the production rate will be utility demand and the comparative costs of using western Canadian or eastern U.S. coal in the Ontario Hydro system. Prairie province utilities will likely use local coal.

Although Canadian production of steam coal did not meet demand in 1976, the imbalance between supply and demand is expected to be restored in the early 1980s and remain positive in the early 1990s. Nevertheless, U.S. coal will likely retain its transportation cost advantages in Ontario markets, with the result that some surplus Canadian coal may be exported. Present long-term contracts for future deliveries of U.S. coal amount to about 13 million short tons per year. Some blending of Alberta and U.S. coal will occur in Ontario, but this is limited by technical constraints.

Uranium. Canada possesses substantial uranium resources. The largest deposits lie in southern Ontario and in northern Saskatchewan. Canada ranks second to the United States in uranium resources in the non–Communist world. Table 3–2 presents the most recent uranium resource estimates from the Canadian Department of Energy, Mines, and Resources. Canada also may possess 1.2 million metric tons of speculative resources in addition to the categories in Table 3–2.

Production capacity may reach 12.3 short tons uranium per year (stu/yr) in 1985 and 15 stu/yr in 1990. Canadian demand, however, has fallen sharply due to a downturn in future reactor orders in Canada. Total operating capacity by 1990 at most will be 14,455 megawatts electricity (MWe).

The Canadian uranium industry developed in response to export demand (the U.S. and U.K. weapons programs) and will remain predominantly export-oriented. The industry received a nearly fatal shock when U.S. military purchases were phased out, starting in 1959. In the 1970s Canada was a leading member of an international uranium cartel arising in large part in response to the slack market resulting from the closure of the U.S. domestic market to foreign uranium. This ban will be lifted entirely by 1984, and U.S. utilities

Table 3-2. Canadian Uranium Resources, Thousands Tons.

	Measured	Indicated	Inferred	Prognosticated Plus Speculative[a]
Up to $130/kilograms uranium (kgu)	73	157	238	. . .
$130 to $200/kgu	4	25	90	. . .
Total	77	182	328	1,800

Source: Department of Energy, Mines, and Resources, *Uranium in Canada: 1979 Assessment of Supply and Requirements*, Ottawa, September 1980.

a. Minable at prices below $200/kgu.

have contracted for significant quantities of Canadian uranium. The prospects for this trade, however, may be influenced by several factors to be discussed later in this chapter.

Electricity.   Electricities across the border have existed since early in this century. Currently, 100 transmission lines, capable of handling 8 gigawatts electricity (GWe) of power, link the two countries. Over 50 percent of this transfer capacity ties Ontario to New York and Michigan. New lines will raise the total transmission capacity to 11 GWe by 1985. At that time, this level would constitute 1.4 percent of U.S. generating capacity, and 10 percent of Canadian capacity.[10] The United States imported nearly 20,000 gigawatts per hour (GWhr) of electricity from Canada in 1977 and over 31,000 GWhr in 1979 (29,000 GWhr net).

Cross-border sales provide several benefits, among which are reserve sharing, diversity exchanges (due to noncoincident peaking), surplus sales, cost reduction, economies of scale in generating plant, and coordinated planning through several regional electric reliability councils. How much electricity will be available for exports will depend upon electricity growth rates. Low growth would normally discourage additions of capacity, but the possibility of sales to the United States, where lead times for construction of new power plants are very long, could enable the "prebuilding" of plants in Canada in advance of domestic need, with the electricity sold to the United States and then gradually phased out as Canadian demand eventually increases.

The Political Environment

Numbers, of course, do not tell all the story. Canada would appear to be relatively well situated, at least in terms of potential self-sufficiency. What has eluded Canada during the 1970s and likely will continue to in the early 1980s is consensus on a national energy policy. Not only does this have adverse consequences for energy development; the absence of consensus between the federal government and the producer provinces saps the political strength of Canada.

Contributing to Canada's energy policy problems is a national political system that is ill-suited to the task of managing regional conflict within the country. Decisionmaking in federal–provincial relations is often the result of direct contacts between political leaders[11], each protecting his own turf. This process gives rise to an energy policy heavily influenced by politics and founded upon bargaining relationships unfolding at two levels: between federal and provincial governments and between consumer and producer provinces. Effective policymaking is often joint policymaking because the necessary policy instruments are shared and because each level has the capacity to frustrate the other. With no clear hierarchy, each side is tempted to tilt the balance against the other. Much of the current conflict between Alberta and the other producer provinces, on the one hand, and the federal government in Ottawa, on the other, can be traced to the current Trudeau government's strongly centralist strategy for strengthening the Canadian confederation.

The efforts of the producer provinces and the federal government to protect and extend their power are the dominant feature of energy policymaking in Canada. The British North America Act of 1867 (BNA) vests the ownership of natural resources and exclusive legislative jurisdiction over them in the provinces where they are located. The federal government by virtue of its jurisdiction over "the regulation of trade and commerce" can regulate interprovincial and international trade. The provinces can charge royalties and levy taxes on energy industries in their jurisdiction; the federal government can also levy taxes and can grant subsidies. However, neither royalties nor taxes can be so high as to prevent the other authority from exercising its valid authority by depriving it of necessary revenues. This principle figures prominently in the current dispute between Ottawa and the producer provinces over oil and gas taxes.

A double-licensing regulatory framework within Canada also reflects this federal–provincial division of power. The Alberta government as early as 1948 established a board to set guidelines for gas sales to customers outside the province and to license export applications (sales to other provinces as well as to the United States were both considered "exports"). Licensing of oil exports was added in 1969. Only gas in amounts surplus to that required to ensure a thirty-year supply (now twenty-five years) for Alberta could be licensed for export. Other producer provinces have similar boards.

A federal National Energy Board (NEB) was established in 1959 to regulate tariffs, tolls, and traffic on the interprovincial oil and gas pipelines and to license all international exports of oil, gas, and electricity. The purpose of the NEB was to strengthen the federal role in the natural gas trade, which previously had largely been preempted by the Alberta board. As was the case in Alberta, regulatory power was extended to oil much later (in 1970). The NEB is not an independent regulatory agency as such but makes recommendations to the cabinet through the minister of energy, mines, and resources. As a result, political considerations can and often do affect the ultimate disposition of NEB advice.

The issues with which the federal political system must contend stem in many respects from an uneven distribution of industry and natural resources that gives rise to sharply divergent regional economic interests. Ontario and to a lesser extent Quebec are the industrial centers of Canada, whereas oil and gas resources are concentrated in the Prairie provinces of Manitoba, Saskatchewan, and Alberta, which have 80 percent of proven oil and gas, as well as in British Columbia and the Northwest and Yukon territories. The provinces of Prince Edward Island, New Brunswick, Nova Scotia, and until recently Newfoundland, which has laid claim to offshore oil deposits, have lacked both.

A dominant underlying force in Canadian regionalism is dissatisfaction with the concentration of commercial influence in central Canada.[12] Issues in the taxation and exploitation of provincially administered natural resources as well as resentment at the slow spread of secondary industry outward from central Canada are sources of conflict between western Canada and Ottawa. The western grievance, dating back to the 1870s, that federal economic policy has enriched Ontario at western expense is evident in Alberta's response to recent federal energy policy initiatives such as the federal export tax on crude oil, oil and gas price controls, and the use of revenues generated by the export tax to subsidize higher priced imported crude in the Atlantic provinces and Quebec. Alberta perceives these initiatives as a continuation of the transfer of real resources from the provincial to the federal treasury and on to consumers in the eastern provinces, and as an unwarranted, even unconstitutional, federal intrusion into areas of provincial prerogative. This grievance is all the more ironic because higher oil and gas prices are shifting purchasing power toward the western provinces, with profound implications for the rate and location of future economic growth in Canada.[13]

The economic regionalism that is central to the politics of energy policy reflects a quite different set of preoccupations from those of

Québécois nationalism. However, regionalism and Québécors nationalism share a common relevance to national energy politics, in that they have encouraged a strong centralist response on the part of the Trudeau government to the questions of constitutional reform and the distribution of political power in Canada. This centralist thrust clashes directly with the countersentiment of greater regional autonomy implicit in much of Alberta's energy policy and apparent in the brief Clark government's approach to a number of energy policy issues in 1979, such as oil prices and Newfoundland's ownership claims.

Another element complicating energy policy is Canadian nationalism and specifically wariness of U.S. domination. The degree of penetration of Canada by U.S. interests is considerable. Seventy percent or more of various sectors of the oil and gas industry are foreign owned, as are 40 percent of coal production and 50 percent of uranium production, although the Canadian share of ownership in the oil and gas sectors has been creeping steadily upward toward 50 percent. Controlling foreign investment and energy exports have been prominant factors in government regulation of the energy trade and more recently in direct government participation in the energy industries.

At their most fundamental level, the economic issues of energy policy in Canada have fallen into two basic categories. The first category of issues focuses on the market price for oil and gas and on the related tax and royalty rates. The rates determine how much economic rent is collected, how much is given directly to the consumer by foregoing its collection, and the allocation among the federal government, producing provinces, and industry of the rent that is collected.[14] The second category of issues focuses on exploration, production, and marketing, especially the pace and location of production activity. The basic political issue is who—the federal or provincial governments or the industry—makes these decisions. Canadian export policy historically has in large part been a function of compromises made over these basic issues at different times.

The Energy Trade

Although a detailed examination of the history of U.S.-Canadian energy relations is beyond the scope of this chapter, it is worth recalling that during the 1950s and 1960s Canadian perspectives on energy relations with the United States were somewhat different from what they are now. Access to U.S. markets provided additional outlets for shut-in oil and gas production capacity in Alberta. The availability of cheaper imported oil, largely from Venezuela, for supplying eastern Canada, the attractive prices Canadian oil and gas could fetch in the United States, and the need for capital to develop the Alberta oil and gas industries made exports to the United States attractive to governments and industry alike. Indeed, the national oil policy announced in 1961 divided Canada into two markets, with those provinces east of Ontario supplied by imported oil and the rest of Canada supplied indigenously. Oil surplus to demand west of the "Ottawa Valley Line" was exported to the United States. Gas supply did not extend eastward beyond Toronto, making sizable quantities of gas also available for export.

Despite the development of oil and gas exports, Canada's attitude toward its energy dealings with the United States was somewhat schizophrenic. On the one hand, both the federal government and the producer provinces sought to secure access to the U.S. market to provide a broader base for developing the Canadian oil and gas industries. Although continentalism was never the declared aim of federal policy, Ottawa on several occasions negotiated with Washington to lift restrictions on U.S. imports of Canadian oil. For its part, the United States was never favorably disposed toward continentalism so long as domestic American producers found it difficult to compete with Canadian crude in the upper Midwest. Despite contrary suggestions from President Nixon's oil import task force, which expressed interest in a continental arrangement, Canadian oil finally was placed under the U.S. mandatory oil import control program in 1970.[15]

At the same time considerable sensitivity within Canada to American influence in the energy sector was evident especially in regard to pipeline construction. The nationality of the industrial consortia building pipelines was at issue as was their direction (that is, how much of the Canadian market they served). Heavy American investment was controversial across the political spectrum in Canada.

By the 1970s the context within which the continental concept had once been considered had changed fundamentally. Growing concern over the resource base and the availability of geographically remote and technologically difficult frontier resources, as well as rising nationalist sentiments changed Canadian perspectives on exports, while the question of foreign domination of the oil and gas industries became more politicized. The events of October 1973 only served to accelerate a trend already underway in Canadian policy. Major Canadian initiatives—such as the 1974 decision to phase out oil exports, the rejection of new gas export license applications beginning in 1970, more direct federal efforts to screen and control foreign investment in Canada, the establishment of a crown corporation, Petro-Canada, to give the federal government a direct role in oil production in certain areas, and the adoption of two-tier pricing schemes, in which exports were priced at substantially higher levels than domestically produced and consumed oil and gas—dramatically altered the state of U.S.-Canadian energy relations.

A brief review of the oil and gas trade statistics for the past two decades indicates a progressively increasing share of Canadian production being allocated to exports, from 23 percent in 1960 to over 50 percent in the early 1970s (see Table 3-3). By the same token Canadian petroleum supplied no higher than 7.66 percent of total U.S. petroleum demand in 1973. A more meaningful measurement in terms of the impact of Canadian exports on American supply security was the Canadian share of U.S. oil imports, 17 percent in 1973, and the much heavier dependence of refineries in the Northern Tier states upon Canadian supply.

Table 3-3 also indicates the increase of Canadian oil imports as, under the impetus provided by the national oil plan, the energy structures of Quebec and the Maritime provinces shifted toward much heavier reliance upon imported oil. By 1975 over 75 percent of Quebec's energy base, and 83 percent of the Maritimes' was in the form of imported oil. Canada was a net exporter of oil until 1975, when imports began to outpace exports.

Gas production and marketing (Table 3-4) share with oil a large export orientation. The percentage of exported gas increased until it reached approximately 40 percent of Canadian production in 1974. As with oil, these exports provided only a very small share of total U.S. consumption (approximately 5 percent). This minor share of the national market, however, obscures more pronounced regional dependencies, particularly in the U.S. Pacific Northwest. Any decline in the availability of Canadian gas and oil could result, then, in substantial regional dislocation.

Table 3-3. Canadian Petroleum Supply, Thousand Barrels per Day.[a]

	1960	1965	1970	1971	1972	1973	1974	1975	1976	1977	1978	1979
Canadian production	532.0	867.1	1,382.1	1,476.0	1,698.4	1,962.9	1,843.3	1,623.1	1,437.3	1,440.2	1,230.0	1,608.0
Imports												
Crude	343.1	395.0	568.9	671.1	769.6	883.7	797.7	844.5	755.3	649.8	617.5	430.0
Refined	96.2	162.5	193.3	158.6	147.6	123.6	86.4	46.3	36.0	45.0	55.3	35.0
Exports												
Crude	113.0	295.6	669.8	750.8	951.3	1,148.0	907.0	707.3	465.1	270.0	463.1	95.0
Refined	9.9	8.6	36.2	52.1	116.4	149.8	134.7	115.6	n.a.	n.a.	n.a.	192.0

Sources: Ministry of Energy, Mines, and Resources, An Energy Strategy for Canada, Ottawa, April 1976, p. 162; National Energy Board, Annual Report (Washington, D.C., 1977), p. 20; U.S. Central Intelligence Agency, International Energy Statistical Review, March 1976, 1977 (Washington, D.C.), p. 10, average over first three-quarters of 1978; Canadian Embassy, Washington, D.C.

a. These figures exclude plant-liquified petroleum gases.

Table 3-4. Canadian Marketable Gas Supply, Billion Cubic Feet.

	1960	1965	1970	1971	1972	1973	1974	1975	1976	1977	1978	1979	1980
Canadian production[a]	443.0	1,051.0	1,868.6	2,071.8	2,362.1	2,520.8	2,498.9	2,520.2	2,458.6	2,576.8	2,600.0	2,600.0	2,600.0
Exports	109.8	404.7	780.2	912.2	1,009.7	1,028.0	959.2	946.9	953.6	1,003.0	881.0	1,600.0	791.0

Sources: Ministry of Energy, Mines, and Resources, An Energy Strategy for Canada, Ottawa, April 1976, p. 163; National Energy Board, Annual Report (Washington, D.C., 1977), p. 20; Canadian Embassy, Washington, D.C.

a. Production figures for 1978–80 are approximate.

BILATERAL ENERGY RELATIONS IN THE 1980s

Despite Canada's apparent rich endowment in energy resources, the course of energy development in that country during the 1980s will be determined much more by political and economic than by technical and geological factors. The economic ground rules governing oil and gas development are unsettled, with industry and federal and producer–province governments locked in a political struggle for control. This struggle will likely continue for some time, with effects on the pace of energy development, the pricing and marketing of energy resources, the regime governing energy investments, and the level of exports to the United States. The energy arena provides a battleground for political and economic forces of fundamental importance to the future of Canada. Understanding the nature of this struggle is essential to U.S. policy and the protection of U.S. interests.

The National Energy Program

At the center of the current conflict stands the National Energy Program (NEP) announced by the Liberal government of Pierre Trudeau in October 1980.[16] The objectives of the plan came as no surprise, as its basic thrust had been apparent for several months, although the exact means chosen to achieve these objectives went beyond what many expected. The Liberal party had compaigned on a platform attacking the oil pricing proposals of the previous Conservative government for imposing an unacceptable burden on consumers while conferring a windfall on the industry and the producer provinces. Had they been implemented these proposals would have raised domestic oil prices to international levels within a few years and would have resolved a long-standing disagreement between the federal government and the producer provinces over pricing policy. The new Liberal government had also issued statements about Canadianization of the oil and gas industries prior to issuing the NEP. These initial actions had already precipitated a serious breach between Alberta and Ottawa and led to corporate reconsideration of major investments in several tar sands plants even before the NEP was officially presented.

The NEP contains a number of highly controversial and frequently complicated measures. Although some modification of individual elements in the NEP may yet occur, it offers a forceful statement of the Trudeau government's position on energy policy and of how it intends to use energy policy to achieve a number of broader economic and political objectives.

The strictly energy-related objectives of the program include reducing oil's share of total energy demand to 10 percent and achieving oil self-sufficiency by 1990. A considerable part of the debate over the program centers on whether these objectives are actually achievable under its proposed regimes for pricing, incentives for frontier development, and control of foreign investment. By far the greatest controversy, however, surrounds those measures stemming from what the Trudeau government considers to be the two most crucial issues in the energy arena: restructuring the distribution of oil and gas revenues between the federal and producer–province governments to give Ottawa a larger share; and increasing Canadian control, not just ownership, of the energy industry. These two issues go beyond mere energy policy. At its most fundamental level the NEP is an attempt by the federal government to assert itself regarding the central question of who will make the economic and political decisions that will shape Canada's future.

The most important elements of the program are as follows:

Pricing

- Continuation of administered prices through the establishment of a blended price scheme yielding an average price from separate conventional, oil sand, and imported crude prices, such that the average price to Canadian consumers will not exceed 85 percent of world levels or the U.S. average price, whichever is lower.

- Encouragement of greater use of natural gas, at the expense of oil, by allowing the gap between gas and oil prices (on a Btu basis) to widen, together with new gas pipeline construction east of Montreal.

Taxation

- A new federal tax on all natural gas, wherever it is sold, to provide a new source of federal revenues.

- An 8 percent tax on all net operating revenues from oil and gas production.
- A tax on oil and gas consumption to finance the federal government's plan to purchase the assets of the Canadian subsidiaries of one or more foreign-owned major oil corporations.

Incentives

- Phasing down and eventual replacement of standard depletion allowances (except for oil sands and heavy oil upgrading equipment) with a system of graduated grants for exploration that increase in size as the level of Canadian control in a company increases and are higher for exploration and development on federal lands than on provincial acreage.

"Canadianization"

- Preferential treatment under tax and incentive programs for Canadian firms, plus a minimal 50 percent Canadian ownership goal at the production stage on federal lands (so-called Canada lands. In addition, a more vigorous role for Petro–Canada in such ventures on Canada lands. Petro–Canada will be entitled to a 25 percent "carried interest" in frontier and offshore developments, in addition to the ownership share it already holds in several frontier, offshore, and syncrude projects.

The NEP does not assume a supply solution to Canada's oil import problem but, rather, views measures to reduce oil demand to levels consistent with anticipated domestic supply as the largest part of the answer. The NEP projects oil demand to be 1.615 million barrels per day in 1985 and 1.475 million in 1990, or nearly 400,000 barrels less than the average daily oil demand in 1979. The estimated level of domestic oil production is 1.355 million barrels per day in 1985, and 1.520 million in 1990. Domestic production in 1979 averaged 1.608 million barrels per day. According to these estimates Canada would have a very slight surplus of domestic production in 1990.

Another key premise of the NEP is that natural gas is plentiful in Canada relative to oil. Some 14.5 Tcf of gas is authorized for export to the United States through 1990, and the NEP projects that a 5.8 Tcf additional surplus (surplus to both domestic demand and existing licensed export volumes) could accumulate between 1980 and 1990. Thus meeting domestic gas demand, which could rise to 2.5 Tcf in 1990, is not a problem as is meeting oil demand. Rather, the problem is the timing of phasing in production from new sources.

A comparison of the NEP with previous energy strategies reveals an important change in emphasis. Both the Liberal party and the Progressive Conservative party, when previously in power, concentrated on reducing oil import vulnerability and encouraging production of frontier and unconventional oil and gas resources. The National Energy Strategy announced by a previous Trudeau government in April 1976 emphasized self-reliance, which was defined in terms of reducing Canadian vulnerability to arbitrary import price changes or prolonged supply disruptions.[17] In practical terms this would have entailed lowering import dependence to one-third of total oil demand by 1985 and preserving natural gas for domestic use until frontier resources could be brought to market. A later study commissioned by the Ministry of Energy, Mines, and Resources emphasized substitution of other energy sources for oil (to reduce oil's share in primary energy supply from 46 percent to 30 percent in 2000 and expand use of electricity).[18] The Clark government (1979–80) committed itself to a net oil import limit of 600,000 b/d by 1985, and a 1 percent annual energy growth rate in order for Canada to achieve self-sufficiency by 1990.

In view of the potential for conflict between the federal government and producer provinces over the issue, the price regimes of the two previous governments merit attention. The strategy of the Trudeau government in 1976 called for gradual movement of domestic oil prices to world levels of the Trudeau government in 1976 and near, if not full, commodity pricing for gas within two to four years; it also called for reduction in the growth of demand, a doubling of frontier exploration and development activity, and construction of new delivery systems for frontier resources. The brief Progressive Conservative government of Joe Clark concentrated primarily upon revising the energy pricing agreement worked out with the provinces in 1976, because at the agreed upon rate of increase ($1 per barrel every six months) the gap between world and domestic prices was actually increasing. The Clark government proposed to raise oil prices at the rate of first $4 per barrel and then $4.50 per barrel every year until the world price or 85 percent of the U.S. price, whichever was lower, was reached. This was expected to occur in 1984.

The NEP departs from these previous strategies in several important regards. The Trudeau government maintains that past policies overemphasized security of supply while paying insufficient attention to the ramifications of energy policy for the balance of political and economic power within the country and the control of the industry. The NEP rejects the premise of the previous, Conservative government that rapid movement of prices of domestic oil, regardless of source, to international levels is the most important step in achieving self-sufficiency and retains a regime of administered prices set according to whether the particular oil is imported, produced from frontier areas or tar sands, or comes from current conventional fields. The NEP proceeds on the belief that the pre–NEP net backs were more than sufficient to make high-risk projects attractive without the price levels contemplated by the Clark government and that the priority for federal policy is to restructure the distribution of revenues and achieve Canadian control of the industry.

The Trudeau government contends that the existing distribution of revenues, in which the federal government receives 10 percent and industry and the producer provinces split the rest, enriches the producer provinces, especially Alberta, disproportionately to the rest of Canada while the federal government provides the incentives to production. More concretely, the federal government found itself with insufficient revenues to finance its energy-related obligations, notably the oil equalization scheme.[19] Moreover, the Trudeau government alleges that a foreign controlled oil and gas industry is exporting capital from Canada and might not invest higher revenues in Canada.

Thus the energy program revises the distribution of revenues to give the federal government a larger share—24 percent—leaving the provinces with 43 percent and industry 33 percent. It would rectify a serious federal budget deficit by generating additional federal revenues through new taxes and moving the compensation payments off-budget by financing them through a new surcharge imposed on refineries. The NEP addresses the foreign control issue through new Canadian ownership and control requirements, a more extensive role for Petro-Canada, and the purchase of the Canadian subsidiaries of one or more major foreign oil companies. It is fair to say that this program was guaranteed to arouse considerable opposition, since it fundamentally revises the rules of the energy game in Canada.

The issues would be complicated enough were they simply economic in character. What makes resolution more difficult is the political struggle between Ottawa and the producer provinces over who makes such decisions and the tendency for both sides to see it in zero-sum terms: One side's loss is the other's gain. Such a perspective does not exactly encourage compromise.

Alberta is intent on protecting jurisdiction over its resources, which it sees as threatened by Liberal policies and is adamant in demanding the prices offered by the previous, Conservative government for what it regards as a rapidly depleting resource. Conventional oil produced in Alberta would, under the NEP, be priced as "old" oil and receive only the current price of C$17.75 per barrel. Syncrude and frontier and offshore oil produced on federal land would be priced much closer to international levels. The Alberta government objects to this arrangement for obvious reasons.

Alberta's immediate response to the NEP was to announce production cuts to force the federal government to accept higher oil prices. Both Alberta and British Columbia maintain that the federal government has no right to tax gas and referral of the issue to the Supreme Court of Canada is likely following consideration in the provincial courts. For its part the federal government perceives the energy area as an important testing ground for Prime Minister Trudeau's strongly centralist approach to national unity and constitutional reform issues. Although a compromise on prices may eventually be worked out, the underlying source of the tension between Ottawa and the producer provinces will not disappear.

The jurisdiction issue also arises in regard to the offshore oil resources east of Newfoundland.[20] The Progressive Conservative Clark government had promised Newfoundland exclusive ownership and control over offshore resources in an attempt to resolve a jurisdictional dispute originating in the circumstances under which Newfoundland, then a separate dominion, joined the confederation in 1949. The Trudeau government, however, has reasserted federal jurisdiction while offering Newfoundland 100 percent of provincial-type revenues until per capita income there reaches the national average. The issue is not simply how to satisfy Newfoundland's revenue needs, however. Newfoundland, with the prospect of economic growth in sight, wants the right to administer and regulate offshore development in order to maximize the economic benefits to its depressed economy, that is, to have the same prerogatives as other producer provinces.

The consequences of the situation with Newfoundland are potentially serious. Mobil Canada, which has important interests in the Hibernia and Ben Nevis permits, has said that although exploration will continue, commercial development will not take place until the jurisdictional dispute is settled. Other oil companies share this attitude. Referral of the issue to the Supreme Court of Canada is likely here as well.

The struggle between federal and provincial governments over political and economic power in Canada is being played out in the energy area because of the economic stakes involved and because the absence of a clear hierarchy of political authority in that sector makes it an ideal battlefield. It is imperative from the perspective of U.S. interests to understand that the conflict runs deeper than simply energy and is not likely to be settled for some time.

The National Energy Program and Foreign Investment

Potentially the greatest irritant for U.S.-Canadian relations to emerge from the National Energy Program is its provisions regarding foreign investment in Canada's oil and gas industries. Of the top twenty-five petroleum companies in Canada, seventeen are more than 50 percent foreign owned and controlled and the latter account for 72 percent of Canadian oil and gas sales. The Trudeau government finds this level of foreign control objectionable on a number of grounds. It maintains that non-Canadian interests receive the lion's share of the financial benefits of higher domestic oil and gas prices and that financing new projects through internally generated funds simply perpetuates the lack of opportunity for new Canadian participation. Moreover, it sees foreign companies as controlling future production decisions as well, because of their predominant position in frontier and offshore areas and their extensive role in syncrude development. Finally, the Trudeau government basically distrusts the multinationals, on the grounds that the necessarily worldwide interests of these companies do not coincide with Canadian national interests and that they cannot be relied upon to treat Canada equitably during a world supply crisis or to maintain a commitment to high-risk and high-cost projects in Canada.

It is very significant that the NEP defines the issue of foreign investment not simply in terms of ownership, which an increase in Canadian owned equity might rectify, but in terms of control: who makes the decisions and on the basis of whose interests.[21] The NEP sets three objectives regarding foreign investment:

- At least 50 percent Canadian ownership of oil and gas production by 1990;

- Canadian control of a significant number of the larger foreign oil and gas firms;

- An early increase in the share of the oil and gas sector owned by the federal government.

Changes in the depletion allowance and the establishment of an incentive payment system geared to a domestic ownership and control test, preferences in granting new export licenses to Canadian owned firms, the imposition of a 50 percent ownership test at the production stage of projects on territory under federal jurisdiction, and more extensive use of the Foreign Investment Review Agency to prevent non-energy investments by oil and gas companies and to block purchase of already discovered oil and gas reserves by foreign controlled firms are intended to help achieve the 50 percent ownership goal.

A more extensive role for state owned and state controlled enterprise is a particularly controversial element of the Trudeau government's strategy to reduce foreign ownership. New crown corporations could be formed to purchase the assets of larger foreign owned companies using funds raised by special charges on all oil and gas consumption in Canada. The role of Petro–Canada would increase by virtue of a proposed 25 percent carried interest in every new and existing right on federal lands. Petro–Canada already holds significant positions in a number of important syncrude, frontier, and offshore projects. The effect of expanding the direct role of the federal government in those projects that will be crucial to Canada's energy future will be to enhance its influence dramatically regarding the pace of development and, perhaps even more important in the eyes of the Trudeau government, its leverage against the producer–province governments and the private sector.

The Trudeau government's efforts to impose greater control over foreign energy investment could have a substantial effect on bilateral relations. The foreign corporate interests in question are predominantly U.S. based, and industry charges that the new policy amounts to little more than expropriation. The proposed mandatory carried interest for Petro–Canada, the intention to buy out one or more major foreign owned companies, the retention of price controls, and changes in the fiscal regime governing energy development have had a chilling effect on corporate expenditure plans, especially on the part of the major oil companies, such as Imperial Oil (Exxon), Shell Canada, Gulf Canada, and Mobil Canada.

The new incentive system favoring Canadian owned and controlled enterprises also raises the thorny question of whether Canada is violating the "national treatment" provisions of the OECD's "Guidelines for Multinational Enterprises." Adherents to the Declaration on National Treatment agree to:

> accord to enterprises operating in their territories and owned or controlled directly or indirectly by nationals of another Member country . . . treatment under their laws, regulations, and administrative practices, consistent with international law and no less favorable than that accorded in like situations to domestic enterprises.

Adherence to the principle of national treatment is an essential prerequisite to a stable international investment regime. Canada claims that the so-called national treatment provision requires only consultation where policies derogate from the rule and that such policies are not precluded by the declaration, a position that the United States does not fully accept.[22] On the face of it Canada's discretionary use of incentives to favor Canadian firms is in conflict with the national treatment provision.

The changes in Canada's treatment of foreign energy investment should be kept in perspective, however. The foreign investment issue is not new. The federal government has exercised control over the establishment of almost all new businesses and the acquisition of existing business by foreign firms since 1973, when the Foreign Investment Review Act was promulgated. Earlier, in 1971, it blocked the sale of a Canadian oil company to outside interests. There also has been continuing concern in some Canadian political sectors at the effect of foreign ownership on the performance of Canadian industry in general, although the intensity of this concern has fluctuated. The return of the Trudeau-led Liberal party to power in 1980 represents a shift toward a more interventionist government strategy in a number of industrial sectors, not just energy.

Moreover, as the Trudeau government is quick to point out, other industrial countries have established state oil companies and imposed in some cases rather rigid restrictions on foreign oil companies operating within their territory. The latest initiatives reflect a conviction that such extensive foreign ownership as found in Canada (over 50 percent in mining, 55 percent in manufacturing, over 70 percent in oil and gas) results in an unacceptable level of foreign control over Canada's future, and that a strong federal government is essential to preserving Canada's political and economic independence. It would be a mistake to view the investment provisions of the NEP as a manifestation of an incipient socialism.

The long-range consequences of these initiatives are not easy to gauge. Achievement of a consensus between the federal government and the producer provinces on energy pricing, which undoubtedly would result in higher domestic prices, could have a salutary effect on the situation, since prices may be of greater importance to the industry over the long run than investment regulations. It is not clear that Ottawa is going to set about buying out foreign oil companies wholesale, as the possibility thereof could just as easily serve the purpose of putting the companies on notice that their actions will be carefully scrutinized. There is no thought of uncompensated expropriation. Petro–Canada's offer of C$1.46 billion for the assets of the Canadian subsidiary of Petrofina S.A. of Belgium has in fact been criticized in some Canadian circles as too generous. Corporate reorganization to establish new, more heavily Canadian owned subsidiaries to acquire interests in frontier areas and thus qualify under the incentive system may be feasible in some cases, as a recent move by Dome Petroleum demonstrates. Finally, some companies may simply feel they can live with the new policies without changes in ownership, despite the smaller grants that would then be available. The head of Imperial Oil, the Exxon subsidiary, recently said as much to a Canadian Parliamentary committee.[23]

The most serious problem from a corporate perspective may not be the substance of federal policy, onerous as the industry may contend it is, so much as the lack of stability and certainty among the policymakers. Changes that are adverse to corporate interests have occurred in other producer countries without the industry's going under. What is essential is a planning environment stable enough to permit high-risk investments necessary to develop resources. The greatest threat posed by the National Energy Program is not expropriation or reduction of revenues per se but continuation of the conflict over who makes the rules, perpetuating an unstable investment environment.

The NEP's treatment of foreign investment becomes doubly important in light of the magnitude of the financial resources needed for the Canadian energy sector. A Canadian government study in 1977 estimated that Canada could meet energy investment demands through the 1980s without a substantial increase in reliance upon foreign funding. This conclusion assumed increased domestic savings and some reallocation of investment capital from other sectors. A recent study by the Royal Bank of Canada, however, has cast a harsher light on domestic investment. With C$1.4 trillion required by the year 2000, according to the report (over C$700 billion in the electric utility sector), foreign investment will unavoidably be required.[24] Even if only 25 percent of the total investment is slated to come from foreign sources, the report warns that energy investors will confront in Canada "difficult and possibly unacceptable levels of risk." The economic prudence of the goal of reducing foreign shareholdings to 50 percent in the energy sector may come to appear increasingly questionable and unrealistic if there is a competing demand for the necessary capital from massive energy investments in the United States and elsewhere.

The Pace of Energy Development

In its effort to address the federal–provincial and foreign investment issues the Trudeau government's energy strategy raises a fundamental question: Can the program achieve its energy objectives, or will the controversy surrounding its major elements result in serious project delays and possibly aggravation of Canada's energy situation? Although it is too soon to answer this question with confidence, a number of points warrant mentioning.

Theoretically the potential inherent in tar sands and frontier oil and gas could enable Canada to satisfy its own requirements and then some. The technical and physical obstacles in many of these areas are substantial, but they are not insurmountable. Several companies warned during the 1978 round of NEB oil supply hearings that frontier and syncrude projects might compete with each other to some extent for necessary financial, labor, and equipment resources. It may not be prudent simply to add projected frontier supplies without considering the interaction of project requirements across producing areas. Nevertheless, although technical problems may pose temporary obstacles, their impact on the pace of development may not be the determining one.

The more fundamental impediments are not technical but political and economic in nature. The political struggle between provincial and the federal governments creates an environment that does not encourage major new investments, certainly of the magnitude contemplated in the energy sector. So long as energy policy is used as a political tool, the stability in the political and economic ground rules necessary for sizable investment will not be present.

The NEP's approach to pricing policy is another potential impediment. The Trudeau government's position is that a replacement cost approach to pricing new sources, based on cost of production plus a "fair" rate of return, rather than an approach based on the price of imported oil, provides sufficient returns to justify new investment. Moreover, not only does the Trudeau government believe that world prices would only give foreign controlled firms a windfall, it believes also that domestic financing of major energy projects would be undesirable, since it would limit new investment opportunities for Canadians.

Finally, the prospective changes in the financial regime governing frontier and syncrude projects and the prospect of a more extensive direct state role in the industry through Petro–Canada and newly purchased subsidiaries of foreign oil companies could have a substantial impact on exploration and development activity.

The previous super-depletion allowance for frontier exploration and development had reduced industry's real expenses to less than 10 cents on the exploration dollar. The new incentive-based grant system may partially offset the loss of this allowance (grants up to 80 cents on the exploration dollar are possible for Canadian companies), but what may be more important to the pace of development is the fact that this system is discretionary. Some foreign owned companies may reorganize to take advantage of it. Other foreign companies reluctant to reorganize may simply sell off their Canadian subsidiaries. Although a more "Canadian" industry might result, the time and resources necessary to recoup the loss of expertise that might result from this could delay resource development in physically challenging regions.

The oil and gas industry's reaction to the pricing, tax, and investment/ownership provisions of the National Energy Program has been to slash exploration budgets, place major capital investment in tar sands projects on hold, and, where possible, shift production rigs and exploration activity to the United States and elsewhere where the financial returns are higher.[25] Among the projects affected are the Cold Lake and Alsands syncrude projects in Alberta and the Hibernia project off Newfoundland. A sizable number of the smaller and more aggressive Canadian gas exploration firms, the very ones the NEP is intended to benefit, have moved rigs and exploration budgets south of the border where returns on decontrolled "over-thrust" gas in the Rocky Mountains are four times those of conventional gas in Canada.

The Canadian oil industry, when it appeared that the previous Conservative government would lift price controls in fairly short order, confidently asserted that Canadian self-sufficiency could be achieved by 1990 through rapid development of frontier and unconventional sources, albeit with a hefty C\$300 billion price tag. Several of the major oil companies (notably Mobil, Shell, and Imperial Oil), however, gloomily forecast in testimony to the NEB in early 1981 that Canadian oil supply could be 400,000–600,000 b/d short of the NEP's target for 1990 as a result of the NEP.[26]

Exports and Current Canadian Policy

Although oil and gas exports to the United States were prominent features of Canadian energy policy until the 1970s, the lead times for production from new sources and the additional uncertainties affecting major new projects discourage any notion that imports from Canada will provide a significant source of future supply for the United States over the next decade. This is true of both oil and gas, despite the potential size of Canadian resources. The principal exception to this picture is electricity, where the potential for significant new exports to the United States is far more promising than for the other energy sources.

The prospects for oil exports are particularly slim. Light crude is available only through exchanges, at approximately 100,000 b/d each way, that were instituted after Canada announced in 1974 that it would phase out oil exports. Although their continuation will avert a shortfall for refineries in U.S. Northern Tier states, this is a temporary solution, and it remains imperative to develop an alternative supply source, presumably a pipeline from the U.S. West Coast, for the Northern Tier. Exports of heavy crude, which have been exempt from the general export phase-out, may also gradually decrease through the mid-1980s. The National Energy Program calls for investment in heavy crude upgrading equipment to make this oil usable in Canada.

Although the physical potential for oil exports in the 1990s might be present if syncrude, Beaufort Sea, and East Coast offshore oil projects all reach their full potential by 1990, the prospects for this to occur are not particularly encouraging, as they will be necessary to replace declining production in conventional areas. It is likely that any Canadian federal government, regardless of party composition, will feel compelled politically to strive for Canadian self-sufficiency. This will leave little if any room for exports.

The picture in the natural gas sector is somewhat different. Gas exports will likely hold at 1.2–1.8 Tcf through 1990 and then will decline under existing licenses. Although recent experience with reserve additions in existing areas and the gas prospects in the High Arctic hold the promise of making continuing exports possible, even at the most optimistic levels Canadian gas would satisfy only 5–6 percent of the total gas needs of the United States. The American Gas Association in late 1980 estimated that 1–2 Tcf/year of Canadian gas might be available in the year 2000.[27] Of course, the importance of this gas on a regional basis will be greater.

The level of gas exports beyond 1990 will be a function of several factors. The development of High Arctic resources will clearly have an important effect on deliverability, although the timing and volume of deliveries are not yet definite. The means of delivery—pipelines and/or liquefied natural gas (LNG) tankers—will be important, since the former would require delivery of larger volumes, and hence larger markets, to be profitable. Transport by LNG tanker would allow the gas to seek markets anywhere. Some LNG will be sold to Japanese customers, and several potential European customers have also shown interest.

Although the industry has argued that exports could help provide a market sufficiently large to allow early production, the Trudeau government has taken the position that Arctic gas is Canada's safety

net and has cautioned that, consistent with that concept, development might not begin as soon as the industry would like if that
would entail substantial new exports and, from the government's
perspective, political controversy.[28] It should be recalled that a previous Trudeau government had been sorely embarrassed in the early
1970s when extravagant estimates of frontier resources subsequently
proved to be unfounded.

At the very least, new export applications will be carefully scrutinized, and license validity periods may be shorter than in the past
(possibly less than ten years). This situation would pose planning
problems for the importing gas utilities and customers in the United
States.

Marketing gas into eastern Canada as a substitute for oil probably
will not have a major effect on potential exports, given the small size
of that market. The NEB estimated in November 1979 that 180 billion cubic feet per year could be sold in eastern Canada by 1990.
The National Energy Program projects only a modest increase in
Canadian gas demand over previously projected levels, since substitution of gas for oil has been emphasized for some time. What must be
kept in mind, however, is the political importance in Canada of maintaining the commitment to expand gas sales in eastern Canada and
the need for U.S. interests to acknowledge this goal when considering the prospects for Canadian gas exports.

Another factor affecting gas export prospects is their marketabil-
ity in the United States. At present about 75 percent of NEB authorized gas export volumes are in fact being taken by U.S. consumers.
Most of the shortfall is occurring in California and the Pacific Northwest, where the gas market is fully saturated. Some expansion in
Canadian gas imports could occur in the Northeast, where gas accounts for only 6 percent of total energy consumption in New England, as compared to an average of 27 percent nationwide. Canadian
gas, which is cheaper than residual fuel oil, could compensate for the
unavailability of additional domestic supplies. A change in the U.S.
gas pricing regime that might preclude the rolling-in of high-priced
Canadian gas with lower cost indigenous supplies could also affect
the attractiveness of imports.

The position of the Trudeau government toward exports is designed to discourage any U.S. thoughts that Canada could once again
become a major U.S. supplier, let alone a participant in a North
American "Common Market," a proposition the Trudeau govern-

ment rejects. The intention not to allow exports to drive Canadian energy policy nor dominate corporate decisionmaking is evident in the Trudeau government's willingness to use its tax powers where necessary to eliminate any encouragement of exports stemming from Canada's two-tier pricing policy, in which exports are priced higher than domestic oil and gas, and in the safety net approach to frontier resources.

Whether this perspective will come into conflict with the need to provide the market to start major projects will be of significant importance, as it is very doubtful that private corporations would accept the withholding of production until a strictly Canadian market was available. Were this to be the case frontier exploration and production might be expected either to slow or to fall into the hands of the state oil company to an even greater extent than now contemplated.

In any event it should be anticipated that Canada will seek full price for its exports to the United States. Oil exports have been priced at appropriate world levels since 1973, while gas is priced on a Btu-parity basis with crude oil imported into Canada. Where lower prices are offered or scheduled price increases passed up, they will occur strictly in order to assure the competitiveness of the commodity in the markets they serve.

The discussion in this chapter so far has concentrated upon oil and gas, since these sectors dominate the bilateral energy agenda. The prospects for future trade in bulk power, uranium, and coal, however, are far less bounded by constraints of a supply and demand nature, and, with the possible exception of uranium, are less prone to be politicized in the way the oil and gas trade has been. As a result, trade in the electricity sector, defined here to encompass both bulk power and coal and uranium, presents a quite different aspect.

As pointed out earlier, with the addition of new high-voltage lines, the cross-border transmission capacity could reach 11,000 MWe by 1985, or 1.4 percent of U.S. generating capacity and 10 percent of Canadian capacity. Regional trade will be extensive, especially in the Northeast.

The sale of electricity generated by surplus capacity, often on an interruptible or seasonal basis, has been common. A more interesting possibility is the construction of Canadian generating capacity that could be dedicated to the U.S. market. Several Canadian utilities—in Quebec, Manitoba, and Alberta—are investigating the construction of new hydroelectric or coal-fired plants dedicated primarily to U.S. markets.[29] Manitoba Hydro estimates that nearly 6,000 MW of hydroelectric power could be produced at sites yet to be developed in that province, and Hydro Quebec is willing to build 1,800 MW of hydro capacity. In both cases sales would not begin before 1989. Only Ontario Hydro, of the large electricity exporters, has shown little interest in dedicated plants, although some experts have suggested that Ontario Hydro build nuclear reactors dedicated to the U.S. market, a highly controversial idea from which the provincial government is likely to shy away.

The prospects for additional electricity sales are not unlimited, however. Canada as yet does not have a fully interconnected power grid, and developing one is a major tenet of more nationalistic political forces in Canada. Further sales may also be constrained by the emergence, because of greater use of air conditioning in Canada, of a seasonal peaking pattern resembling that in the United States. Finally, while declining electricity consumption has made surplus capacity available for export, dedication of new capacity to the U.S. market, where Canadians see themselves as bearing the environmental costs for projects benefiting Americans, could encounter public acceptance problems. Imposition of a federal electricity export tax is also possible.

American utilities hypothetically should be able to get as much Canadian uranium as they want. With at most 14,445 MW of domestic nuclear capacity in service by 1990, the Canadian uranium industry will continue to sell the bulk of its output on the export market. The uranium export supply test announced in September 1974, reserving for domestic use enough uranium to ensure a thirty-year reserve for each reactor to start operation in the following ten-year period, will be irrelevant in determining the exportable surplus, and Canadian production capacity will exceed annual Canadian requirements by a factor of five to seven during the 1980s.

Among irritants and potential impediments to bilateral uranium trade is price. Despite current "softness" and declining real prices in the world uranium market, price may be a major point of contention with Canada. Since December 1976 all new Canadian uranium contracts have contained a clause for annual price renegotiation at the prevailing market price, determined by either spot prices or an escalating floor price, whichever is higher. In practice, Ottawa sets the price each year, leading some customers to believe that the contract is virtually worthless on this point. A second irritant is the extra-territorial application of U.S. antitrust law to Canadian subsidiaries of U.S. firms that participated in the international uranium cartel in the 1970s. Finally, provincial government action may also impede Canadian production, especially in regard to royalty rates and, in the case of British Columbia, to temporary uranium mining bans based on environmental considerations (five years in this situation). The possible consequences of these developments is that U.S. utilities may not regard Canadian supplies as secure.

Coal exports from the United States to Ontario will probably retain their cost advantage over western Canadian coal in large part because of their lower transportation costs. This cost differential does not affect users in the Prairie provinces. Utilities in these provinces will probably build coal-fired capacity using low-sulfur local coal. Ontario Hydro, the largest utility customer of U.S. coal, has begun blending U.S. coal with low-sulfur Alberta coal in order to reduce emissions. In 1980 Ontario Hydro planned to import 11 million imperial tons of U.S. coal and to use 2.7 million tons of Alberta coal. Nevertheless, the National Coal Association expected U.S. coal exports to Canada to grow by 2 million tons by 1983.[30]

CONCLUSIONS

The prospects for any significant increase in oil and gas supply from Canada are not promising. Exports may be increased temporarily as Canada seeks to defray the high cost of introducing new energy projects into the domestic supply system. The unsettled state of political relations within the country and the potentially adverse effect of major elements of federal energy policy on the pace of oil and gas development may jeopardize or at least substantially delay the achievement of Canadian domestic energy objectives, let alone create the conditions for substantially increased oil and gas exports to the United States. The electricity sector may offer an exception to this prospect, but even there potential impediments to exports exist.

In any event, given the lead times needed to develop frontier, offshore, and unconventional oil and gas resources, the impact of new production areas will not be felt before the late 1980s at the earliest.

This situation would not change even if the Progressive Conservative party formed the next government and reintroduced a more market-oriented approach to prices and eased the investment measures.

Rather than concentrate on increasing exports, bilateral energy relations in the 1980s will have to cope with a number of challenges arising as exports decline:

- Facilitating both the adjustment to supply problems in the oil and gas sectors and the integration of new supply from unconventional and frontier sources;

- Taking maximum advantage of the complementarity of oil and gas transportation needs of both countries, where present; and

- Promoting the efficient utilization of productive capacity.[31]

Aside from possible increases in electricity exports, the biggest benefit of coping successfully with these challenges will be to remove one more country from dependence on the world oil market and to back the oil currently imported by Canada out into the world market. The quantities involved are limited, certainly so in relation to U.S. imports, but an industrial country's achieving a measure of self-sufficiency is of great economic and political importance.

Declining export volumes, rising prices, and the huge investment requirements may strengthen the relationship of energy to other items on the bilateral agenda. Indeed, there is fear in Canada that energy supply questions could overshadow a very broad agenda of bilateral issues in which many problems remain to be solved. One linkage that may become more evident is that between energy and the overall pattern of U.S.-Canadian trade, in which the United States pays for its oil and gas imports from Canada with manufactured goods, a trade pattern that Canadians resist. Another linkage involves foreign investment and Canadian control over the economy. The NEP's provisions in this area have already drawn protests from the United States and Europe.

Realistic expectations regarding supply from Canada are particularly important for the United States, since one of the consequences of the declining availability of Canadian oil and gas will be the need for replacement sources for those regions affected: the U.S. Pacific Northwest, California, and the so-called Northern Tier states. The completion of the Alcan pipeline, the construction of a Northern

Tier oil pipeline, and the development of other oil and gas supplies take on added importance in this context. The changing supply relationship does not preclude important forms of cooperation, such as research and development of tar sands and unilateral efforts to reduce the cross-border transmission of airborne pollutants, but these measures should not be undertaken on the premise that more exports will be available as a result.

Although the issue has not been discussed in this chapter, it is essential that the United States recognize the importance for bilateral cooperation of completing the Alaskan natural gas pipeline. Failure to complete the U.S. portion of this project would be a blow to bilateral relations. The prebuilding of the Canadian portion of this line, which has proceeded on the basis of assurances from President Carter and the U.S. Congress that the Alaskan portion would be built and Canadians compensated for their expenses, is politically very controversial within Canada, and collapse of the project would be a very serious development. The U.S. clearly confronts a dilemma here, in view of both the political importance of the project and its somewhat shaky economics as presently constituted. Nonetheless the onus is on the United States to honor its commitment to Canada.

Planning for alternatives to dwindling Canadian supplies of oil and gas appears to be a more prudent course of action for the United States than predicating policy toward Canada in the energy sector on the assumption that new U.S. initiatives can elicit substantially higher exports. Such assumptions are likely to be invalid so long as the political framework for energy policy in Canada is battled over and export policy remains a major federal weapon in this battle. The United States must avoid intruding upon this struggle, which reaches to the very foundation of the political and economic structure of Canada. Despite its resource endowment Canada is not in a position to extricate the United States from its energy predicament.

NOTES TO CHAPTER 3

1. National Energy Board (NEB), *Canadian Oil Supply and Requirements*, September 1978, p. 3.
2. *Oil and Gas Journal* (February 25, 1980): 64–65 and (April 13, 1981): 75–78.
3. NEB, *Canadian Oil Supply and Requirements*, p. 58.

4. NEB, *Reasons for Decision*, November 1979, pp. 7-8.
5. NEB, *Canadian Natural Gas Supply and Requirements*, February 1979, p. 19.
6. Ibid., p. 18.
7. *Oil and Gas Journal* (February 25, 1980): 64-66 and NEB, *Canadian Natural Gas*, p. 34.
8. *Oil and Gas Journal* (February 25, 1980): 66.
9. NEB, *Canadian Natural Gas*, pp. 38-39.
10. U.S. Department of Energy, *United States-Canada Electricity Exchanges*, February 1979, DOE/ERA-0053, chap. 1.
11. See Richard Simeon, *Federal-Provincial Diplomacy: The Making of Recent Policy in Canada* (Toronto: University of Toronto Press, 1972, p. 39, and Wallace D. Koehler, "The Impact of Canadian Energy Policy on Changing Federal-Provincial Relations," *The American Review of Canadian Studies*, 7 (Spring 1977): 1-32.
12. See the essays by Walter Gainer, Eugene Forsey, and A.E. Safarian, in H. Edward English (ed.) *Canada-United States Relations, Proceedings of the Academy of Political Science*, 32 (no. 2, 1976).
13. See Judith D. Maxwell, "Energy Bargaining in a Regional Context," in J. Maxwell (ed.), *Policy Review and Outlook, 1978: A Time For Realism* (Montreal: C.D. Howe Research Institute, 1978).
14. Ted Greenwood, *Canada's Energy Policy and Exports to the United States*, paper delivered at the Conference on North American Energy Policy, Carleton University, Ottawa, October 2-4, 1975.
15. James W. McKie, "United States and Canadian Energy Policy," in Cambell Watkins and Michael Walker (eds.), *Oil in the Seventies: Essays on Energy Policy* (Vancouver: The Fraser Institute, 1977), pp. 251-54.
16. Ministry of Energy, Mines, and Resources (EMR), *The National Energy Program*, October 1980.
17. Ministry of Energy, Mines, and Resources, *An Energy Strategy for Canada*, 1976, sec. IV.
18. Ministry of Energy, Mines, and Resources, *Energy Futures for Canadians*, 1978.
19. The subsidy paid to refiners using imported oil is an on-budget expense. The proceeds from the oil export tax and a small gasoline tax, theoretically designed to finance this scheme, are added to the federal government's general revenues. Because of declining exports and import costs much higher than anticipated, the subsidy exceeds returns from the tax by over C$3 billion.
20. Newfoundland was a separate dominion, the constitution of which was suspended in 1934 in favor of direct rule from London. The constitution was revived at the date of union with Canada in 1949, even if only for a split second. Newfoundland maintains it carried ownership of offshore

resources with it into the confederation. The Supreme Court of Canada ruled in 1968 that British Columbia (and by inference other provinces) did not own offshore resources. Newfoundland argues this does not apply in its case because of the special circumstances of its entry.

21. EMR, *National Energy Program*, p. 19.

22. The Canadian position on this point was stated by the minister for external affairs, Allen MacEachen, before the OECD council of ministers on June 21, 1976.

23. *Wall Street Journal*, February 18, 1981.

24. *World Business Weekly* (June 23, 1980).

25. *Oil and Gas Journal* (February 9–16, 1981).

26. *Oil and Gas Journal* (January 26, 1981).

27. American Gas Association, *Gas Energy Supply Outlook: 1980-2000*, October 1980.

28. EMR, *National Energy Program*, p. 44.

29. *Energy Daily*, July 28, 1980.

30. *Coal Week* (October 29, 1979).

31. This discussion draws upon Paul Daniel and Richard Shaffner's "Lessons from Bilateral Trade in Energy Resources," in C. Bergie and A. Hero (eds.), *Natural Resources in U.S.-Canadian Relations*, vol. 1 (Westview 1980).

4 INVESTMENT RELATIONS BETWEEN CANADA AND THE UNITED STATES

Gary Clyde Hufbauer
Andrew James Samet

Multinational enterprise has grown at explosive rates since World War II without systematic international rules. Between 1950 and 1975 the agenda of commercial negotiations was dominated by tariff cutting rounds of the General Agreement on Tariffs and Trade (GATT). Between 1975 and 1979 the agenda of the Tokyo round was dedicated to limiting nontariff trade barriers. These efforts were largely successful, but they will be undermined if national governments control the investment and production decisions of multinational enterprises. Such controls can create the same distortions that arise when nations control trade directly.

The absence of systematic international rules does not mean that laissez-faire prevails at the national level. Both Canada and the United States pursue policies aimed at controlling direct foreign investment.[1]

- Both Canada and the United States have enacted statutory limits on the entry of foreign multinational corporations in certain sectors of their economies.

- Canada exercises control over the establishment of almost all new business and the acquisition of existing business by foreign firms

The authors are associated with the International Law Institute, Georgetown University Law Center. Sperry Lea provided valuable comments on an earlier draft of the chapter.

under the Foreign Investment Review Act of 1973.[2] The United States screens a select few cases of foreign investment in this country through the Committee on Foreign Investment in the United States (CFIUS).[3]

- Both Canada and the United States and provincial and state governments use incentives to attract foreign investment. Trade, tax, cash grants, and other incentives are made available to attract new firms.

- Canada has institutionalized a process for obtaining "commitments" from direct foreign investors to improve the economic benefits that Canada derives. These commitments, made to the Foreign Investment Review Agency (FIRA), which administers the 1973 act, look increasingly like performance requirements— specific target levels for export, value added, and employment. The United States extracts no such commitments from foreign investors.

Incentives and performance requirements and hostile tender offers threaten to cause the greatest tension in Canada–U.S. relations.[4] Nations that feel the impact of foreign investment incentives and performance requirements are tempted to respond in kind. The danger of a competitive spiral is particularly acute for Canada–U.S. relations, both because of geographic, economic, and cultural proximity and because of a great deal of industry lies close to the border. Governments of both nations, especially state and provincial governments, have adopted the practice of offering ad hoc inducements just sufficient to persuade the multinational enterprise to select the local site. Efforts by Canada to obtain its fair share of North American automotive investment and production create many of the same problems.

Some Canadians view direct foreign investment, particularly by U.S. multinational enterprises, as causing or perpetuating serious structural difficulties within the Canadian economy. Direct foreign investment is widely believed to inhibit Canada's sovereignty and its ability to implement effective industrial policies. A consensus has accordingly developed that more government intervention is required to assure Canadian control over the Canadian economy.

Officially Canada continues to insist on its openness to direct foreign investment, but national concern over the role of multinationals was evident early in the 1960s. The growth of U.S. investment in

Canada (partly the result of Canadian tariff policies), aroused sufficient anxiety to spawn various inquiries during the late 1960s and early 1970s.[5] Nonintervention was officially abandoned with the creation of FIRA in 1973.

In the United States meanwhile policy pronouncements continue to stress the global benefits derived from the free flow of investment capital. For example, in 1977 the Economic Policy Group, the top Carter administration panel on economic matters, restated the American commitment to avoiding governmental interference in international investment:

> The fundamental policy of the United States Government toward international investment is neither to promote nor discourage inward or outward flows or activities.
>
> The Government, therefore, should normally avoid measures which could give special incentives or disincentives to investment flows of individual companies regarding international investment. Whenever such measures are under consideration, the burden of proof is on those advocating intervention to demonstrate that it would be beneficial to the national interest.

However, the oil embargo of 1973–74 and the specter of large U.S. investments by members of the Organization of Petroleum Exporting Countries (OPEC) prompted members of Congress to introduce numerous bills to control inward foreign investment.[6] As a result some laws were passed to strengthen information gathering activities, and CFIUS was established by President Ford in 1975.

Meanwhile other factors have moved U.S. policy away from the traditional two-way open door. For example, labor unions express concern over the job displacement and loss of income that overseas U.S. investment may cause. Some economists question the premise that the foreign operations of U.S. multinational corporations benefit the U.S. economy.[7] The fact that other governments negotiate investment decisions with multinationals raises the possibility that outcomes might be tilted against the best interests of the United States.[8] The net result is a slow but visible U.S. movement toward more interventionist policies.

These themes underlay hearings conducted by the commerce, consumer, and monetary affairs subcommittee of the U.S. House of Representatives in the 1970s.[9] The critical report published by the subcommittee in 1980, "The Adequacy of the Federal Response to Foreign Investment in the United States," is a manifesto for intervention.[10] Among other suggestions, the subcommittee recommends that the United States establish an agency similar to Canada's FIRA to control inward foreign investment.[11]

Meanwhile only a few investment issues surfaced in Canada–U.S. relations from the commencement of FIRA in 1974 until problems arose in the automotive sector in 1978. An exception to the general tranquility was the issue of "cultural investment." Parliament enacted laws to deny a tax deduction for advertising in the Canadian editions of *Time* and *Reader's Digest*[12] and to advertising placed by Canadians with U.S. border television stations.[13]

On the whole, relations were so smooth during the mid–1970s that renewed discussion of the free trade option emerged. The Canadian standing Senate committee on foreign affairs published a report advocating examination of a free trade arrangement with the United States.[14] This theme was picked up by the short-lived Progressive Conservative government of Prime Minister Joe Clark. Likewise both the U.S. Trade Act of 1974 and the U.S. Trade Agreements Act of 1979 called upon the president to examine the possible negotiation of expanded North American trade agreements.[15]

But the constitutional crisis now gripping Canada has not only placed freer trade on a back burner, it has rekindled other difficulties for investment relations. The politics of Prime Minister Pierre Elliott Trudeau are decidedly more nationalistic than those of Joe Clark. Trudeau used the issue of foreign investment to attract electoral support in 1980. Since then Trudeau has carried through on some of his election commitments.

Trudeau's first step was the appointment of Herb Gray as minister of industry, trade, and commerce. Gray is a spokesman for the nationalistic wing of the Liberal party and author of the report that led to the creation of FIRA. In a June 1980 speech in Montreal, Gray outlined the industrial policy that Canada will follow under his leadership:

1) To capitalize on Canada's energy base in order to build a world competitive industrial sector;
2) [T]o ensure that the Federal Government is an active player in industrial development rather than just passive referee;
3) [T]o strengthen Canada's research and technology capacity;
4) [T]o encourage independent Canadian enterprise; and,
5) [T]o expand Canadian control of the economy while increasing the benefits for Canadians from foreign investments already here.[16]

On October 28, 19780, Trudeau's government presented a federal budget. The accompanying National Energy Program (NEP) drastically altered the investment climate in the Canadian petroleum industry.[17] The energy measures are designed, inter alia, to increase the domestically owned percentage of the Canadian oil and gas industry to 50 percent by 1990 from its current level of 30 percent. Likewise the NEP aims to increase the federal government participation in and revenues from the petroleum industry.

The NEP has met with stiff opposition from Canadian oil and gas producing provinces, and from both Canadian controlled and foreign controlled firms. For example, Premier Peter Lougheed of Alberta, which produces 85 percent of Canada's oil and gas, claims that he can find nothing to support in the NEP:

> it forces us to sell off our rapidly depleting provincial crude oil at less than half the value. Second, it forces us to sell natural gas at very, very substantial discount on value. Third, it has a federal royalty at the wellhead on a provincially owned resource. Fourth, it has a discriminatory federal export tax on natural gas. Fifth, it punitively taxes an industry that is centered in our province, with a multitude of jobs jeopardized as a result. And sixth, it's an ill-conceived approach in the sense that it's negative to both the rest of Canada and to Canada's economic future.[18]

The NEP has attracted little support among Canadian controlled petroleum companies.[19] The Petroleum Incentives Program and Canadian Ownership Ratio provisions are criticized as too bureaucratic. A particularly damaging source of criticism is signaled by a newspaper advertisement by the Independent Petroleum Association of Canada claiming that the federal policy designed to help them may actually drive them out of the country. The overall industry cash flow is expected to drop 15 to 25 percent under the NEP.[20] Those criticisms have led to some modifications of the original program.

Since the bulk of foreign investment in the Canadian petroleum industry is U.S. controlled,[21] the NEP promises to create long-term tension in Canada–U.S. relations. The program clearly discriminates against foreign firms operating in Canada, in contravention of guidelines of the Organization for Economic Cooperation and Development (OECD). Any new efforts by U.S. firms to invest in oil and gas companies in Canada will be rebuffed by FIRA.[22] Petroleum has now become a key sector in terms of investment access. So far however U.S. oil and gas companies have maintained a low profile in the

Canadian energy debate. Perhaps they remember the halting efforts of the Trudeau government to increase Canadian ownership in the petroleum industry in 1975, and perhaps they hope that the federal government will yield to provincial and Canadian controlled industry opinion.

These Canadian developments come at a time when U.S. policy is also in a fluid state. Canadian actions therefore may have a far greater impact on future U.S. foreign investment policy than is generally recognized. The Carter administration sought to hold the line against greater government intervention in the investment field, and an open investment environment was recently endorsed by Treasury Secretary Donald Regan.[23] Pressure to establish a more activist federal policy has mounted with the growth of foreign investment in the United States and the perceived policy activism of foreign nations. U.S. sympathy toward nationalist policies in Canada may be limited by calculations of American investment interest injured, trade redirected, and jobs lost. Remarks by Reagan administration officials critical of Canadian FIRA and NEP policies indicate that little sympathy may be expected from Washington.[24] Investment relations have entered a period of tension.

In the remainder of this chapter the main elements of the investment relationship will be analyzed. First, international efforts to discipline government intervention and to regulate multinational enterprise will be examined. In particular, the work of the OECD and the GATT code on subsidies and countervailing measures will be discussed. Next, the efforts of each country to oversee the foreign investment process will be reviewed. The incentive policies of Canada and the United States will be summarized and investment incentives in the automobile sector will be analyzed. The chapter closes with recommendations for U.S. policy.

INTERNATIONAL CODES AND THEIR BILATERAL IMPLICATIONS

Few international agreements specifically shape national policies toward international investment. A GATT for investment was called for by Don Wallace, Jr., when he commissioned an article published in 1970 by Paul Goldberg and Charles Kindleberger that set forth proposals for the supervision of multinational enterprises.[25] Despite extensive negotiations the 1970s ended with little progress toward a multilateral investment regime.[26]

Nevertheless, the fabric of international discipline is beginning to emerge. Over the years a network of bilateral tax treaties and commercial treaties has served to create a more certain environment concerning rights of establishment, national treatment, and taxation of multinational enterprises. In recent decades some international discipline has been established over the growing national use of investment incentives and performance requirements. OECD played the initial role in the development of international guidelines. As early as 1961 the OECD adopted the Code of Liberalization of Capital Movements, which requires signatories to authorize transactions involving international direct investment to or from other OECD countries.[27] (Canada is the only OECD member country that does not adhere to this code.) Subsequently the OECD inaugurated two committees to examine international investment issues: the Committee for Invisible Transactions (CIT), which since 1970 has held periodic sessions on international direct investment, and the Committee on International Investment and Multinational Enterprise (CIME), which dates from 1975.

The OECD Accords of 1976

In 1976, as a result of the work of the CIME, the OECD adopted its "Guidelines for Multinational Enterprises," containing its declarations on national treatment and on international incentives and disincentives.[28] The first part of the Guidelines, a five-part document, is a voluntary, weakly phrased code of conduct for multinational enterprises. The second part, the Declaration on National Treatment, provides that member nations will

> accord to enterprises operating in their territories and owned or controlled directly or indirectly by nationals of another Member country . . . treatment under their laws, regulations and administrative practice, consistent with international law and no less favorable than that accorded in like situations to domestic enterprises.

The principle of national treatment stands in tension with many Canadian policies. The two latest examples are the NEP and the government's desire to strengthen the commitments process of FIRA into genuine performance requirements. Canada and other countries that shared the same concerns about maintaining the option to adopt discriminatory policies were able to "arrange for a 'general' exception to the rule."[29] When the 1976 OECD accords were ratified, Canada's foreign minister noted that "elements of differentiation in treatment between Canadian and foreign controlled enterprises" existed in Canada. He further stated that Canada would "continue to retain its right to take measures, affecting foreign investors, which we believe are necessary given our particular circumstances."[30] In the view of the Canadian government its adherence to the OECD's Declaration on National Treatment merely requires that Canada offer consultations on policies that derogate from the rule, not that Canada is bound to revoke existing nonconforming policies or to forego future policies with the same effect. The Decision of the Council on National Treatment tends to support Canada's interpretation. It provides that

> Measures taken by a Member country constituting new exceptions to "National Treatment" (including measures restricting new investment by "Foreign-Controlled Enterprises" already established in their territory) taken after the date of this Decision shall be notified to the Organisation within 30 days of their introduction together with the specific reasons therefore and the proposed duration thereof.

By contrast, the United States does not believe that the mode of Canadian acceptance entitles it to a reservation from the national treatment rule.

The third part of the OECD document, the Declaration on International Incentives and Disincentives, merely states that member countries should

> recognize the need to strengthen their cooperation in the field of international direct investment; and they recognize the need to give due weight to the interests of Member countries affected by . . . incentives and disincentives to international direct investment.

This declaration commits its adherents to nothing.

Likewise the fourth part of the 1976 Guidelines and a subsequent decision of the council merely provide for consultations within the framework of the CIME at the request of a member country concerned by the investment incentive or disincentive actions of another member nation.

The fifth declaration provided for a review, which took place in 1979–80 and resulted in the establishment of a medium-term work program on incentives and disincentives under the supervision of the CIME. The program includes a working group on investment incentives and one on performance requirements.

In years to come the OECD initiative may be regarded as a first step in the evolution of a meaningful international framework. But for the foreseeable future OECD pronouncements will have little effect upon U.S. investment relations. The simple fact is that the OECD declarations can be ignored by governments bent on a particular course. The United States, however, is attempting to use the CIME to bring pressure upon Canada over the National Energy Program.[31]

The GATT Code on Subsidies and Countervailing Measures

A more promising achievement is the Code on Subsidies and Countervailing Measures signed in the Tokyo round of multilateral trade negotiations in 1979.[32] Both Canada and the United States participated in the negotiation of this code. The United States insisted that it would accept a material injury test in its countervailing duty statute only if Canada and other major trading nations would restrict their national subsidy policies. The injury test adopted by the United States means that the industrial subsidies of code signatories are not per se subject to countervailing duties (which had been U.S. law prior to the code and still is for nonsignatories) but will be subject to such duties if they lead to exports that demonstrably injure the trading interests of another signatory. The United States insisted that prohibited export subsidies be listed in detail.

The code may serve two important functions. First, it arguably prohibits virtually any subsidy to an industry that is extended in exchange for an export commitment by that industry. Second, it obliges governments granting subsidies to avoid "causing serious prejudice" to competing industries of other signatories of the code. Any subsidy that promotes investment and ultimately affects trade raises a potential claim of serious prejudice to another signatory's industry.

The code, however, provides only a starting point in the discipline of investment incentives and performance requirements. It merely sanctions an old remedy, namely countervailing duties, for "injurious" trade impacts that surface long after a firm has been lured to invest in the nation offering the best deal. It would be far more effective if subsidies could be disciplined at the time they were offered, rather than years later when trade impacts are determined in a semi-judicial forum.

The code recognizes that subsidies

> are widely used as important instruments for the promotion of social and economic policy objectives and further that the agreement does not intend to restrict the right of signatories to use such subsidies to achieve these and other important policy objectives.

Canada was one of the nations that fought to have this clause placed in the code. The federal government is committed to use industrial subsidies as a means of redistributing wealth among Canadian provinces. For example, the federal Department of Regional Economic Expansion (DREE) extends grants and loans to firms that select a site in an area of Canada designated as industrially depressed. Although most DREE grants only affect the site selection of an industry that is already committed to a Canadian location, the DREE program can also act as an incentive for industries that were considering either a U.S. or a Canadian site. The famous Michelin case is probably the best example. The French tire manufacturer rejected a possible U.S. location in favor of one in Nova Scotia after being offered a C$14.4 million DREE grant coupled with a C$45 million provincial low-interest loan. The United States imposed countervailing duties on Michelin exports to the United States (still collected at the rate of about 1 percent). These exports account for about 80 percent of the production from the Nova Scotia plant. A second Canadian based Michelin plant is now in operation, and a C$56 million federal grant was approved in 1980 toward the construction of a third plant. The countervailing duty has had no perceptible impact on the Michelin's Nova Scotia operation, but it did result in prolonged acrimony in Canada–U.S. investment relations.

The federal government has also used the DREE program in its power struggle with the provinces. Through the use of federal monies, the federal government has enlisted the support of the poorer provinces in its effort to preserve federal fiscal powers. Thus the Canadian government will continue to view international constraints upon the use of industrial subsidies as inimical to its bureaucratic and political interests.

Nevertheless the code may serve as the basis for supplementary efforts to discipline the use of investment incentives. In their effort to negotiate an agreement on investment incentives in the automotive industry, Canada and the United States attempted to adopt the format of the code as an outline. Although the effort was suspended in 1979, the code provided a starting point from which to approach these negotiations.

INVESTMENT CONTROL POLICIES

For most of the post–World War II period Canada has attracted more foreign direct investment than any other nation. The largest percentage of this investment has come from the United States. In the 1970s, however, the United States experienced a rapid increase in direct foreign investment and seems to have become the number one host nation. Nevertheless, the impact of foreign investment on Canada will continue to be far more important than it is on the United States simply because the Canadian economy is approximately one-tenth the size of the U.S. economy. Table 4–1 indicates the size of direct foreign investment in Canada and the United States from 1970 to 1980.

Canadian investments in the United States are concentrated in real estate and manufacturing.[33] Canada also has important investments in the U.S. petroleum industry and in insurance.[34] Although none of Canada's investments account for a significant proportion of any U.S. industry, some observers place Canadian direct investment at closer to U.S.$20 billion rather than the reported figure of U.S.$7.5 billion.

U.S. investment, as a proportion of foreign investment in Canada, has shrunk from its high of 85 percent in 1950 to about 80 percent today.[35] But U.S. investment still dominates entire sectors of the Canadian economy. Industries of high foreign ownership include automotive, mining, smelting, chemicals, pulp and paper, rubber, petroleum, textiles, electronics, and machinery.

The scope of U.S. investment in Canada explains Canadian concerns about the role of U.S. multinational enterprises. Conversely the size of U.S. investment in Canada makes the U.S. government apprehensive about possible adverse Canadian federal and provincial policies.

Although neither Canada nor the United States screens outward direct foreign investment, both have policies that shape its inward

Table 4-1. Accumulated Direct Foreign Investment in Canada and in the United States.

Year	Total (at Book Values, C$ Billion)	Per Capita, C$
IN CANADA		
1970	32.9	1,525
1975	40.1	1,767
1980 (est.)	61.4	2,558
From the United States		
1970	26.1	1,210
1975	32.3	1,423
1980 (est.)	49.5	2,063

Year	Total (at Book Values, US$ Billion)	Per Capita, US$
IN THE UNITED STATES		
1970	15.9	65
1975	27.7	130
1980 (est.)	65.5	294
From Canada		
1970	3.3	15
1975	5.6	26
1980 (est.)	9.8	44

Sources: Statistics Canada Daily, October 8, 1980, Cat. #11-001E, and U.S. Department of Commerce, Office of Foreign Investment in the United States.

flow. Both seek to assure that direct investment does not compromise their economic and political sovereignty. Since inward investment has been of far greater concern to Canada, it is natural that Canada employs more comprehensive control policies.

In Canada, four types of policies inhibit the process of foreign investment[36]:

● Federal and provincial nationalizations;

● The prohibition from foreign investment in "key sectors";

- The use of tax policy; and,
- The operation of the Foreign Investment Review Agency.

In the United States, the controls are confined to:

- The prohobition of foreign investment in "national security" sectors; and,
- The use of tax policy.

The United States has an armory of additional potential control mechanisms, but in practice, these have had little significance. One is the Committee on Foreign Investment in the United States (CFIUS), which screens inward investments in which a foreign government is significantly involved. Another is the presidential power to freeze foreign investments under the International Emergency Economic Powers Act[37] or to seize foreign investments under the Trading with the Enemy Act.[38] But these acts can only be invoked in a national emergency (as when Iranian assets were frozen) or war. Likewise Canada could act in a national emergency to freeze or seize foreign investments under the War Measures Act,[39] or by a special act of Parliament. For example, although no moves against Iranian investment were taken by Canada, a freeze could have been imposed under the Iranian Economic Sanctions Act of 1980.[40]

Nationalization

Nationalization of industry is simply not on the American economic agenda. By contrast, Canada regards nationalization as a viable, if undesirable, tool of investment policy. This policy alternative has two parts: the actual expropriation of industry, and the use of crown corporations.

Expropriation is rarely used at the Canadian federal level, although parts of the NEP may be an exception. Provinces, however, have been less hesitant to expropriate foreign investments. Two recent examples are potash in Saskatchewan and asbestos in Quebec. The attempted expropriation of the Asbestos Corporation owned by General Dynamics has been a long and contentious process. Although it has not provoked a clash in Canada–U.S. relations, many members of Congress have spoken out against it.[41]

The process of nationalization is more often accomplished by the creation of crown corporations, at both federal and provincial levels. The creation of Petro–Canada in 1975 was an important first step in the nationalization of the Canadian petroleum industry.[42] Other crown corporations exist in the radio, television, and rail and air transport industries at the federal level and steel and mining at the provincial level. Created inter alia to preclude foreign investment from dominating important industries, crown corporations have increasingly become a tool to diminish the role of foreign investment.

"Key" or "National Security" Sectors

The concept of reserving certain sectors from foreign investment is a milder alternative to nationalization. The restraint placed upon foreign ownership in certain sectors can be accomplished by statute, or by less formal means.[43]

In Canada, foreign owners have been effectively barred from participation in the rail, water, and motor carriers industries under federal jurisdiction.[44] Other statutes bar foreign participation in the air transport industry[45] and in the broadcasting industry.[46]

Canadian law also requires that a majority of the directors of insurance,[47] loan,[48] and trust[49] companies be resident Canadian citizens. The banking industry has been sheltered, and at least 75 percent of bank directors and shareholders must be Canadian citizens.[50] The United States was precluded from participating in the Canadian banking industry when Mercantile Bank, Canada's only foreign controlled bank (it is Dutch), was acquired by First National City Bank of New York. Canada passed a bank act in 1967 that required the sale of a controlling block of Mercantile's equity shares to Canadian citizens.[51] In 1980, however, a new bank act[52] provided improved but still limited investment opportunities for foreign banks.

Canada restricts mining[53] and oil and gas[54] leases on federal lands to companies incorporated in Canada that are at least 50 percent Canadian owned or listed on a Canadian stock exchange. These restrictions will be tightened by the NEP, and new investment is prevented, de facto, by FIRA.

In the United States, federal laws limit or prohibit foreign investment[55] in broadcasting,[56] aviation,[57] and maritime industries.[58] Although the foreign acquisition of a defense production facility is not prohibited, the U.S. Defense Department can deny a company contracts if it believes a security problem will arise.[59]

Foreign investment in energy resources on federal lands is governed by a number of statutes. The Mineral Lands Leasing Act of 1920 controls the leasing of federal lands for the production of coal, oil, shale, and natural gas.[60] Foreign owned corporations are eligible for leasing rights provided they are chartered in the United States and provided further that the investing nation affords reciprocal rights to U.S. owned corporations carrying out like activities in their country.[61] The discriminatory nature of the Trudeau government's NEP have sparked action in the U.S. Congress to examine the possibility of denying comparable rights to Canadian owned corporations active in the United States energy industry.

Tax Policies

Tax policy reflects many concerns. Occasionally international investment is at the forefront of those concerns; usually is is affected by the backwash of policies adopted for other reasons.

The former Finance Minister Walter Gordon, a Liberal, is noted for his proposals that Canada use its tax policy as a disincentive to foreign investment. In 1963 Gordon proposed the enactment of a takeover tax of 30 percent on block sales of shares of Canadian corporations to nonresidents.[62] Gordon's proposals met with limited success, but his legacy influenced future tax policies. For example, discriminatory tax laws encourage foreign owned corporations to increase the equity owned by Canadians through the provision of a lower withholding tax on dividends paid by "domesticated" corporations.[63] Moreover, Canadian controlled corporations pay income tax at a lower rate.[64] The tax laws are also used to prohibit the establishment of new foreign owned periodicals in Canada, by denying a tax deduction to advertisements placed in them.[65]

Canadian complaints about U.S. tax laws tend to focus on the operation of the Domestic International Sales Corporations (DISC) legislation.[66] The DISC provides an indefinite deferral for a portion of corporate income tax earned on export profits. By making export earnings more attractive from a tax standpoint, the DISC encourages U.S. corporations to forego foreign investment. Most Canadian criticisms of DISC are directed at its export stimulation effects. But it would be ironic if Canadians were to criticize the DISC, or U.S. duty-free zones, while seeking to diminish U.S. investment in Canada by the use of discriminatory tax laws.

Canadians also criticize U.S. tax regulations that affect transactions between parent companies and their foreign subsidiaries.[67] Regulations under section 482, for example, establish transfer prices between related companies according to a set of criteria that, in Canadian eyes, favors U.S. tax receipts. Likewise, regulations under sections 861–864 stipulate that certain expenses for interest, and home office costs, must be offset against foreign source income even though the expenses were incurred in the United States.[68]

The sporadic efforts of the Kennedy, Johnson, and Carter administrations to end "deferral"[69] could, if ever realized, adversely affect U.S. investment abroad. "Deferral" refers to the fact that the income of a foreign subsidiary of a U.S. corporation is subject to U.S. income tax only when the income is remitted to U.S. shareholders as a dividend. Deferral has provided an important advantage to U.S. investors in Canada because of the lower Canadian corporate tax rates and because greater depreciation, investment, and research deductions are allowed under Canadian tax laws. Another tax issue is the proposal to index capital gains realized by U.S. taxpayers on shares held in U.S. companies to eliminate the inflation component of such gains. Canadians claim that such indexing could have a depressing impact upon Canadian issues traded on U.S. markets, gains in which would not be indexed.[70]

To some extent national differences in tax policy are harmonized in bilateral tax treaties. After lengthy and complex negotiations, Canada and the United States concluded a tax convention in 1980. This treaty will make significant changes to the 1942 convention once ratified.

The Background to FIRA

The most significant investment control policy a nation can implement is a comprehensive screening process including the authority to exclude investments. In Canada FIRA plays this role. The Liberal government elected in 1980 appears likely to strengthen the role of FIRA. As Thomas Franck explains: "The shift toward government control over foreign investment in Canada is a response to two related but distinct issues: Canadian independence and unity."[71]

The flow of U.S. investment into Canada has exacerbated the historical struggle of Canada to remain a sovereign and confederated entity. U.S. policy was the cause of some of the evolving resentment. For example, the changes in U.S. tax policy in 1963 and 1968, to which Canada felt compelled to seek exemptions, convinced many Canadians that the influence of U.S. direct investment in Canada was unacceptable. The Nixon import surcharge "shock" of 1971, from which Canada was not exempted, was another example. By the early 1970s the vulnerability of Canada to U.S. economic policies seemed to require some mechanism to reassert Canadian control.

Likewise many Canadians perceived inward foreign investment as complicating their efforts to maintain an identity distinct from their southern neighbors. Criticism of U.S. multinational enterprises often tended toward polemics, with indictments for everything from the inability of Canada to increase its manufactured exports to the renewed outbreak of separatist agitation in Quebec.[72] Anti–American arguments were further stimulated by the Vietnam War and the civil strife that gripped the United States.

These political and social arguments, combined with the argument that multinational corporations were compromising Canadian industrial policies, yielded the quest for the third option,[73] proclaimed by the Trudeau government in 1972. This refers to the decision of the Canadian cabinet to reject the other two foreign policy options of continuing the status quo with the United States or of consciously moving closer to it. Instead, the government sought to increase Canada's economic relations with Western Europe and Japan and other nations that rim the Pacific.

In 1973 the Foreign Investment Review Act was passed. Some analysts claim that it was designed not so much as an economic measure but as an instrument to bring a "sense of well-being resulting from an increase in national independence and pride."[74] At the same time it was presumed that a screening process would increase the net benefits of inward investment to Canadians, would facilitate the pursuit of national industrial policies, and would bring greater Canadian control over the domestic economy.[75]

But in 1973 Canadians were not prepared to accept economic hardship in exchange for intangible benefits. The issue of foreign investment, while important, was less important than other economic issues.[76] Consequently the initial powers given to FIRA were limited.[77]

Canadian opinion on the FIRA screening mechanism has since divided into three basic views: (1) the traditionalists, who welcome inward investment as a boon and regard FIRA intervention as harmful; (2) the moderates, who believe that foreign investment is generally beneficial but that some screening is necessary; and (3) the nationalists, who deplore uncontrolled foreign investment and regard a strong government role as the sine qua non of a viable industrial policy.

A proponent of the traditionalist view is Stephen Globerman of York University.[78] Globerman believes that restrictions on direct foreign investment in Canada "impose net economic costs upon Canadians."[79] He traces the inefficiencies in the economy to a high protective tariff and a high degree of concentration in domestic industry. These inefficiencies result in greater production costs, lower rates of new product innovation, and smaller exports as a percentage of production.[80] Globerman sees FIRA intervention as likely to result in even less competition for domestic firms, and even greater inefficiency. He would prefer that the government reduce tariffs and strengthen its antitrust legislation. In the past Globerman has been joined in his skeptical attitude by a number of provincial governments, including Newfoundland, Nova Scotia, New Brunswick, and Manitoba.

A moderate approach is articulated by I.A. Litvak and C.J. Maule, who view FIRA screening as likely to yield benefits if it competently assesses the impact of investment proposals against a "checklist" of relevant issues.[81] The Progressive Conservative government of Joe Clark was prepared to streamline FIRA's operations in line with a moderate approach.

The nationalist school, led by Herb Gray and illustrated by H. Lufkin Robinson,[82] applauds FIRA, seeks to see it strengthened, and wants greater government involvement in investment decisions. It stigmatizes foreign investment as leading to a branch-plant economy, with decisions made at a foreign head office that has little regard for Canadian interests. Further, the branch plants supposedly succumb to the "miniature replica effect": the Canadian subsidiary reproduces the parent's full line of products for a much smaller Canadian market.[83] Thus, too much product differentiation frustrates the development of a Canadian line of products that might be competitive on a world scale. The nationalist school advocates the greater use of investment incentives and performance requirements, a longer list of key sectors, and greater patriation of foreign investment.

The Operation of FIRA

While the creation of FIRA is often thought to mark a new departure in Canadian policy, much of FIRA's activities were performed by the Canadian government before the 1973 act was passed. For example, the Canadian government used policies ranging from "moral suasion" to direct incentives in exchange for performance commitments.[84] Consequently "FIRA in some respects did not make all that basic a change in doing business in Canada."[85]

FIRA began reviewing the foreign acquisition of Canadian firms by "noneligible" persons on April 9, 1974. For the purpose of acquisition reviews, the purchase of more than 50 percent of a corporation's voting shares yields "irrefutable" control, while the acquisition of 5 percent or more of publicly traded shares, or 20 percent of the voting shares of a nonpublicly traded corporation, results in "rebuttable" control. On October 15, 1975, FIRA's mandate was expanded to include a review of new Canadian establishments by ineligible persons who did not have an existing business in Canada to which the new establishment would be related. The threshold for review of the establishment of a new business or the acquisition or control of a corporation is gross assets of more than C$250,000, and gross revenues of more than C$3 million. FIRA approval is not required for real property purchases of less than C$10 million, or 250,000 square feet of floor area.

An investment proposal that requires FIRA approval passes through four main steps.[86] The compliance branch examines the proposal to assure that it falls within FIRA's mandate before forwarding it to the assessment branch, where the agency negotiates with the investor to assure that the proposal conveys "substantial benefit" to Canada. The assessment branch reports to the minister of industry, trade, and commerce, who decides whether or not to recommend the proposal to the cabinet, whose final approval of the proposal is required.

For the United States, the most worrisome facet of the process is the exaction of performance commitments during the negotiating process. Although the commitments that an investor makes are labeled "voluntary," they are in fact a prerequisite for approval. The investor may initially select from a checklist of negotiable commitments, including: capital expenditures for plant expansion; purchasing materials and services based upon a "Buy Canadian" preference, allocating larger expenditures for research and development in Canada, appointing more Canadians to boards of directors, reinvesting earnings in Canada, and maintaining or enlarging employment in the business.[87] Once the commitments have been accepted and the proposal approved, they become a legally enforceable obligation upon the investor.

The Speech from the Throne on April 14, 1980, states that: "The Foreign Investment Review Act will be amended to provide for performance reviews of how large firms are meeting the test of bringing substantial benefits to Canada." This initiative, at the prompting of Herb Gray, would expand the mandate of FIRA to include a monitoring role over all direct foreign investments.

In addition, the Speech from the Throne suggests that amendments will be introduced in Parliament to require that major acquisition proposals by foreign companies be publicized prior to approval. Further, the government has pledged to assist Canadian companies subject to takeover offers by non–Canadians. A recent example of this policy was federal opposition to the takeover of McIntyre Mining Company by Superior Oil Company and the encouragement of a rival offer from Brascan. Despite opposition to these policies from some segments of the business community,[88] the government continues to support a more active FIRA.

The U.S. Response to FIRA

While the United States did not welcome the creation of FIRA, the official attitude was one of accommodation. Then ambassador to Canada, Thomas Enders indicated that FIRA would not become a problem in Canada–U.S. relations, provided that it did not discriminate against U.S. investors.[89] But the change in Canada's attitude was not overlooked by private firms. Since FIRA's funding investments in Canada by U.S. firms have mostly been financed by retained earnings rather than by new capital inflows. The number of U.S. commitments in Canada seems to be declining.[90] Although other factors, such as tariff cuts, may underlie these trends, the operation of FIRA has certainly had an impact. The newest proposals to expand the mandate of FIRA along with the NEP will further curb the expansion of U.S. investments.

Meanwhile, the United States has become concerned about the adverse trade impact of FIRA's performance requirements. Despite FIRA's approval rate in excess of 80 percent, about one-half of the proposals are the subject of extensive negotiations. A five-year report of the 1,613 proposals approved by FIRA (from 2,089 filed applications) claimed that over 50,000 jobs, $4 billion in investment, and $70 million in research and development were among the benefits accruing to Canada under the review process.[91] It is impossible to know what these figures would have been in the absence of FIRA or how quickly any distortions introduced by FIRA will be offset by market mechanisms. But the ability of FIRA to commit investors to maintain specific employment levels and to increase the level of investment or the export percentage of total sales might well have adverse effects for U.S. interests.

For example, FIRA claims that Brown Boveri (Canada), a Swiss owned corporation, which acquired the electrical division of Canron Limited of Canada in 1975, undertook to allow all products from the Canadian plant to be sold worldwide and gave the Canadian subsidiary exclusive rights to manufacture Brown Boveri traction motors and controls for sale in North America.[92] Consequently no U.S. investment could be made by Brown Boveri to serve the American market for these products. Other instances in which investors have accepted commitments to increase exports to the U.S. market include that of a Finnish corporation exporting rock drilling equipment and Hauserman Limited's agreement to increase its Canadian subsidiary's exports to the United States.[93]

Efforts of FIRA to extend the processing of resources in Canada and to favor Canadian suppliers in procurement activities can also have significant trade impacts contrary to U.S. interests. FIRA's efforts in this direction are reinforced by "offset" and "coproduction" requirements when Canada purchases U.S. military equipment and by laws such as the National Pipeline Act that set "Buy Canada" specifications for the Canadian leg of the Alaskan pipeline. Likewise the NEP procurement law for energy industry goods and services will be discriminatory and may lead to a formal U.S. charge against Canada under the GATT.[94]

The widely accepted view of FIRA as a bar to U.S. investment misses a significant part of its impact. The trade effect of FIRA, especially given the proposals to increase performance requirements, may eclipse the investment problem. The requirement for U.S. owned and third-country firms to apply nonmarket considerations to their purchasing, export, and research efforts directly conflicts with GATT policy.[95]

The extraterritorial reach of FIRA was affirmed in a recent case decided in Canada's federal court, *Attorney-General of Canada v. Dow Jones & Company, Incorporated.*[96] Dow Jones, a U.S. corporation, acquired another U.S. corporation, Richard D. Irwin Incorporated, that had a wholly owned Canadian subsidiary. The acquisition was made through a new Dow Jones subsidiary established for tax purposes. The Canadian court held that the change in control of the Canadian subsidiary was subject to FIRA review. Thus a transaction taking place solely in the United States could be complicated by an adverse FIRA ruling on the transfer of control of a Canadian subsidiary.[97]

U.S. Response to Inward Foreign Investment

While the policy of the United States toward inward foreign investment has been one of neutrality, events in the 1970s precipitated a movement away from that policy. The most important event was the OPEC oil embargo of 1973–74, which led to an exaggerated concern that oil-producing nations would use their revenues for acquiring companies in the United States. In reaction to these fears, over seventy foreign investment bills and resolutions were introduced during the 93rd and 94th Congresses.[98] Although no laws actually restricting direct foreign investment were passed, a number of laws were adopted to improve the government's data collection system. These include the following:

• The Foreign Investment Study Act of 1974 (PL No. 93–479) which directs the secretaries of commerce and treasury to conduct a comprehensive overall study of foreign direct and portfolio investment in the United States;

- The International Investment Survey Act of 1976 (PL No. 94–742), which directs the president to set up a regular and comprehensive data collection program on foreign investment and to conduct benchmark surveys of direct and portfolio investment at five-year intervals;

- The Domestic and Foreign Investment Improved Disclosure Act of 1977 (PL No. 95–213, title II), which requires expanded disclosure to the Securities and Exchange Commission of beneficial owners of more than 5 percent of specified kinds of securities;

- The International Banking Act of 1978 (PL No. 95–369), which regulates some activities of foreign controlled banks in the United States.

- The Agricultural Foreign Investment Disclosure Act of 1978 (PL No. 95–460), which establishes a nationwide system for monitoring farmland holdings.

Despite this legislation, both Congress and the General Accounting Office claim that U.S. data collection on inward investment remains inadequate.[100]

On May 7, 1975, President Ford established the Committee on Foreign Investment in the United States, which is composed of representatives from the Departments of Treasury, State, Defense, and Commerce, the Office of the U.S. Trade Representative, and the Council of Economic Advisors. The Committee is responsible for monitoring the impact of foreign investment in the United States and for coordinating the implementation of U.S. policy on inward investment. Reading its mandate narrowly, CFIUS met only about ten times and discussed only about a half-dozen proposed foreign government investments. It has taken a very limited interest in private foreign investment.

Canadian initiatives in the investment field have deeply affected Congressional thinking. For example, in 1976, Congress held a series of hearings on "Canadian Foreign Investment Screening Procedures and the Role of Foreign Investment in the Canadian Economy."[101] In 1979 the General Accounting Office was asked to prepare a report on the question "Should Canada's screening practices for foreign investment be used by the United States?"[102] In 1980 the U.S.

House of Representatives committee on government operations recommended the following course:

> Congress should create an FDI [foreign direct investment] registration and
> screening agency, similar to the agencies in Canada, Mexico, and in many
> other countries. This agency would (1) examine the costs and benefits to the
> United States for specific FDI transactions, (2) impose, if necessary, reason-
> able conditions on the prospective foreign investor, such as a joint venture
> requirement, so as to extract "substantial benefit" to the U.S. economy, and
> (3) bar harmful investments, where the harmful aspects cannot be alleviated
> through other measures.[103]

The reliance upon the Canadian experience by the committee in for-
mulating these recommendations is striking. Trudeau's proposals to
expand the mandate of FIRA may similarly prompt future Congressional initiatives toward controlling inward direct investment.

Meanwhile U.S. Treasury officials have continued to argue against
any additional legislative authority for CFIUS to screen foreign investment.[104] They maintain that there is no need for greater authority, that the mere establishment of greater authority might lead to
the delay of foreign investment proposals for no justifiable reason,
and that new initiatives in the United States could have unfavorable repercussions abroad both for U.S. investments and for the general investment climate.[105] As Treasury Secretary Donald Regan
has stated: "We want a generally open foreign investment policy.
We think it is in our best interest. And we intend to continue that
policy."[106]

There is no congressional consensus yet for investment restrictions, but if foreign investment in the United States continues to
grow at a significant rate, congressional initiatives will be strengthened. And if it becomes clear that the new FIRA mandate is detrimental to U.S. investors in Canada, or is seen to have a harmful trade
impact, the argument for U.S. controls will be reinforced.[107]

Canadian policymakers have probably not considered the impact
that their example might have on ending the U.S. policy of neutrality toward inward investment. On the other hand, U.S. policies that
deter Canadian outward direct foreign investment are not likely to
upset the Canadian federal government.

INVESTMENT INCENTIVE POLICIES

Federal, provincial, and state governments in Canada and the United States maintain incentive programs designed to influence private investment decisions. Investment incentives come in a variety of forms that may be grouped into three broad categories:

1. Tax and fiscal incentives: tax exemptions, abatements, and preferential assessments and accelerated depreciation allowances;

2. Direct financial assistance: loans, loan guarantees, grants, subsidies, bonds, equity participation, discounts on public services and utilities, the provision of infrastructure, employment training, and free land or low rent tenancy;

3. Information services: marketing and export assistance, site selection assistance, feasibility studies, ·assistance in complying with licensing and other regulatory paperwork, and general encouragement through overseas offices, missions, and seminars.

Incentive programs are normally used to influence the distribution of capital within a nation—between states or provinces—and not to "steal" investment capital from abroad. But the domestic impact of incentive programs is not always distinguishable from the international impact.

Incentives can have an international impact when they are used by a government in a direct effort to influence the international site choice of a firm establishing a major new plant. The classic case is the Michelin tire operation in Nova Scotia.

Perhaps more important quantitatively but less visible politically, investment incentives can influence a multinational corporation's allocation of capital expenditures between its various national operations. Thus an established multinational corporation with existing plants in Canada and the United States may shift the allocation of its capital budget to take advantage of grants, tax reductions, and other assistance programs.

In both countries various levels of government may become involved in bidding games designed to assemble the most attractive incentive package. International competition is often a by-product of domestic competition, where states compete against states and provinces against provinces. However, competition among the provinces has so far been less severe than among the states, because there are fewer provinces, their industrial bases are more specialized, and because Ontario and Quebec have much larger economies than the other provinces.[108] But competition among the provinces may increase with the growing economic power of western Canada.

How effective investment incentives are and whether they rationalize or distort investment decisions remain open questions. Information services may actually improve the efficiency of capital allocation.[109] The OECD commends the use of fiscal incentives for "positive adjustment," namely the channeling of factors of production from industries of declining demand and efficiency into those of increasing demand and efficiency.[110] But many economists assert that fiscal investment incentives are in fact distributed in a highly political manner, thus decreasing the efficient distribution of capital.[111] And some studies indicate that incentives do not significantly influence the overall investment pattern and consequently are an ineffective subsidy.[112]

Incentives in the United States

In the United States, the financial assistance programs run by the federal government exert little if any impact on international investment decisions for two main reasons: the "neutrality" of successive administrations toward direct foreign investment and the eagerness of state development authorities to take on the task.

The federal direct financial assistance incentives currently available to private investors include the Housing and Urban Development Department's Urban Development Action Grant Program and the Commerce Department's Economic Development Administration programs. Most foreign investors are not making use of these federal incentives.[113]

Although the federal government provides relatively little direct financial assistance, it does provide important tax incentives. These include the investment tax credit and accelerated depreciation programs. But the biggest tax incentive is the tax-exempt industrial development bond (IDB). The bonds are issued by state, county, and city governments, and the proceeds are used to finance plant, equipment, and other infrastructures necessary for particular invest-ments.[114] The interest income paid on these bonds is exempt from federal income tax. Consequently the interest rates are lower than would otherwise be necessary, and private firms benefit from a lower cost of capital.

The revenue cost to the U.S. Treasury of IDBs is estimated at about $1 billion for fiscal year 1981.[115] The volume of new bonds issued has grown rapidly in recent years and is estimated to have been $7 billion in 1979. Despite the general $5 million legal limit on IDBs used to finance small-scale commercial enterprises, there is no ceiling imposed on IDBs issued for housing, port facilities, air-ports, sports stadiums, power plants, and pollution abatement equip-ment.[116] For example, between 1975 and 1979, $2.7 billion of IDBs were issued to finance port facilities, an important infrastructure item for many private firms.[117]

The IDB ceiling was raised to $10 million in 1978. At the same time domestic criticism has been directed at IDB issues that are used to finance small-scale enterprises.[118] Congress may ultimately curb the use of IDBs for nonindustrial purposes, but anything short of an elimination of tax-exempt financing for large-scale infrastructure and competitive industrial projects would not satisfy Canadian offi-cials concerned with the subsidy impact of the bonds.

In comparison to the quasi-entitlement nature of federal incen-tives, state government incentives are often aimed at winning a par-ticular investment. State incentives have grown dramatically since 1965,[119] largely prompted by interstate competition. But some states do compete with Canadian provinces. The U.S. federal government has proved incapable of controlling the state programs. The General Accounting Office reports that a majority of state development agen-cies are opposed or neutral to the idea of a national code of conduct limiting state assistance programs.[120] The Advisory Commission on Intergovernmental Relations (ACIR) recently concluded that there is neither a need nor a means by which the federal government could discipline state incentives.[121] Under the Carter administration, the U.S. Treasury Department did not share the conclusions of the ACIR. The Treasury viewed the proliferation of state programs both as a hindrance to efficient resource allocation and as a cause of inter-national irritation.[122]

Incentives in Canada

In Canada investment incentives are available from both the federal and provincial governments. They are concentrated on selected areas and sectors and entail a greater degree of government involvement than in the United States.

Although Canada remains concerned with the level of U.S. direct foreign investment, both the Canadian federal government and the provincial governments have encouraged U.S. firms to invest selectively. And they back up their encouragement with incentives. A cautious welcome mat is supported by public opinion polls that show a diminished Canadian hostility toward U.S. investment.[123]

Federal incentives are designed to implement two basic policies: the pursuit of an "industrial" strategy emphasizing Canada's manufacturing sector[124] and the development of Canada's "regions" in a manner orchestrated by the federal government.[125] Federal tax incentives include corporate tax credits for the purchase of buildings, machinery, and equipment; additional tax credits for investment in all manufacturing and most processing sectors; and accelerated depreciation for capital assets in the manufacturing sector. Recently the Canadian government has concentrated on providing special incentives for research and development.[126] The total package of tax and direct financial incentives is among the most generous in the world and can reduce research and development costs by as much as 85 percent.[127]

Possibly as a result of the unified Canadian tax structure that operates for all provinces except Quebec, the federal government has taken the lead in implementing both tax and financial incentives. However, Ontario and Quebec have used their taxing authority for investment incentive purposes. And Alberta has served notice that it intends to withdraw from the cooperative tax program administered by the federal government, citing as one reason a desire to take a more active role in tax policy for development purposes.

Most direct financial incentives are distributed by the Department of Regional Economic Expansion. DREE provides loans, loan guarantees, and grants to private projects that are regarded as having the potential to create jobs in the areas designated under the program, which include almost all of Canada except for Alberta, British Columbia, and southern Ontario. Each province has concluded a general development agreement with DREE as the primary method by which to distribute the incentives and to coordinate the selection of eligible investments. By contrast with the United States, the DREE program entails considerable cooperation between the Canadian federal and provincial governments. Other federal financial assistance programs that may have an international impact are coordinated by the Enterprise Development Corporation. The corporation stresses incentives for technological, product, and process development.

In its October 1980 budget the Trudeau government signaled an intention to maintain and even expand the federal role in the investment and development process. One new program likely to have a significant impact is a C$350 million allocation to be spent over four years for industrial restructuring and manpower retraining. Much of the expenditure will be distributed in the form of regional development assistance through the DREE. A new C$4 billion Western Development Fund was planned.

The provinces also offer incentives designed to complement federal programs.[128] All of the provinces have established crown corporations to administer their own incentives programs that include loans and loan guarantees. Some provinces also provide grants and equity participation. The growth of provincial programs is the result of competition among the provinces and across the border.[129]

Canada has been quick to criticize state incentives in the United States, but it seems likely that the two major Canadian provinces are using incentives of even broader scope. Ontario, home to over 50 percent of Canada's manufacturing sector, established a temporary Employment Development Fund (EDF) to stimulate job-creating investment through the provision of direct financial grants.[130] For the fiscal year 1979–80, C$200 million was authorized for the fund. Furthermore, Ontario has recently established the Board of Industrial Leadership and Development (BILD) to coordinate the province's economic develoment and incentive programs. BILD, which will absorb the EDF, will provide risk capital amounting to some C$1.5 billion over the next five years to selected sectors, such as high technology and automotive parts manufacturing.[131] Ontario's hopes to raise one-half the total from the federal government and the private sector have so far met with limited success.[132] Quebec also has a variety of incentive programs, many operating at increased levels to compensate for the unfavorable political climate.

The growth in both Canadian and American investment incentive programs reflects a continued conviction that incentives, like performance requirements, can enable governments to alter the capital allocation decisions of multinational enterprises. The conviction persists despite academic studies questioning the effectiveness of incentives. A recent Canadian study expressed skepticism that incentives had significantly improved Canada's manufacturing sector.[133] U.S. studies generally conclude that such factors as labor costs, the level of unionization, transportation costs, access to raw materials and markets,[134] risk diversification, exchange rate levels, climate and the quality of life,[135] are more important explanations of investment decisions.

However reliable these studies may be, it is unlikely that competing governments in North America will passively condone even the hint that some other government's incentives might cause the loss of an important plant. The incentives that are provided by one government authority will thus provoke offsetting offers from others. The taxpayer will pay dearly, and governments will become more and more involved in industrial decisions.

CANADA-U.S. AUTOMOTIVE RELATIONS

The North American automotive industry furnishes the most prominent example of bilateral Canada-U.S. tension stemming from investment incentives.

Several factors distinguish the automotive industry from other sectors of the North American economy. Most significant is the 1965 Canada-U.S. Automotive Products Trade Agreement (the "auto pact"). Because of the pact Canada considers the automotive industry as "North American" despite the high degree of U.S. ownership. Another distinguishing factor is the concentrated structure of the automotive industry and the huge size of the three North American manufacturers. The advantages of size enable the major firms to play off different governments to get the best deal for their investment capital. Finally the Canadian media focused considerable attention upon the issue of whether Canada would obtain a fair share of the new capital expenditures by the industry during the 1980s.[136]

Antecedents of the Auto Pact

The Canadian automotive industry of the early 1960s was an inefficient branch-plant operation that generated staggering current account deficits with the United States of about $600 million annually, suffered from productivity of only 60–65 percent and wages of only 70 percent of U.S. levels and resulted in higher retail prices.[137] In an effort to spur the industry Canada introduced a duty remission scheme in 1962. Under the scheme a Canadian manufacturer could earn a remission of the duty on imported engines and transmissions measured by the amount that it increased the Canadian content in either vehicles or parts exported over the level of the base year (1962). In early 1964 a countervailing duty petition was filed by the Modine Manufacturing Corporation of Wisconsin claiming that the duty remission scheme constituted a "bounty or grant" under the U.S. Tariff Act of 1930 (section 303). Although the major manufacturers, automotive unions, and the U.S. government, did not initially oppose the remission scheme, independent parts producers such as Modine saw it as a threat to their livelihood.[138]

Negotiations on automotive trade commenced soon after Modine's action. Both nations sought to reduce Canada's trade deficit in automotive goods and to avoid the imposition of countervailing duties. The talks led to the signing of the Automotive Agreement on January 16, 1965.

Essentially, the pact provides for free trade between the two countries in original equipment parts and in almost all newly manufactured vehicles. It excludes trade in some specialized vehicles, tires, parts, and accessories.

The United States implemented the pact by providing duty-free entry of the designated products from Canada. In restricting duty-free entry to Canadian shipments, the United States derogated from the "most favored nation" principle of the GATT and had to apply for an Article XXV waiver. Canada meanwhile implemented the pact on a theoretically nondiscriminatory basis but in a manner that confined duty-free importation privileges to the "designated manufacturers" of the United States.

When the pact was signed Canada secured five safeguards that not only confined duty-free entry to U.S. producers but also established a base level for the Canadian production of automotive products.

Among the safeguards are the following:

- The privilege of importing automotive products on a duty-free basis was confined to Canadian manufacturers (unlike the United States where any importer can bring in Canadian products duty free).

- Manufacturers have to ensure that the ratio between net sales value of any class of vehicle *produced* in Canada and the net sales value of vehicles of that same class *sold* in Canada is the higher of 75 percent or the ratio between production and sales prevailing in the base year.

- Manufacturers must ensure that the amount of Canadian content—"in-vehicle" Canadian value added (CVA)—is at least equal to the value in the base year (August 1963–July 1964).

In the letters of agreement exchanged at the time of the auto pact's signing, the manufacturers entered into two other commitments with the Canadian government:

- In each model year the increase in value added in Canada would amount to at least 60 percent of the growth of the value of cars sold in Canada and at least 50 percent of the growth in the value of commercial vehicles sold in Canada.

- The amount of CVA produced in Canada, starting with the model year beginning in August 1967, would be increased by a further $260 million annually.

Although some of the safeguards goals were met quickly, the assembly ratio provision in the pact and the manufacturers' assurances on the CVA-to-sales ratio remain subjects of controversy. The CVA-to-sales ratio requires manufacturers to either rely on Canadian parts producers or to make the capital investments in Canada necessary to meet the target. The commitment continues to represent a form of investment guarantee for Canada, and to affect the pattern of North American automobile investment and trade.

The Aftermath of the Pact

Throughout the remainder of the 1960s and 1970s the United States adopted the position that a termination date must be set for the safeguards. Congress, labor, and industry increasingly blamed the operation of the safeguards for the fact that the U.S. balance of trade with Canada under the pact went into deficit beginning in 1969. U.S. Secretary of the Treasury John Connally labeled the safeguards as the "principal irritant" in Canada–U.S. relations in 1972.[139] Canadian negotiators have steadfastly refused U.S. efforts to end the safeguards and have stated only that they are obliged to consider the end of the safeguards at some undefined future time. Despite U.S. assertions, nothing in the pact states that the safeguards must be terminated.

Canada has preferred to emphasize a clause of the first article of the pact referring to the participation of both countries in the industry on "a fair and equitable basis." It has attempted to convert this language into a guarantee that Canada should have a set share (usually suggested as a ratio of 1:10) of the production, employment, investment, and research undertaken in the North American market. Nothing in the pact would warrant such an interpretation, but that does not stop Canadian officials from demanding a set share.[140]

According to the Reisman Commission, the auto pact has "rescued" Canada from a highly inefficient automotive industry[141] and yielded the benefits of more jobs, investment, wage parity, and cheaper prices. Nevertheless, these gains have lost their luster in the face of growing Canadian deficits (even though the deficits are not attributable to the pact), the inability to establish significant Canadian equity interests in the automotive industry, and the dearth of automotive research and development in Canada. Consequently demands for renegotiation of the pact are now common in Canada. One of the first official acts of Herb Gray, upon taking office in 1980, was to fly to Washington for consultations on the pact.

The depressed condition of the industry today, however, is hardly conducive to mutually acceptable amendments to the 1965 agreement. The United States assented to the pact in the belief that the Canadian market would maintain a positive real rate of growth and produce a continuing surplus in U.S. automotive trade with Canada.[142] These projections proved wrong. Canadian threats to renegotiate the agreement come at a time when the finances of the automotive industry are exactly the converse of those in 1965. It is most unlikely that the United States would be willing to transfer more of the burden of the industry's problems to American workers.

Indeed, the problems of the industry are so severe that one Canadian newspaper has suggested that they have made "Canada's Auto Pact as obsolete as a Detroit gas guzzler."[143] The downturn in the industry is threatening to render the dispute between Canada and the United States over the pact's safeguard provisions academic. Both Chrysler and Ford have had difficulties in meeting pact obligations, and General Motors may not be far behind in seeking some relief.[144]

New Round of Investment Incentives

Although Canada has not declared any intention to abrogate the pact, several government actions taken in the last few years can be regarded as unilateral efforts to alter the present division of benefits—and hardships. Besides continuing to claim that the safeguards guarantee Canada a fair and equitable share of the industry, several specific actions in the late 1970s reflect a more interventionist Canadian policy.

• Canada's grant in 1978 of C$68 million to Ford Motor Company of Canada to locate a C$535 million V-6 engine plant in Windsor, Ontario. The grant was a joint effort of the federal government and the government of Ontario (C$40 million from the federal government and C$28 million from Ontario). This grant represented the first time that the federal government provided a direct grant to obtain a capital investment outside of the DREE framework. It reflected the pressure on the federal government to create some type of balance in capital investment incentives as between Ontario and Quebec.

• Canada's incentive offer, valued at more than C$400 million, to the General Motors Corporation of Canada to locate an aluminum foundry in Quebec. The cost of the subsidy, which would have been provided by DREE and the province of Quebec, was to be divided on a ratio of 75:25. In the end, the offer was not accepted by GM.

• The Canadian Duty Remission Scheme announced on June 26, 1978, as an agreement between the government of Canada and the

Volkswagen Corporation. The scheme represents an incentive for foreign manufacturers to buy more Canadian parts if they want Canada to reduce the duty on imports of U.S. produced vehicles. The scheme has been offered to other producers such as Honda, Mercedes, Toyota, Nissan, and Fiat.

• New performance requirements obtained from the Chrysler Corporation in exchange for C$200 million of bail-out loan guarantees provided by the federal government. Also, the Ontario government provided a C$10 million grant for the establishment of a research and development (R&D) facility related to aluminum and plastic applications. Among the commitments that have already been breached by Chrysler Canada were the investment of C$1 billion in Canada in 1980–83 (Chrysler has announced that it will fall short of the goal by C$400 million); the maintenance of the historic ratio of U.S. to Canadian jobs (11 percent of U.S. total) for 1982–86; and more reliance on Canadian parts and R&D activities.

The subsidy for the Ford plant provoked the most controversy and led to bilateral negotiations on the entire incentives question. In early 1978 Ford approached the Canadian government with a request for assistance to meet the increased cost of plant location in Canada and to match the incentives (estimated at U.S.$5–10 million) offered by Ohio, a competitor for the proposed plant.[145] The initial Ford request was for around C$30 million. At the same time two other developments influenced the Canadian response to the Ford proposal. First, a grant to General Motors for an aluminum foundry in Quebec was offered, though not accepted, under the DREE. Second, a Canadian intergovernmental body was meeting to discuss a possible automotive investment incentive program for non–DREE areas; the proposed corporation was to provide assistance in amounts one-third to one-half those available from the DREE, with the same 75:25 division of cost between the federal and participating provincial governments.[146] This program was intended to benefit southern Ontario, one of the few Canadian regions ineligible for DREE assistance.

For several months in 1978 the governments of Canada and Ontario participated in negotiations as to how the cost of any incentive to Ford would be apportioned.[147] A final total incentive offer of C$68 million was agreed upon in July. Its acceptance was announced on August 3, 1978, the same day that a U.S. delegation was on its way to Ottawa to argue against the grant. Secretary of the Treasury

W. Michael Blumenthal had previously communicated the opposition of the United States to the Canadian Cabinet. U.S. officials, Ohio officials, and U.S. labor unions vainly lobbied Ford to refuse the grant.

Only weeks before the completion of the Ford "deal," the Canadian government announced, again despite U.S. opposition, a duty remission scheme. The U.S. views this scheme as an export subsidy, since the amount of duty reduction is determined by the value of automotive components purchased in and exported from Canada. The U.S. interpretation of GATT Article XVI and the provisions of the Subsidy/Countervailing Measures Code is that the remission of import duties is permissible only if the exported item contains components that can be physically traced to prior imports. Although no countervailing duty or section 301 petitions have been filed, the extension of the Volkswagen scheme to other foreign producers both in the United States and abroad makes it a continuing irritant. The Reisman Commission opposed the scheme and advocated as an alternative that vehicles made by producers not presently enjoying duty-free entry as "designated vehicle importers" under the auto pact be granted an equivalent status if the Canadian value added reaches a level of 60–75 percent through the purchase of Canadian parts or the use of components manufactured in Canada.[148]

The bilateral negotiations on investment incentives that began on August 4, 1978, were initiated by the United States pursuant to Article IV(A) of the auto pact, providing for negotiation and consultation on investment problems, and pursuant to the 1976 OECD Declaration on International Incentives and Disincentives. The participants had little trouble agreeing in principle that the nascent mugs game, as it came to be known, of investment incentives competition should be halted. But the conclusion of a formal bilateral accord proved impossible. Negotiations continued throughout 1978 and most of 1979, when they were suspended without agreement.

The working group negotiations hinged on several premises:

1. The intended agreement should involve some type of linkage to the Subsidies/Countervailing Measures Code of the GATT, the GATT itself (Article XVI), and the Canada–U.S. Automotive Products Trade Agreement (Article IV).

2. A specific list of incentives, by name at the federal level and by generic description at the subfederal level, would be established.

The planned use of incentives on this list would trigger a notification/consultation procedure.

3. In order to initiate the notification/consultation procedure it was proposed that

    a. Any investment incentives given to the North American automotive industry by governments in either country would be presumed to operate directly or indirectly to increase exports or reduce imports.

    b. "Serious prejudice" could result from investment incentives to the automotive sector notwithstanding the fact that no trade flows would be involved at the time the incentive question was raised.

One sticking point concerned the forms of retaliatory countermeasures available to each government if consultations failed. Canadian negotiators could not envision a scenario in which they would threaten countervailing duties against an automotive manufacturer that accepted an incentive in the United States, especially from a subfederal level of government. Hence Canada preferred to avoid any specification of countermeasures, even under GATT auspices.

Another sticking point was that the Canadians were not satisfied with the explanations of U.S. negotiators that they lacked the power to commit the fifty states. Canada maintained that the United States had to provide full particulars on all forms of subfederal incentives, a commitment that the U.S. negotiators felt unable to make. Canada meanwhile suggested that it could commit the provinces through an exchange of letters. Canada rejected the U.S. offer of a "best efforts" agreement to bind the subfederal governments.

The most difficult sticking point was the refusal of Canada to include DREE grants or grants made for R&D purposes under any agreement. DREE is a totem in Canadian politics designed to generate political magic with the poorer provinces. Thus Canada was not willing to deal away its right to use DREE monies in the automotive industry, despite the heavy burden the program might place on an already strapped federal budget.

Finally, Canada rejected the effort of the United States to lead the negotiations toward some consensus on leveling-down incentives or providing for a standstill formula. Canada contended that the equalization of investment incentives would not necessarily provide for equality in "bidding" power, as conditions in Canada might require a larger money expenditure to provide the same level of "real" incentive.

The present Canadian federal attitude toward investment incentives probably accords with the views expressed by Jack Horner, the minister of industry, trade, and commerce in the last Liberal government. Horner condemned competitive subsidization as a "costly no-win proposition," but reaffirmed during the negotiations in 1979, that:

> pending their successful outcome, the Canadian government will not stand by while investment is lost as a result of incentives available in other countries. To offset the effect of such incentives, special federal assistance will be considered when such aid is beyond the financial capability of the province concerned and when existing federal programs do not apply.[149]

This position presages further battles in the bidding war between Canada and the United States. The mugs game is far from under control.

RECOMMENDATIONS

Canadian–U.S. investment relations are complicated in their own right. And they are intertwined with industrial policy, trade, energy, and cultural relations.

The essential question facing both nations is this: Can the relative bilateral economic harmony that has prevailed since World War II be maintained? In the realm of investment relations it increasingly appears that the unilateral policies of both nations and reactions to each other's initiatives will disturb this harmony.

The challenges posed to U.S. negotiators will remain complicated by the power struggle between the Canadian government and the provinces. But Canada's constitutional difficulties should not prevent the United States from adopting a clear policy aimed at protecting its own economic interests. The encouragement of a strong Canadian central government as the most viable long-term negotiating partner need not conflict with the vigorous protection of U.S. investment interests.

U.S. investment policy will need to focus on three levels:

• The United States should continue to enlist Canada's active participation in the design of international rules governing investment by multinational corporations.

- The United States should continue its efforts to convince Canada that both federal and subfederal investment incentives should be disciplined when they have a transnational impact. This goal requires that the United States make an effort to gain cooperation from the fifty states to discipline their incentive programs, either by way of a standstill or an advance notification system.

- The United States should continue to respond to investment problems generated by Canadian policy concerning, for example, the NEP, FIRA, and auto incentives. Canada will continue to claim that such policies are consistent with her bilateral and international obligations. Whatever the legal merits of Canada's position, the United States cannot passively accept economically damaging Canadian policies.

Although overall investment relations can be expected to remain stable, tension may be expected if the new NEP and FIRA policies are not modified. U.S. displeasure about these programs has been communicated to Canada with little effect. More impact has been made by internal Canadian opposition to the effects of the NEP. The cost of Canadianization and economic sovereignty may be prohibitive for Canada in the 1980s. One Canadian observer, questioning the resolve of the Trudeau government with regard to the NEP, has stated that "Ottawa is moving so slowly on Canadian ownership that buzzards are circling."[150] A Canadian consensus, however, still favors the manipulation of direct foreign investment to serve Canadian needs. This manipulation imposes costs on the United States and needs to be addressed.

There is significant U.S. opinion that Canada is "getting away with something." FIRA acts to screen U.S. investments, while Canadian investment capital moves freely in the United States. U.S. business is beginning to demand an official response to Canadian investment policies. As an angry president of the Hobart Corporation, the subject of an unsuccessful takeover effort by Canadian Pacific, stated before the Senate committee on the judiciary:[151]

> Should we stand idle and watch our economy come under the control of foreign investors? Some nations have constructed barriers that have often proven impenetrable to U.S. foreign investments, including friendly ones. Without question, Canadian law and governmental policy would prohibit this transaction in reverse.... Should Congress permit American companies to stand vulnerable to the sort of raid underway by Canadian Pacific, reaching out from all of the protections of fortress-Canada?

The next question is then: What type of response? The response will be made in the context of U.S. policy toward foreign investment. Further nationalistic actions by Canada will strengthen the growing opinion that the United States should move against foreign investment in the United States. If this view prevails the first step will entail the creation of a more effective bureaucratic structure. Perhaps CFIUS will be overhauled to monitor the impact of NEP and FIRA on U.S. investment and trade interests. The United States does not need a review agency like those of Canada and Mexico, but it does require a policy body that can respond to the initiatives of other countries.

One U.S. response could involve reciprocal restrictions on Canadian investment in the United States. Options now being considered by the U.S. Congress include removing Canadian access to federal lands under the Mining Lands Leasing Act of 1920 and imposition of a moratorium against foreign investment in the U.S. energy industry. In some cases a complaint leading to trade action might be appropriate.[152] A policy of retortion is complicated by the fact that innocent parties, including subsidiaries of U.S. multinational enterprises, would suffer. Moreover, the Canadian government is unlikely to be upset by restrictions on the entry of Canadian capital into the United States, although it would find trade restrictions distasteful.

In considering retaliatory action the United States must be careful not to overreact. Any U.S. initiative should come only after a quantitative assessment of the impact of any suspect Canadian policy. And U.S. responses should be sensitive to unresolved Canadian complaints about U.S. policies and actions.

Finally it may be expected that the Trudeau government will continue to indulge the Reagan administration's talk of freer North American trade in the hope that such discussions will forestall any U.S. response to the NEP or FIRA. In fact, while a true free trade accord could harmonize relations, it stands little chance of realization.

NOTES TO CHAPTER 4

1.   "The essential distinction between direct investment and portfolio investment is that the former involves legal control of the underlying real asset. Foreign direct investment is largely represented by equity capital in the form of shares of incorporated subsidiaries and affiliates. Portfolio invest-

ment covers purchases of public issues of bonds and debentures of corporations and governments as well as minority holdings of securities." The distinction between direct and portfolio investment is taken from A.E. Safarian, *Foreign Ownership of Canadian Industry* (Toronto: McGraw-Hill, 1966), and is adopted by Stephen Globerman, *U.S. Ownership of Firms in Canada* (Washington, D.C.: National Planning Association; and Montreal: C.D. Howe Institute, 1979), p. 6.

2. Foreign Investment Review Act, 1973–74, c. 46, s. 3, SI/74–43; 1976–77, c. 52, s. 128, s. 31, Act in force 9.4.74; see SI/74–52, and 15.10.75; see SI/75–99.

3. Executive Order No. 11858, May 7, 1975.

4. Speech of C. Fred Bergsten, American Law Institute/American Bar Association, New York, February 28, 1980, p. 5.

5. For example, Task Force on the Structure of Canadian Industry, *Foreign Ownership and the Structure of Canadian Industry* (Watkins Report) (Ottawa: Queen's Printer, 1968); *Report of the House of Commons Standing Committee on External Affairs and National Defence* (Ottawa: Queen's Printer, 1970); *Foreign Direct Investment in Canada* (Gray Report) (Ottawa: Government of Canada, 1972).

6. Arlene Wilson, *Foreign Investment in U.S. Industry*, (U.S. Congress: Congresssional Research Service–Major Issues System, 1980), p. 2.

7. C. Fred Bergsten, Thomas Horst, and Theodore H. Moran, *American Multinationals and American Interests* (Washington, D.C.: The Brookings Institution, 1978).

8. Ibid., p. 493.

9. "Operations of Federal Agencies in Monitoring, Reporting on, and Analyzing Foreign Investments in the United States," Hearings before a Subcommittee on Government Operations, U.S. House of Representatives, 95th, 96th Cong., pt. 1–5.

10. Twentieth Report by the Committee on Government Operations, U.S. House of Representatives, 96th Cong., 2d sess.

11. Ibid., pp. 160–163.

12. Amendment to Income Tax Act, s. 19, 1974–75–76, 106, ss. 1, 2; 1977–78, s. 12.

13. Amendment to Income Tax Act, s. 19.1 added, 1974–75–76, c. 106, s. 3 in force 22.9.76, see SI/76–122; 1977–78, c. 1, s. 13.

14. *Canada–United States Relations–Volume II: Canada's Trade Relations with the United States*, the Standing Senate Committee on Foreign Affairs (Ottawa: Queen's Printer, 1978).

15. See section 612 of the Trade Act of 1974 (19 U.S.C. 2486), as amended by sec. 1104 of the Trade Agreements Act of 1979. In 1974 Congress only urged that the option of closer trade ties with Canada be explored; the 1979 act amended this option to include all North American countries.

16.   Speech of Herb Gray, in Montreal, June 3, 1980, quoted in "Quarterly Report of the Foreign Investment Review Agency," Second Quarter, April–June 1980, p. 1.

17.   The proposed NEP legislation, the Canada Oil and Gas Act (Bill C–48), is still being debated before Parliament.

18.   "If Ottawa Reassess Its Stand, So Will We," *The Financial Post* December 20, 1980, 1.

19.   See, for example, excerpts of remarks of John D. Porter, managing director of the Independent Petroleum Association of Canada, *The Financial Post* March 28, 1981: p. 24.

20.   See "Federal Budget Update," Greenshields Research Report (Toronto: November 4, 1980), and "Basic Report: The Canadian Oils," Wood Gundy Company (Toronto: December 2, 1980).

21.   Minister of Energy, Mines and Resources, "The National Energy Program" (Ottawa: Supplies and Services, 1980), p. 20. The minister puts the foreign controlled share of all industry sales at 71.7 percent, almost all of which is U.S. controlled.

22.   For example, Getty Oil Company was refused approval by FIRA of its acquisition of 86 percent of Canadian Reserve Oil and Gas Limited. Getty acquired the Canadian interest as a result of a purchase of the firm's U.S. parent company. *The Washington Post*, March 20, 1981, p.D.2.

23.   Speech at the *National Journal*'s Conference on Foreign Investment in the United States Economy, Washington, D.C., May 4, 1981.

24.   Hyman Solomon, "Ronnie's Visit," *The Financial Post*, March 7, 1981, p. 1. U.S. Special Trade Representative Brock suggested that if Canada wants continued access to U.S. trade and investment markets, it must offer "quid pro quo" access to U.S. firms. Also, U.S. State Department Assistant Secretary Elinor Constable testified before a congressional committee that Canada is one of "the most restrictive of industrialized nations" on investment policy.

25.   Paul M. Goldberg and Charles P. Kindleberger, "Toward a GATT for Investment," *Law and Policy in International Business* 2 (Summer 1970): 295–323.

26.   As A.E. Safarian notes, "Some governments look upon such codes to improve the international environment for such enterprises, others see the codes as a way to regulate them more effectively. For this and many other reasons, national policies are likely to continue to remain dominant with international approaches playing a supplementary role." In "Multinational Policy and Multinational Enterprises," *International Journal* 34 (Winter 1978–79): 110.

27.   *International Direct Investment* (Paris: OECD, 1979), p. 1.

28.   *International Investment and Multinational Enterprises* (Paris: OECD, 1979 ed.), pp. 11–13. Also, for a thorough discussion of the guidelines, see Philip Coolidge, George C. Spina, and Don Wallace, Jr. (eds.), *The*

OECD Guidelines for Multinational Enterprises: A Business Appraisal (Washington, D.C.: Institute for International and Foreign Trade Law, 1977).

29. "The OECD Guidelines for Multinational Enterprises," *Journal of World Trade Law*, 12 (July–August 1978): 347.

30. Statement of Allan J. MacEachen, Secretary of State for External Affairs, OECD Minister's Meeting, June 21, 1976.

31. David Fouquet, "OECD Puts Canada in the Dock," *The Financial Post*, June 6, 1981, p. 20.

32. "Agreement on Interpretation and Application of Articles VI, XVI, and XXXIII of the General Agreement on Tariffs and Trade," April 12, 1979, MTN/NTM/236.

33. "Canadian Direct Investment in the United States" (Washington, D.C.: U.S. Department of Commerce International Trade Administration, July 1980), p. 3.

34. Ibid., p. 4.

35. "Canada's International Investment Position," Statistics Canada, 1975, Cat. No. 67–202.

36. "Canadian Foreign Investment Screening Procedures and the Role of Foreign Investment in the Canadian Economy," Hearings before the Subcommittee on Inter–American Economic Relationships of the Joint Economic Committee, U.S. Congress, 94th Cong., 1st and 2nd sess., "Written Statement of Thomas M. Franck," p. 152.

37. Public Law No. 95–223, 91 Stat. 1625 (1977), title II.

38. Act of Oct. 6, 1917, chap. 106; 40 Stat. 411.

39. Revised Statutes (R.S.), 1970 chap. W–2.

40. Iranian Economic Sanctions Act, 1980, chap. 39.

41. In one two–day period nine Senators went on record in opposition to the expropriation action. *Congressional Record*, 96th Cong., 1st Sess., S. 5547–50, May 9, 1979, and S. 5670, 5704, May 10, 1979.

42. Petro–Canada Act—1974–75–76, c. 61; s. 2, SI/75–124; s. 15, 1976–77, c. 10, s. 53.1; s. 29 (consequential amendments).

43. This section on Canadian restraints relies heavily on the "Written Statement of Thomas M. Franck," note 36 supra, pp. 152–156.

44. National Transportation Act, R.S., 1970 chap. N–17, sec. 27.

45. Aeronautics Act, R.S., 1970 chap. A–3, sec. 14(e), (f), (1).

46. Broadcasting Act of 1967–68, R.S., 1970 chap. B–11, sec. 3(b).

47. R.S., 1970 chap. I–15, sec. 6(4).

48. R.S., 1970 chap. L–12, secs. 44–48.

49. R.S., 1970 chap. T–16, secs. 37–41.

50. Bank Act, R.S., 1970 chap. B–1, secs. 18(3), 53(1).

51. Ibid.

52. Bank Act 1980, c. 40 (Part 1, section 2). Act in force 01/12/80 except s. 201(5) and 202(7), see SI/80–203.

53.   Canada Mining Regulations, SOR/61–86, sec. 45(2), SOR/62–249, sec. 20, and SOR/66–80.

54.   Canada Oil and Gas Regulations, SOR/60–182, sec. 32(3).

55.   Two good sources on U.S. restrictions are Marans, Williams, and Griffin (eds.), *Foreign Investment in the United States* (Washington, D.C.: The District of Columbia Bar, 1980); and, Committee to Study Foreign Investment in the U.S., *A Guide to Foreign Investment under United States Law* (New York: Section of Corporation, Banking and Business Law, American Bar Association, 1979).

56.   10 U.S.C. secs. 2272(f), 2279 (1970). Standards are set pursuant to Executive Order No. 10,865, February 20, 1960. Also see Radovan S. Pavelic and Stefan M. Lopatkiewicz, "Federal Restrictions in Participation by Foreign Investors in Defense and other Government Contracts," in *Foreign Investment in the United States*, p. 253 and "Government Contracting," in *A Guide to Foreign Investment under United States Law*, pp. 195–200.

57.   Act of June 19, 1934, chap. 652, 48 Stat. 1064, as amended, 47 U.S.C. sec. 310 (Supp. IV 1974). Also see David M. Phillips and John C. Jost, "Foreign Investment in U.S. Communications," in *Foreign Investment in the United States*, pp. 423–469, and "Communications," in *A Guide to Foreign Investment under United States Law*, pp. 178–82. Alien ownership commercial communications satellite systems is limited by Communications Satellite Act of August 31, 1962, 76 Stat. 419, as amended, 47 U.S.C. secs. 701–44 (1970).

58.   30 U.S.C. sec. 181 (1970). Also see J. Eugene Marans and David M. Phillips, "Federal Restrictions on Foreign Direct Investment in Energy," in *Foreign Investment in the United States*, pp. 474–75, and "Energy," in *A Guide to Foreign Investment under United States Law*, pp. 170–172.

59.   However, a congressional report suggests that the State Department has so far "stymied" the reciprocity provisions of the 1920 act, "Adequacy of the Federal Response," note 10 supra, p. 137. A hearing was held on May 7, 1981 before the House committee on the interior on H.R. 2826, a bill introduced to place a moratorium on acquisition and mergers by aliens in lands under the 1920 act. While relevant to the NEP, the hearing was actually sparked by a challenge to Canadian reciprocal rights under the act by St. Joe Minerals Corporation when resisting a takeover attempt by Seagrams Corporation.

60.   Act of August 23, 1958, sec. 1401, 72 Stat. 806, 49 U.S.C. secs. 301–1542 (1970). Also see Jon Paugh and David M. Phillips, "Federal Restrictions on Aviation and Aeronautics," in *Foreign Investment in the United States*, and "Air Transportation," in *A Guide to Foreign Investment under United States Law*, pp. 175–178.

61.   See David M. Phillips and George A. Quardino, "Federal Restrictions Affecting Foreign Investment in the Maritime Industries," in *Foreign*

Investment in the United States, and "Maritime Activities," in *A Guide to Foreign Investment under United States Law*, pp. 159–69. Shipping Act of September 7, 1916, chap. 451, sec. 1, 30 Stat. 728, 46 U.S.C. secs. 801–842 (1970). Merchant Marine Act of June 29, 1938, chap. 858, 49 Stat. 1975, 46 U.S.C. (1970), 46 U.S.C. sec. 316, 1241(b) (1970).

62. House of Commons Debates, 26th Parliament, 1st sess., 1006 (1963), quoted in Thomas Franck, "Written Statement," p. 156.

63. See Income Tax Act, s. 125, 1974–75–76, c. 26, s. 81; 1976–77, c. 4, s. 49; 1977–78, c. 1, ss. 59, 101(f), c. 32, s. 32; 1979, chap. 5, s. 38, and s. 125.1 added, 1973–74, c. 29, s. 1; 1974–75–76, c. 26, s. 82; 1976–77, c. 4, s. 50; 1977–78, c. 1, s. 60.

64. Amendment to Income Tax Act, 19–20–21, c. 63, sec. 126.

65. Amendment to Income Tax Act, s. 19, 1974–75–76, c. 106, ss. 1, 2; 1977–78, c. 1, s. 12.

66. Robert L. Perry, "Industrial Gaps Left as U.S. Withdraws," *The Financial Post*, April 25, 1981: 21.

67. R.P. Kaplan, "Transborder Skirmishes," *The Tax Executive*, 31 (1979): 113.

68. Ibid., p. 115.

69. See H. David Rosenbloom, "Current United States Foreign Tax Reform Proposals," *Canada–United States Law Journal* 2 (Summer 1979): 145–150.

70. See Robert D. Brown, "Recent Tax Developments and Issues Affecting Canada–United States Transnational Business Activities," *Canada–United States Law Journal* 2 (Summer 1979): 143.

71. "Written Statement of Thomas Franck," p. 147.

72. For example, see Kari Levitt, *Silent Surrender: The Multinational Corporation in Canada* (1970).

73. *"Foreign Policy for Canadians"* (Ottawa, 1970), and "Canada–U.S. Relations: Options for the Future" *International Perspectives* (Autumn 1972).

74. A.E. Safarian and Joel Bell, "Issues Raised by National Control of the Multinational Corporation," in *Multinational Corporations and Governments*, p. 74.

75. For a discussion of the origins of FIRA see Peter Morici, Arthur J.R. Smith, and Sperry Lea, *Canadian Industrial Policy* (Washington, D.C.: National Planning Association, 1981), pp. 76–89.

76. Don Munton and Dale H. Poel, "Electoral Accountability and Canadian Foreign Policy: The case of foreign investment," *International Journal* 33 (Winter 1977/78): 222–23.

77. Ibid., p. 241.

78. Globerman, *U.S. Ownership*, p. 43.

79. Ibid.

80. Hearings, Joint Economic Committee, p. 72.

81. "Canadian Outward Investment: Impact and Policy," *Journal of World Trade Law* 14 (July/August 1980): 313.

82. *Canada's Crippled Dollar* (Toronto: James Lorimer, 1980), pp. 98–102.

83. H. Edward English, *Industrial Structure in Canada's International Competitive Position* (Private Planning Association of Canada, 1964), p. 37.

84. Safarian and Bell, "Issues Raised," p. 69.

85. Hearings, Joint Economic Committee, p. 34.

86. Much of the subsequent explanation on the operation of FIRA is adopted from General Accounting Office, "Should Canada's Screening Practices for Foreign Investment Be Used by the United States" (ID–79–45) September 6, 1979.

87. Ibid., pp. 8–9.

88. See Robert Gibbens, "Publication of Bids Opposed," *The Globe and Mail*, August 27, 1981, p. B2.

89. Thomas Claridge, "Canada Told to Resist Using Investment Laws against U.S. Firms," *The Globe and Mail*, April 30, 1976, p. B2.

90. Robert C. Perry, "Canada Waking up to Reality over Foreign Control," *The Financial Post*, March 8, 1980, p. 5. U.S. nonfinancial businesses decreased from 4,404 in 1976, to 4,288 in 1977. Also see Robert C. Perry, "Tomorrow's Branch Plants," *The Financial Post*, April 25, May 2, 9, 1981. Perry discusses changes in the U.S. ownership role in Canada's manufacturing sector and explains why U.S. corporations are leaving Canada.

91. FIRA, *Five Year Summary Report*, 1974–1979 (1980).

92. Ibid., p. 7.

93. Cable of the U.S. embassy in Canada, November 24, 1979.

94. Hyman Solomon, "US warns NEP may violate GATT," *The Financial Post*, February 14, 1981, p. 1.

95. Cable of the U.S. embassy in Canada, November 24, 1979.

96. Peter R. Hayden, "FIRA Rules Cover Outside Takeover," *The Financial Post*, August 9, 1980, p. 13.

97. Getty Oil Company recently faced such a problem; see note 22 supra.

98. Wilson, *Foreign Investment in U.S. Industry*, p. 5.

99. U.S. General Accounting Office, *Foreign Direct Investment in the United States — The Federal Role* (ID–80–24), June 3, 1980, p. 6.

100. Ibid., p. 9, and "Adequacy of the Federal Response," p. 49.

101. Hearings, Joint Economic Committee.

102. General Accounting Office, *Foreign Direct Investment*.

103. "Adequacy of the Federal Response," p. 41.

104. "Operations of Federal Agencies," p. 65, Part III.

105. Ibid.

106. Speech at the *National Journal*'s Conference on Foreign Investment in the United States Economy, May 4, 1981.

107. According to one Canadian observer, the Trudeau cabinet has not yet endorsed the fundamental FIRA changes championed by Herb Gray. See

Stephen Duncan, "Gray Unlikely to Get the Tougher FIRA He Wants," *The Financial Post*, March 21, 1981, p. 8.

108. Globerman, *U.S. Ownership*, pp. 70–71.

109. "The Role of State Development Agencies in U.S. Positive Adjustment," prepared by the U.S. Delegate to the OECD High Level Group on Positive Adjustment, p. 22, and see Gary C. Cornia et al., "State–Local Fiscal Incentives and Economic Development," *Urban and Regional Development Series No. 4*, Academy for Contemporary Problems, Columbus, Ohio, June 1978.

110. "Role of State Development Agencies," p. 2.

111. Ibid., p. 22.

112. Ibid.

113. U.S. Department of Housing and Urban Development Office of Community Planning and Development, "The Impact of Foreign Direct Investment on U.S. Cities and Regions," February 27, 1979.

114. General Accounting Office, *Foreign Direct Investment in the United States*, p. 29.

115. Robert J. Samuelson, "Industrial Revenue Bonds—Economic Boon or Public Ripoff?," *National Journal* (October 18, 1980): 1,749.

116. Ibid., p. 1,750.

117. Ibid.

118. Ibid., p. 1,749.

119. Ibid., p. 1,746. Table: "The States Grow Generous," Source: Industrial Development Research Council.

120. General Accounting Office, *Foreign Direct Investment in the United States*, p. 67.

121. Ibid., p. 33.

122. Bergsten speech.

123. See survey results in Harold von Riekhoff, John Sigler, and Brian Tomlin, *Canada–United States Relations* (Washington, D.C.: National Planning Association, and Montreal: C.D. Howe Institute, 1980), p. 84.

124. In the budget of May 1982, former Finance Minister John Turner outlined the government's industrial strategy, which called for the development of Canada's lagging manufacturing sector through the use, inter alia, of tax and fiscal incentives. This goal remains relatively constant.

125. The Regional Development Incentives Act, R.S., 1970, chap. R–3, and amendments.

126. J. Peter Johnson, *Government Financial Assistance Programs in Canada* (Toronto: Price Waterhouse, 1980), p. 89.

127. Ibid., p. 90.

128. Ibid., p. 125.

129. Andrew H. Malcolm, "Ontario Welcoming Concern from U.S.," *The New York Times*, March 12, 1978, p. 17.

130. Johnson, *Government Financial Assistance Programs*, p. 252.

131. Deborah Dowling, "Ontario Goes the Super-Board Route," *The Financial Post*, December 27, 1980: 8.

132. Deborah Dowling, "Ottawa May Not Be Partners in Ontario BILD Programs," *The Financial Post*, May 23, 1981, p. 6.

133. J. Douglas May, "Investment Incentives as Part of an Industrial Strategy," *Canadian Public Policy*, 5 (Winter 1979): 79. May discusses, inter alia, the results of Canada's Tax Measures Review Committee.

134. General Accounting Office, *Foreign Direct Investment in the United States*, pp. 34–35.

135. Michael R. Gordon, "With Foreign Investment at Stake, It's One State against the Others," *National Journal* (October 18, 1980): 1,745.

136. David Leyton–Brown, "The Mug's Game: Automotive Investment Incentives in Canada and the U.S.," *International Journal*, 35 (Winter 1979/80): 171.

137. *The Canadian Automotive Industry: Performance and Proposals for Progress*, Inquiry into the Automotive Industry, Simon Reisman, Commissioner (Minister of Supply and Services Canada, October 1978), p. 36.

138. Ibid., p. 23.

139. Ibid., p. 43.

140. *Commons Debates*, 31st Parliament, 1st sess., vol. 2, November 15, 1979, pp. 1,384–85. See statements of Mark MacGuigan, now secretary of state for external affairs.

141. *Canadian Automotive Industry*, p. 232.

142. R.J. Wonnacott and Paul Wonnacott, *Free Trade between the United States and Canada* (Cambridge, Mass.: Harvard University Press, 1967), p. 382, quoted in Charles Stedman, "Canada–U.S. Automotive Agreement: The Sectoral Approach," *Journal of World Trade Law*, 8 (March/April 1974), p. 178.

143. Patricia Best, "Auto Pact up to the Brink," *The Financial Post*, January 24, 1981, p. 1.

144. Ibid.

145. Leyton–Brown, "Mug's Game," p. 172.

146. Ibid., p. 173.

147. Ibid., pp. 172–76.

148. *Canadian Automotive Industry*, p. 245.

149. Remarks of Jack Horner to the Windsor Chamber of Commerce, March 14, 1979, p. 5.

150. Roderick McQueen, "The Twitch and Squawk of Big Oil," *Maclean's* (June 1, 1981): 44.

151. Remarks of David B. Meeker, President and Chief Executive Officer, Hobart Corporation, before the U.S. Senate Committee on the Judiciary, February 16, 1981.

152. Hyman Solomon, "Border–TV Issue Surfaces Again," *The Financial Post*, May 16, 1981, p. 3. An unfair trade practice finding was made against Canada under Section 301 of the U.S. Trade Act of 1974 (19 U.S.C. 2411 (1976)), with regard to Canada's Bill C–58, denying tax deductions to Canadian advertisers on U.S. border TV stations. Congress failed to pass the "mirror-image" law recommended by President Carter that would have denied comparable U.S. tax deductibility to U.S. advertisers using two Ontario radio and TV stations. The issue remains alive, however, and the dispute may spread to the growing cable TV industry, in which there is heavy Canadian investment in the United States. For a fuller treatment of the issue of media investment see Isaiah A. Litvak and Christopher J. Maule, "Bill C–58 and the Regulation of Periodicals," *International Journal*, 36 (Winter 1980–81): 70–90.

5 CANADA-U.S. TRADE RELATIONS
Prospects and Problems in the 1980s

John M. Volpe

A movement toward closer links between Canada and the United States since World War II[1] can be seen in merchandise trade patterns. Substantially increased trade interdependence has developed because of geographical propinquity, similar levels of affluence, a concurrence of consumer tastes and life styles, and until recently the complementary nature of the two economies. These and other long-term influences have been reinforced by diverse recent elements, including the vast increase in transactions between American parent companies and their Canadian subsidiaries, the Canada-U.S. Automotive Agreement of 1965, and progress in reducing barriers to trade, chiefly through successive rounds of negotiations of the General Agreement on Tariffs and Trade (GATT) but also in other important ways. The extent of the bilateral trade relationship is well known: Each country is the other's largest trading partner, bilateral trade having grown substantially both absolutely and relative to Canadian and American trade in other markets. The scope of Canada-U.S. trade ties vitally affect the economies of both countries.

During the 1970s certain problems in this trade relationship arose as a consequence of similar national policies adopted by the two countries to meet new internal and external challenges they faced in common, their altered national perceptions of the bilateral relationship, and the growth of government intervention within and the substantial interdependence between their respective economies.

153

Policymakers on both sides of the border wrestled with actual or expected changes in the bilateral trade account due directly or indirectly to such influences as developments in energy and automobile products trade (both perennial Canadian–U.S. trade issues); Canadian import quotas on U.S. egg sales and the proliferation of bilateral trade barriers on North American livestock and meat; the temporary U.S. import surcharge; the U.S. Domestic International Sales Corporations (DISC); multilateral trade negotiations; the services trade dimensions of Canadian "cultural nationalism" as found, for example, in the cross-border advertising issue (and the linking of this issue by the U.S. Congress with the U.S. tax convention); the Canadian Foreign Investment Review Agency (FIRA); the operations in Canada of U.S. multinational corporations; and industrial incentive policies and programs adopted or contemplated by both countries.

Some bilateral trade issues have disappeared but others still exist, some in different forms. Bilateral trade problems can be expected to command attention during the 1980s, given the scope of the commercial relationship between Canada and the United States, the growing tendency of both countries to act unilaterally, and the increased politicization and linking of issues. The need to deal with the issues will become even more urgent as both countries face what is perhaps the most uncertain international and domestic economic environment of the postwar period.

External Developments

Until the 1970s, Canadian–U.S. relations proceeded for the most part in a spirit of close cooperation and accommodation. Although the asymmetry of the relationship occasionally resulted in periods of uneasiness for some Canadians, it was generally accepted that a special relationship existed between the two countries in terms of the policies each pursued regarding the other and in the degree to which the two economies had become interdependent. From the early 1970s, in contrast, it has become evident that the bilateral relationship has entered a new and more difficult phase, shaped by a series of external and internal challenges and by the reordering of national priorities to face these challenges.[2]

The increased ability of producers in the European Community and Japan to compete on relatively equal terms with their North American counterparts and the growth of high-technology manufacturing in the newly industrialized countries such as Brazil, Mexico, and Taiwan have created a more competitive world trading and investment climate.[3] The international rivalry for markets, natural resources, and capital will become even more intense in the 1980s because of the projected decline in world economic growth rates and the rise of nationalistic and protectionist sentiments around the globe. These pressures are compounded by key issues such as world-wide inflation and the relative ease with which it is transmitted from country to country, balance-of-payments adjustments problems and the accumulation of debt in deficit countries, the high cost of energy and uncertainty with respect to future prices and supplies, and the demands of the developing countries for greater participation in and benefits from the integrated international economy without their subscribing to GATT rules governing world trade.

Against this background of a more competitive trading environment, increasing nationalism and protectionism, and the persistence of certain global economic problems, the accelerated growth of post-war world economic interdependence means that policies adopted by one country to solve national problems often have a considerable impact on other countries. Because of the growth in economic interdependence, the industrialized countries have tended to become more similar in terms of the broad structural characteristics of their economies and have exhibited a narrowing of differences in productivity levels, real wage levels, and related factors. As a result, trade flows among the industrialized countries are increasingly sensitive to small adjustments in domestic output and prices, temporary technological advantages, skill differences, and other factors that can be and often are affected by selective government intervention.

In the Canada–U.S. relationship, government economic programs at the provincial or state level as well as the federal level often create bilateral trade conflicts because of the substantial interdependence of the two economies. Research has demonstrated that the business cycles of both countries are closely related in timing and duration, indicating, because of the asymmetry of the relationship, the sensitivity of the Canadian economy to developments occurring in the United States. Although knowledge of existing linkages is still limited,[4] the probability is quite high that government economic programs, even when focused on domestic problems, will "spill over" and thus irritate the bilateral relationship, particularly in trade but also in other areas. Trade conflicts may become more complex in the foreseeable future because the U.S. government at the federal level (not the state level) is backing away from regulating and redirecting production and consumption patterns between domestic and foreign markets while, in Canada, government has become even more influential in shaping and redirecting economic decisions.[5]

The Current Economic Environment

The economic outlook for the second half of the 1980s is guardedly optimistic for improved economic performance in both countries. If realized, the improved performance should contribute positively toward reducing the number and intensity of bilateral trade issues. Both countries must continue to respond to well-entrenched problems of inflation,[6] unemployment, regional and other income disparities, poor productivity, low levels of investment, and market disruptions caused by domestic and international forces. These problems have a significant effect on bilateral trade relations, of course. At the same time adjustments to be made to rapidly changing world economic conditions will color the environment within which bilateral trade occurs.

Prospects for improved economic performance in Canada, given the relatively open nature of the economy, depend heavily on the success of the United States in responding to its problems. The nature of the bilateral economic relationship is such that declines in U.S. economic growth rates, particularly during recessions, are quickly transmitted to Canada in the form of reduced Canadian exports and ensuing Canadian current account problems. With its export sector comprising 28 percent of the economy, Canada cannot entirely divorce its external economic policies from developments in the U.S. economy.

The comprehensive economic program pursued by the administration of President Ronald Reagan in the form of broad tax reductions designed to reduce marginal tax rates on income and to remove impediments to work, save, and invest; massive cuts in the growth of federal spending; reforms to reduce regulatory impediments to the private sector; and closer coordination between the administration and the Federal Reserve Board to restrain the growth of monetary aggregates have been put forward to increase economic growth and reduce inflation. To the extent these U.S. goals are attained, Canadian economic growth should be stimulated.

The debate in Canada over shaping the nation's economic future could well lead to further bilateral trade issues. In general the Liberal government of Prime Minister Pierre Elliott Trudeau appears to believe that Canada is too decentralized and that further moves in this direction would make the nation ungovernable. The political strains that have ensued (in the form of federal–provincial, French–English, and Canada–U.S. issues) will make bilateral relations more difficult in the decade ahead. Federal–provincial disputes over Canada's National Energy Program (NEP) have heightened uncertainty over tax burdens and other factors influencing investment in the energy sector and have deferred, perhaps for a long while, the impetus the energy investment boom was expected to have on the Canadian economy. Other key Canadian initiatives that directly or indirectly affect bilateral trade patterns and issues are the move toward greater Canadian ownership in energy and high-technology manufacturing, increased federal control through the FIRA over the activities of foreign (mainly U.S.) companies through the imposition of performance requirements affecting exports, local content, local research and development (R&D) and the like, and the desire to become less dependent on the U.S. market through trade diversification.

The State of Bilateral Relations

Besides the effects of global as well as domestic economic developments on trade relations between the United States and Canada, certain bilateral economic issues in trade, investment, energy, the environment, or other areas have an effect.[7] The need to resolve these issues or at least mitigate their impact is made more urgent by the differing philosophies of the U.S. and Canadian governments with respect to the role of government in responding to the external and internal challenges outlined before.

In a suitably bland and uncontroversial statement[8] issued preparatory to President Reagan's visit to Ottawa in mid–March 1981, the U.S. State Department's public affairs office characterized Canada–U.S. relations as "close and friendly," conducted "in an atmosphere of mutual confidence between two nations whose unparalleled degree of interdependence "will inevitably bring clashes of interests" which must be resolved "to the mutual satisfaction of both countries." Although little progress toward resolving current bilateral concerns resulted from President Reagan's meeting with Prime Minister Trudeau,[9] State Department officials noted optimistically that discussions on a host of actual and potential bilateral issues continue at various levels of both governments.

Canadian officials appear less sanguine. Their apprehensions stem in part from the fact that Canadians tend to be less comfortable with a Republican than with a Democratic administration. They also stem from the fact that although the attitude of the Reagan administration and its policies toward Canada remain unclear, there has been a stiffening U.S. response to what are seen to be Canada's new, more nationalistic trade and investment policies. U.S. Special Trade Representative Brock, for example, recently suggested that Canada must offer quid pro quo access to U.S. firms if it wants continued access to U.S. trade and investment markets. Deputy Assistant Secretary of State Elinor Constable, in a statement prepared for a committee of Congress, echoed a similar theme.[10]

The most outspoken comments by an American official were made on July 9, 1981, by David R. Macdonald, deputy U.S. trade representative, before the subcommittee on oversight and investigation of the U.S. House of Representatives' committee on energy and commerce. Referring to the operations of FIRA and to Canada's NEP, which, he noted, is being enforeced in many cases by FIRA, he said:

> Canada clearly does not desire new investment from the United States, at least not in the same way that this country welcomes foreign investment; and the American investment which is now there is not secure. . . . In addition to being discriminatory, the National Energy Program also incorporates certain elements which we consider to be expropriatory in nature. From an international standpoint, Canada's FIRA and the NEP are very serious derogations from the OECD's 1976 Declaration on National Treatment, even taking into account the interpretive statement made by the Canadians at the time of their initial adoption of this declaration. . . . Certain aspects of the operation of FIRA are, we believe, clearly in violation of the GATT.

In short, there is evident and justifiable disquiet in U.S. official and business circles over the implications of present Canadian economic programs and policies for American trade and investment. The official Canadian reaction has thus far been one of redoubled assertiveness. At the same time Canadians tend to view the Reagan administration as adopting a hard-line stance in global affairs, in contradistinction to the Carter administration's accommodating attitude.

Put another way, many Canadians expect that the U.S. approach in international relations will now be based more on strategic alignments than on economic rivalry.[11] This shift, it has been argued, will alter U.S. perceptions of current bilateral issues and of Canadian initiatives in the foreseeable future.[12]

In addition, the differences between President Reagan and Prime Minister Trudeau in philosophic approach toward the role of government in the economy suggest that bilateral issues may be harder to resolve to the mutual satisfaction of both countries in the near future. President Reagan, following with much greater vigor the market-oriented economic philosophy espoused in the mid-1970s by Presidents Nixon and Ford, has been pressing for government withdrawal from the economic system at the same time that Prime Minister Trudeau is indicating a greater role for the government in the economy. Such differences in approach could exacerbate current bilateral trade and other problems and resurrect previous bilateral concerns over trade-related issues such as industrial strategy.[13]

It is obviously premature to assume that, in the near term the Canadian and American governments will adjust their perceptions · and positions in a way that will bring forth the responses necessary to remove or mitigate current bilateral commercial problems. In the meantime the possibility exists that changes in Canadian and American views of the bilateral relationship, together with the impact of external international developments on the relationship, may be redirecting Canada-U.S. relations once again. This "redirection" exercise, coming at a time when the bilateral relationship can arguably be described as "less accommodating" than it has been in recent years, may make it more difficult to resolve commercial policy issues in the foreseeable future.[14]

Assessing Future Prospects and Problems

With the foregoing in mind, the task of this chapter is to discuss future trade prospects and problems for the United States in its relations with Canada. Existing trade patterns and expected changes in such patterns will be reviewed. The purpose here will not be to recite the numbers but rather to see what is and what is likely to be. Because for at least the next several decades the United States will continue to be by far Canada's major trading partner and because more than one-quarter of Canada's gross national product (GNP) is generated by export trade, anticipated developments with respect to Canada's international competitive position are important for identifying potential shifts in Canadian policymaking. Future patterns of Canada–U.S. trade influence trade policy and vice versa. Yet some insight on the "stability" of future bilateral trade flows can come from evidence of growth rates of bilateral merchandise exports and imports by key sectors.

MERCHANDISE TRADE: TRENDS AND ISSUES

Canada ranks as the world's sixth largest trading nation, and its volume of trade per capita is among the highest in the Organization for Economic Cooperation and Development (OECD).[15] Thus its trade relations have a substantial influence on Canada's economic growth prospects, and its economic future is closely tied to the economic performance of its major trading partners, particularly the United States.

U.S. policymakers in both public and private sectors, though slow to recognize the importance of international markets to the achievement of domestic and international goals, now understand that foreign trade is a significant component of the U.S. economy. U.S. exports and imports as a percentage of GNP and as a proportion of the total output of goods have risen markedly in recent years and will rise even further if past trends toward greater international interdependence continue as expected.

At the same time, that foreign trade has played an increased role in the economies of both countries, each country's share of world exports and of manufactured goods exports has been falling for well over a decade.[16] Many of the reasons for this trend were stated earlier. For the foreseeable future both Canada and the United States may continue to face lower growth rates of income, output, employment and productivity, in part because each country in its own way has become less competitive technologically and in part because other countries have become more so. Technological advances are widely recognized as major determinants of international trade patterns. Although the United States continues to be the technological leader of the industrialized world, its leadership role and therefore its preeminence in high-technology trade is being threatened by the rapid gains being made in other industrialized and some developing countries. For its part, Canada simply has not kept pace with world technological advances.

Table 5–1 depicts two-way trade over a recent period.[17] Trade shares between Canada and the United States have remained high since World War II even though each country has commanded a smaller share of world trade. Thus Canada and the United States continue their extensive trade ties, with Canada much more dependent on U.S. trade than the United States on trade with Canada. Approximately 70 percent of Canada's export and import trade is with the United States.[18] Over one-fifth of U.S. exports and imports are with Canada. The United States trades as much with Canada as it does with the European Community and about twice as much as it does with Japan.

It is important to note the concentration of bilateral merchandise trade in several industrial categories. In the end-product category, automotive products constitute the major trade item in both directions, amounting to two-thirds of Canadian exports to the United States and close to 50 percent of U.S. exports to Canada. Total two-way trade in automotive products fell over C$3 billion in 1980, reflecting the massive decline in automotive sales in both countries. For the United States other important end-product exports to Canada include chemicals and industrial machinery.[19]

Two-way trade patterns traditionally reveal the net exporting of natural resources and semiprocessed goods from Canada to the United States and the net exporting of fully manufactured goods in the reverse direction. Nevertheless, in terms of its worldwide trade, raw and semiprocessed materials constitute a smaller percentage of Canada's total trade with the United States than with its other trad-

Table 5–1. Canada's Trade with the United States, C$ Billion.

	Exports	Imports
1976	25.2	25.8
1977	30.4	29.8
1978	36.7	35.4
1979	43.4	45.4
1980	46.7	48.2

Source: Canadian Embassy, Washington, D.C.

ing partners, whereas its highly manufactured goods constitute a larger percentage.

Certainly for some time to come Canada will continue to be a net exporter of natural resources and semiprocessed goods to the United States.[20] Exports of petroleum and natural gas as a percentage of total Canadian exports to the United States, however, can be expected to decline as Canada continues its policy of reducing its reliance on imported sources of energy. Canadian exports to the United States in the end-product or fully manufactured goods category can be expected to increase in percentage terms, particularly as tariff reductions negotiated during the latest GATT round are phased in. For its part, the United States can be expected to retain its net export position in bilateral manufactured goods trade.

The trade patterns noted are a reflection of each country's comparative advantage—Canada in natural resources, resource-intensive industries, and capital-intensive industries, and the United States in human-capital-intensive, high-technology manufactured goods. If this pattern continues, Canadian trade surpluses will remain concentrated in exports whose growth, in terms of long-run elasticity of demand, is quite low, while the country's deficits will grow in highly manufactured goods, whose income elasticity of demand is quite high. This development would not auger well for the Canadian merchandise trade balance,[21] particularly if world competition from mineral and resource-based nations intensifies, as does the emphasis in the industrialized world on the continuation of high-technology exports.

Policy Considerations

Although Canada maintains a large proportion of its total trade with the United States, it has not been conspicuously successful in penetrating markets in the developing world, and its share of world exports has fallen. Generally speaking, it is caught between low-cost-labor and high-technology countries. In terms of its trade relations with the United States, Canada must also determine what the costs to interdependence will be if it pursues trade growth areas in other countries and what the potential is for the development of such areas. Canada is not favorably positioned for the longer run in terms of its individual trade surpluses and deficits with other nations. As noted earlier, a more competitive and rapidly changing world environment and slower growth rates in the United States over the past decade, as well as structural problems in the Canadian economy (such as poor R&D performance, the inability to achieve economies of scale in certain lines of manufacturing, and the Canadian tariff structure and provincial protectionism) are all contributing factors. Unless international conditions change in ways unforeseen at the present time, therefore, Canadian government policy in the future must be directed toward redressing current account deficits and attracting foreign capital inflows of even greater magnitude.

One final and more general point is in order. Greater bilateral economic interdependence and the convergence of Canadian and American industrial structures have created a more contentious North American climate. Interdependence—or, more accurately, Canadian dependence on the U.S. market and capital—has made it difficult for Canada to pursue an independent monetary and fiscal strategy, gaining the benefits from interdependence while at the same time shielding itself from some of the costs. With regard to the convergence of industrial structures, Canadian economic growth over the 1960s and 1970s was led by exports of manufactured goods, much of which went to the American market. The growth of the Canadian manufacturing sector has resulted in increased competition with the United States in a number of areas, such as electronics, petrochemicals, and aerospace, and a broad range of consumer goods. Whereas the Canadian economy has developed along lines highly complementary to the American economy, supplying industrial raw materials and semi-manufactured goods, a new effort at increased competitiveness in manufacturing, particularly in the production of advanced, high-technology products is now underway. Thus with its government long committed to strengthening the nation's manufacturing base, Canada is a major competitor of the United States and yet at the same time fundamentally complementary and interdependent.

What are the implications of such trends and of actual and potential policy responses for the future Canada–U.S. trade relationship? The Trudeau government has embarked on a program of increasing efficiency and output in Canada's energy and manufacturing sectors through domestic policies and programs designed, broadly speaking, to Canadianize the nation's economy. From a Canadian perspective, the key issues of the National Energy Program (NEP) are taxation, production levels, and ownership. The NEP was put forward in October 1980 to achieve a pricing system that ensures a fair return to the government and adequate exploration incentives to Canadian firms in order to meet Canada's energy needs. With respect to ownership, the NEP attempts to provide an increase in Canadian ownership levels to 50 percent of the country's oil and gas industry by 1985.[22]

The United States is concerned that Canada's NEP is contrary to international undertakings and practices in trade, investment, and energy policy. In the case of trade, the "Buy Canadian" provisions of the NEP may run counter to OECD declarations[23] and to Canada's undertakings in Article 3 of the GATT, which provides for nations granting equal treatment for domestic and imported products. Put another way, there is an inducement in the NEP for Canadian oil companies to give preferential consideration to Canadian suppliers of equipment that goes into the production of energy. This can mean discrimination against foreign suppliers of like equipment.[24]

U.S. concerns with respect to the NEP's impact on investment and energy policy also have significant trade implications. On the investment side the NEP is alleged to discriminate between foreign and Canadian ownership. Prior to the takeover of Husky Oil and Pacific Petroleum by Canadian firms, over two-thirds of Canada's oil and gas extraction was foreign controlled; these subsidiaries exported three-fifths of their total exports to parent firms and imported at least 75 percent of their total imports from parent or affiliated companies. On energy policy the NEP would keep Canadian energy prices lower than would otherwise be the case.[25] Although energy costs represent only a small fraction of total costs for many manufacturing industries, some concern exists that lower energy costs for Canadian manufacturers will provide an unfair trade advantage, particularly in bilateral but also in multilateral trade.[26] On the other hand, it should be noted that funding the NEP will increase the cost of capital to Canadian manufacturers, thus making it more difficult for high-technology industries to compete and for industry across the board to modernize. This can only add to the competitive disadvantage of Canadian industry in bilateral and multilateral trade.

A number of developments are underway to Canadianize the manufacturing sector, with perhaps the most important being the recent statement by Prime Minister Trudeau and Minister Herb Gray of the Department of Industry, Trade, and Commerce, indicating a more forceful and interventionist role for Canada's FIRA. Canada created FIRA in response to concerns over the degree of foreign (mainly U.S.) control over domestic industry.[27] FIRA reviews and approves or disapproves mergers and acquisitions by foreign firms in Canada, as well as new foreign investment in the country, according to whether the proposed investment is of "significant benefit" to Canada. FIRA has required some foreign firms to accept minimum Canadian employment targets, to undertake a certain amount of research and development in Canada, and to buy Canadian goods and services.

Some specific export requirements have been levied on prospective investors as a condition of investment approval. FIRA has also sought to reduce Canadian imports or to increase local processing and value added, actions that could amount to a nullification or impairment of benefits accruing to the United States under the GATT, including the benefits of Canadian tariff concessions negotiated by the United States. In addition, there have been occasions when a change in ownership of the U.S. parent company has triggered a FIRA review of the Canadian assets involved and the imposition of employment and research and development requirements as a condition of approval of the ownership change. The United States is also disturbed about isolated cases where FIRA has imposed constraints on an otherwise unaffected Canadian affiliate as a result of a parent company merger outside Canada.[28]

Possible distortion of trade and investment by performance requirements levied on foreign investors by FIRA is a matter of concern to the United States.[29] Both government and business in the United States are troubled by what they see as a departure from the preferred "national" treatment concept, which FIRA represents, and have registered their concern with the Canadian government on numerous occasions. Although Canada does not subscribe to the principle of "national treatment" of new investment, it signed the 1976 OECD investment declaration, which calls for national treatment of existing investment. Should the Canadian government implement the announced intention by Prime Minister Trudeau to empower FIRA to examine the activities of established foreign controlled enterprises, the United States would have further grounds for concern.

Canadian attempts to increase Canadian ownership of industry, particularly in high-technology areas,[30] affect trade both directly, in terms of bilateral exports and imports, and indirectly, in terms of transfers such as research and development between U.S. parent firms and their Canadian subsidiaries. The bond between parent firms and their foreign subsidiaries is obvious: Parents have a strong bias toward trading with subsidiary firms. Thus any substantial reduction in U.S. ownership of Canadian manufacturing would no doubt reduce the nature and extent of bilateral trade interdependencies. The Canadian argument is that Canadian owned firms are more aggressive in exporting abroad than are Canadian subsidiaries of U.S. firms because of various constraints placed on the subsidiaries by U.S. parents. In any event part of the unwritten reason for Canada's reducing U.S. ownership levels is to encourage trade diversification, particularly the establishment of stronger ties with Mexico, countries of the Pacific rim, the Caribbean and other developing countries, but also with the European Community and Japan.

It has been argued that parent companies provide their subsidiaries with advantages in the way of technology transfers and research and development benefits that reduce the cost of exporting by Canadian subsidiaries. That is to say, since the U.S. parent firm probably does not charge its subsidiary the full cost of such "overhead functions" as technology transfers and R&D, the subsidiary in effect enjoys an export subsidy. In seeking to enhance the capabilities of domestically owned firms, the Canadian government has provided research and development grants, tax write-offs, and investment credits for companies involved in research.

Several general conclusions can be drawn from the foregoing.[31] First, the NEP and a strengthened FIRA could provoke retaliation from the United States, with consequences not only for investment but also for bilateral trade. Although U.S. policy affecting inflows and outflows of capital has not changed significantly, public reaction to more restrictive foreign investment policies, not only in Canada but elsewhere, could precipitate a hardening of U.S. official attitudes. Reagan administration officials state that there will be no departure from existing nonrestrictive U.S. investment policy.[32] Yet numerous bills before the current Congress deal with the treatment of foreign investors under U.S. securities and tax laws. Moreover, the International Investment Survey Act of 1976 provides for the collection of data on the nature and extent of foreign ownership and control of U.S. business. The act is an expression of concern in the U.S. Congress over the possibility of foreign control of the U.S. economy and of unwarranted plant closings. Restrictive legislation could follow if the U.S. Treasury Department were to maintain a noninterventionist stance. Such legislation could adversely áffect Canadian investment in and therefore trade with the United States, particularly in communications industries but also in other high-technology areas.

Second, the Trudeau government's strategy of achieving efficiency, specialization, Canadianization of the economy (with generous help from crown corporations) and greater diversification of trade and other external contacts—in short, government intervention—can lead to more bilateral trade conflicts. This will be particularly so the more Canada resorts to government intervention to favor domestic over foreign owned entities.

The third conclusion will be more fully developed in a subsequent section. Suffice it to say here that, up to now, one rationale in the United States for a freer trade arrangement (in whatever form) with Canada assumed the exchange of U.S. high-technology goods (and enhanced access for Canada in the U.S. high-technology market) and U.S. capital for Canadian energy and materials in both raw and semi-processed form. If the United States is only partially successful in reducing energy dependence and enhancing high-technology output, the scope for bilateral trade could well be reduced as each nation more closely approaches the other's areas of comparative advantage. Finally, the possible adverse trends for foreign investment noted previously[33] could have serious consequences for bilateral trade cooperation in such areas as defense production sharing, where national security matters command significant attention.

SPECIFIC TRADE CONCERNS

Tariffs

Although the Tokyo round of GATT negotiations provided for a further reciprocal reduction in industrial (and to a less extent agricultural) tariff barriers, important barriers to bilateral trade in this area persist.[34] In addition, gradual tariff reductions in the Canada–U.S. relationship can lead to or may mitigate future bilateral trade concerns in the following ways:

1. Tariff reductions may provide an effective counterweight to the perceived increase in Canadian vulnerability to the U.S. economy

and may lessen the potential for reduced economic interdependence mentioned earlier.

2. The possibility of bilateral trade conflict remains in sectors where tariffs remain relatively high.

3. Because tariffs have been an important component of Canadian manufacturing growth, their reduction will no doubt require further rationalization of Canadian industry, requiring government involvement in financial and other forms of assistance (this point is reinforced by some studies that conclude that previous tariff reductions have not brought about the expected increase in rationalization and industrial competitiveness.

4. Tariff reductions are not likely to reduce the amount of study and discussion of possible free trade arrangements with the United States.

Although it is difficult at this stage to assess the significance tariff reductions[35] will have for the Canadian economy, some observations will be made.

The tariff reductions agreed to by each of the participating countries in the latest GATT round of multilateral trade negotiations, except as otherwise expressly specified in a particular country's schedule, began with the first reduction in 1980, with cuts to follow over each of the next eight years. There is nothing to prevent a country from speeding up the rate of its reductions, of course. After the final cuts have been made in 1987, U.S. tariffs will average about 4 percent, and 90 percent of Canada's exports to the United States will enter at tariffs of 5 percent or less. Including items covered by the Canada–U.S. Automotive Agreement, close to 50 percent of Canadian exports will not be subject to U.S. duty. The Canadian tariff on dutiable U.S. imports will average about 9 percent, and about 65 percent of U.S. goods will enter Canada free of duty.

The highlights of the impacts in various sectors are as follows: The negotiations achieved a substantial degree of harmonization between U.S. and Canadian forest product duties. For dutiable pulp, paper, and stationery products, the trade-weighted average U.S. tariff will fall from 3.8 percent to 0.8 percent. For dutiable wood products the trade-weighted average will drop from 6.1 percent to 0.8 percent. Substantial harmonization was also achieved for nonmetallic minerals, nonferrous metals, and data-processing equipment. As a consequence tariffs will either be removed entirely or else be at very low levels for raw materials and industrial materials. Canada made large tariff cuts in consumer electronics products and household appliances and fabricated metals products. The United States appreciably lowered its tariffs on some organic and inorganic chemicals. Certain plastics and fertilizers have been granted duty-free entry into the United States and, for all participating countries, civil aircraft, engines, component parts, and related avionic equipment will be duty-free items. Overall, tariff cuts will apply to about 80 percent of Canada's dutiable farm sales in the United States. Canada will grant tariff-free status to some forty-three commodities and will cut tariffs substantially on certain other products. Most of these cuts will be reciprocated by the United States.

The general effect of the Tokyo round of negotiations is to reduce further the relative importance of tariffs as a conditioning factor in Canada–U.S. trade relations. Some observers, such as Rodney de C. Grey, Canada's chief negotiator during the Tokyo round, claim that even before the latest GATT round a switch had been made from a tariff-centered commercial policy system to a system of contingent protection, including, in particular, countervail systems. However, in certain industries tariffs remain important; these are worth identifying for they could form the basis for further bilateral trade liberalization. One such industry is industrial chemicals. Although U.S. and Canadian tariffs on large-volume commodity chemicals in the inorganic chemicals sector will be largely eliminated, this will not be the case in other sectors. For example, tariff reductions will be marginal or nonexistent in the organics and specialty chemicals sector and the petrochemical sector. The Canadian Chemical Producers' Association has expressed particular concern about the lack of improved access to petrochemical export markets. Given the substantial capacity expansion (actual and prospective) in this Canadian industry, the status of trade conditions in petrochemicals is potentially of considerable bilateral interest.

Another broad industrial category where tariffs remain potentially important is industrial machinery. Under existing legislation, Canada levies a 15 percent duty on virtually all forms of industrial machinery but remits the duty if the machinery is not made in Canada. As a result of the multilateral trade negotiations, this legislation will be liberalized. Approximately one-quarter of all classes of machinery will be duty-free regardless of whether a similar machine is available from a Canadian manufacturer. The duty on other machinery will be reduced to 9.2 percent or duty free if not made in Canada. Additionally, the average weighted duty on machinery subject to the "Made in Canada" provision is not to exceed 5.25 percent.

Notwithstanding this liberalization the tariff remains a significant trade barrier, particularly for certain categories of computer controlled industrial machinery. Since there is a large potential growth in demand for this category of output, the possibilities for further trade liberalization should be carefully considered. Although tariffs on both sides of the border were essentially unchanged for textiles, clothing, and footwear, the potential importance of these industries in the bilateral context is not as significant as industrial chemicals and machinery because existing tariffs largely protect domestic producers in Canada and the United States from third country imports.

Nontariff Barriers

Whereas previous multilateral trade negotiations had largely dealt with multilateral and reciprocal reductions in industrial tariff barriers, the Tokyo round sought to negotiate international codes of conduct in trade in the areas of government procurement, product standards, customs valuation, subsidies, and countervailing duties, licensing, and aircraft and procurement standards. It also sought to develop internationally acceptable dispute settlement procedures for managing areas of trade conflict.

With regard to subsidies and countervailing duties, the subsidies code tightens the prohibition on export subsidies for nonprimary products (including an illustrative list of prohibited subsidies) and limits the use of export subsidies for agricultural products. Signatories agree not to use even legitimate domestic subsidies in a manner that harms the interests of trading partners. The code provides a two-track remedy system: A country may unilaterally impose countervailing duties against subsidized imports that are injuring domestic producers and it may also bring an international complaint against a subsidy practice that is interfering with its exports to the subsidizing country itself or to third country markets. In accordance with the list of the kinds of subsidies that are expressly prohibited to all the signing countries under the terms of this agreement, subsidy programs such as DISC would be ruled out. It is less clear how research and development subsidies will be treated under the agreement and, particularly for Canada, how regional expansion subsidies will be handled. With respect to countervailing duty measures, a significant gain for Canada was accession by the United States to the stipulation that injury be proven and public disclosure of decisions taken be made before countervailing duties are applied.

The standards code attempts to minimize technical barriers to trade by establishing open procedures for the development and application of health and safety standards. It encourages the use of international standards wherever appropriate, the acceptance of standards certification, and the specification of standards in terms of performance rather than design.

The key purpose of the customs valuation agreement is to establish uniform rules to be followed by all signatory countries in determining the dollar value of imported goods for customs purposes. Signatories are obliged to use as the value for duty the price at which goods move in international trade—the transaction value or the price shown on the invoice. However, the agreement establishes a set of tests to determine if the transaction price in a sale between related parties can be accepted as the valuation price. If it cannot, value will be determined by one of a variety of other methods. Under the code the United States will drop its American selling price (ASP) valuation for certain chemicals and footwear but will raise duty rates to compensate. Whereas the United States converted to the new valuation code in 1980, Canada will not do so until 1985. However, Canada reserves the right to raise tariff rates to compensate for the lower values for duty that may result under a new valuation system. (Canadian importers have long argued that the "fair market" concept underlying Canada's customs valuation system results in tariffs and duties far in excess of the nominal levels because the value for duty under the fair market system is often higher than the actual transaction value.)

The agreement seeks to reduce the trade-restricting effects that can result from the administration of import licensing requirements by requiring greater clarity of licensing requirements. It imposes the obligation that normally only one authority be dealt with in obtaining a license, and it simplifies licensing procedures.

The government procurement code requires open, nondiscriminatory bidding procedures for government contracts worth over $190,000 from entities covered by the code. Bids and opportunities must be made public. Losing bidders must be given access to information as to the name of the winning bidder, the reason for its selection and in most cases, the amount of the winning bid. In order to encourage wider acceptance, the United States will apply current "Buy America" preferences to bids from countries that do not subscribe to the procurement code for two years from the date the multilateral trade negotiation agreement was initialed. After that grace period such countries would be excluded from bidding on U.S. government contracts.

In one way or another the various provisions of the agreement touch upon the major nontariff barriers that have been identified in the Canada–U.S. context. The U.S. nontariff barrier cited most frequently by Canadian officials and businesses as harming Canadian exporting is the administration of U.S. customs. Exporters complain of long delays before an official ruling by the U.S. customs administration can be obtained concerning a tariff classification. Similarly, a number of countries have indicated that the Canadian practice of using fair market value as the basis for calculating the duty payable on imports is a nontariff barrier to trade. The derivation of a "synthetic" fair market value from accounting data is suggested as leading to uncertainties and to potential discrimination. The customs valuation agreement, by establishing uniform classification rules and procedures, should mitigate some of these concerns. In addition, the provisions regarding product standards may alleviate some concern expressed by U.S. exporters about the expenses and difficulty of obtaining approval for electrical equipment to be sold in Canada.

Government purchasing policies are probably the most important nontariff barrier to Canada–U.S. trade and potentially the most intractable. Although the Canadian government is not bound by a specific "Buy Canadian" act, general statutes contain a residence requirement that, combined with economy of purchasing stipulations, normally provide a premium of up to 10 percent in the cost of Canadian content in comparison to foreign content.

The "Buy America" act has been identified by several Canadian industries (particularly the transit equipment industry) as a substantial barrier to trade. The most notable example is the U.S. Surface Transportation Assistance Act of 1978 (STAA), which established a 10 percent domestic price preference on all contracts funded under the act. Orders for transit equipment are usually placed by municipalities to meet individual needs and are of a size that the Canadian industry can easily handle. The recently invoked act requires that the equipment for any U.S. transit program supported by U.S. federal funds must contain 51 percent U.S. content. Negotiations are expected between Canada and the United States on whether Canadian companies will be exempted from this restriction. With regard to STAA, Canada seeks an overall waiver, claiming that the Canada–U.S. Automotive Agreement should automatically exempt buses. The U.S. federal government is against exempting Canada from this restriction until U.S. railway car manufacturers obtain greater access to Canadian markets. On a more general level it is expected that a balanced agreement for federal expenditures in the transportation sector will not provide reciprocal commercial opportunities because Canada's expenditures for public transportation are small in comparison with U.S. expenditures. To make the agreement more acceptable to the United States, provincial purchases would have to be included.

Purchasing policy at lower levels of government are also significant in certain industries. City and state governments generally apply either formal or de facto preferences in their purchasing policies, as do provincial governments. For most industries this is not a dominant concern, but it is alleged to be an important factor in a number of industries, including telecommunications equipment, aerospace, electronics, wire and cable, electric generating equipment, business forms, and, most recently, steel and steel-related products. In reviewing this list, it is readily apparent why local content purchasing requirements are an important policy issue for the present decade. The industries involved are generally of the high-technology type with good growth potentials. Government policymakers will be particularly loath to suffer decreased employment in such industries unless there is a clear likelihood of offsetting employment gains in equally desirable industries.

Direct regulation of output and trade in agriculture and crude energy sources is extensive in Canada–U.S. trade. Very little basis exists for anticipating any significant relaxation of such regulation. Marketing boards, energy boards, agricultural quotas and subsidies, natural gas export and import permits, and the like are by and large permanent fixtures of the North American environment. However, their significance as nontariff barriers should not be ignored.

Other Trade Issues

It is impossible in this chapter to consider all the relevant Canada–U.S. trade issues in detail. One specific area of contention not covered by the discussion of conventional tariff and nontariff barriers does warrant attention, however.

A specific and well-publicized manifestation of Canada–U.S. conflict is to be found in the exchange of "cultural" services. Canadian Bill C–58 disallowed tax deductions by Canadian companies of expenses associated with advertising on U.S. border broadcasting stations. However, Bill C–58 is certainly not the only manifestation of Canadian cultural nationalism. Steadily increasing Canadian content requirements on radio and television can be viewed as a form of nontariff barrier to the import of recorded U.S. performance. Generous tax write-offs granted by the Canadian government for investing in feature film production might be considered a form of export bounty. The burgeoning satellite communications technology, fiber optics, videodisks, and other new ways to transmit fixated performances across national borders will most certainly heighten bilateral conflict in an already contentious area.

Such conflicts will not be easy to resolve. Nationalist sentiment is fervid when the preservation of Canadian culture is at stake. The one issue that all national parties agreed upon in the last Canadian election was that the federal government had to stimulate Canadian cultural industries. This doctrinaire position apropos protection of Canadian cultural resources will make a compromise in this area extremely difficult. In addition, rapidly changing communications technology threatens to render existing international agreements on cultural property rights progressively more obsolete. Complex trade issues may need to be negotiated in an environment where legal rights and obligations are somewhat vague.

Such "sectoral" issues of a nontraditional sort are emerging as major bilateral trade issues, and they raise concerns relating to nontariff barriers that are not effectively addressed under GATT provisions. Subsidies, quotas, and taxes in cultural and related communications industries may well be among the most contentious bilateral issues of the decade. A comprehensive review of existing and proposed measures in this area is needed, as is a careful appraisal of their likely effects and a consideration of how the most pernicious adverse effects of cultural nationalism can be mitigated consistent with the overall growth of these sectors in the two countries.

Policy Considerations

Review of existing tariff and nontariff barriers inevitably leads to consideration of policy choices open to both countries in terms of the direction the North American relationship should take in this decade. Canada has been of tremendous importance to U.S. interests and will become even more important in the 1980s. Certainly some of the best economic opportunities for the United States can be found closest to home.

No nation was able to achieve all that it sought in the Tokyo round of multilateral trade negotiations, so there is a need to try to obtain freer access to markets through bilateral discussions in the years ahead. Moreover, it is clear that it will be years before new multilateral trade negotiations are undertaken and even longer before such negotiations can be expected to yield positive results. This belief reinforces the point that progress toward removing or at least reducing existing trade barriers, particularly nontariff barriers, can proceed only on the basis of new bilateral initiatives. Reviewing new initiatives seems appropriate, in addition, because of the rapid and forceful change the global economy has been undergoing for over a decade and because of the need to develop more secure trading and economic conditions for the North American economy to meet increased uncertainty with respect to the supply of a broad range of commodities.

Further North American Trade Liberalization

Over the past several years, the popular but by no means new idea of linking the United States and Canada (and Mexico) in a North American common market—or other institutional arrangements involving greater degrees of economic cooperation and freer trade than presently exist—has received increasing attention.[36]

As examples, former presidential aspirants, Senator Ted Kennedy, Governor Jerry Brown, and former U.S. Treasury Secretary John Connally advocated a "North American Economic Community" in their campaign platforms. President Reagan, in his nominating speech, called for a North American economic and military partnership with Canada and Mexico. Several prominent U.S. business figures have also endorsed the common market approach, and the National Governors' Association has made North American trade one of its primary areas of focus. Finally, the North American Trade Caucus of the U.S. Senate, formed in early 1980 and chaired by Max Baucus of Montana, was convened "to pursue more actively a policy of strengthening trade relationships on the [North American] continent." (Several members of the U.S. Congress requested that the House of Representatives establish a similar group to "study the prospects for greater integration of trade on this continent.") The Senate Caucus is studying North American trade with a view toward recommending ways of furthering U.S. cooperation with Canada and Mexico.

An amendment by Senator Max Baucus to the Trade Agreements Act of 1979 called for a study by the executive branch of "the feasibility of entering into trade agreements with countries in the northern portion of the western hemisphere." Begun under the Carter administration the interagency study was completed July 26, 1981, and transmitted to the Congress by President Reagan on August 4. It observes that "great disparities in levels of economic development, resources, and economic philosophies . . . preclude realistic expectations of a fully integrated regional trade compact in the short term." It suggests improving trade relations with Mexico and Canada separately, rather than on a regional basis. With respect to Canada it proposes a more formal consultative mechanism for exploring opportunities for increased trade cooperation and rationalization of industry. Finally, it expresses the intention of the executive branch to consider, with the governments of Canada, Mexico, and countries in or bordering the Caribbean, the formation of a commission of private businessmen and heads of state enterprises "who could identify realistic opportunities for further expansion of trade."

In Canada, Minister of Finance John C. Crosbie, then in office, suggested that free trade with the United States was an option Canada should seriously consider during the next few years. He also recommended exploring several other trade liberalization strategies, including development of a North American common market encompassing Canada, the United States, and Mexico. Liberal Senator George Van Roggen, Chairman of the Canadian Senate's Foreign

Affairs Committee, also favors a Canada–U.S. free trade pact.[37] Former Canadian Prime Minister Joe Clark, while rejecting outright the idea of a common market in energy, cited four areas where Canada and the United States could cooperate with no threat to the sovereignty of either country. These areas are joint stockpiling of oil, bilateral research and development of alternative sources of energy, protecting the environment from acid rain, and energy conservation.

Renewed interest in reshaping North American trade relations has emerged in part as an extension of various calls for a greater sharing of energy resources. Indeed, some observers have stated that endorsement by some prominent Americans of the common market approach is mainly for the purpose of increasing the flow of oil and natural gas from Canada and Mexico to the United States, inasmuch as U.S. consumption of oil and gas was far exceeding domestic supplies and traditional foreign suppliers were becoming or had the potential to become unreliable sources. This recent criticism aside, implementing some form of free trade arrangement between Canada and the United States has been the subject of debate on both sides of the border for the last hundred years.

When considering the options for future changes in the Canada–U.S. trade environment, certain approaches would appear to be nonstarters based upon existing political and sociological considerations. Specifically, aside from whatever economic misgivings might be raised, the current political climate in Canada would not sustain a commitment toward complete free trade with the United States. Notwithstanding studies suggesting that the primary effect of free trade would be to encourage intraindustry specialization, the Canadian government has insisted on production guarantees even in the case of a trade agreement limited to an individual industry like the auto pact. In short, the Canadian government probably would not risk significant contractions in certain key sectors attendant on a full free trade agreement.

Within certain boundaries the concept of implementing more limited trade liberalization strategies is somewhat more plausible. The Canadian government has made it clear that a North American common market is not desirable. Nor is the concept of a North American agricultural common market very plausible. Government regulation of production and marketing of agricultural output is an institutional feature of all western economies. Given the fairly close correspondence of U.S. and Canadian agricultural production functions, the potential gains from free trade in agricultural products may be relatively limited, compared to issues of political sovereignty and income maintenance for farmers.

Several specific industries have been identified in various places as candidates for sectoral agreements between Canada and the United States. These include the chemical, computer, major appliance, nonferrous metals, specialty steel, forest products, and machinery industries (see Van Roggen committee report). It is not possible to evaluate the potential effects of sectoral agreements in any or all of these industries without much more detailed study. However, certain a priori conditions may be stipulated as prerequisite to any successful bilateral sectoral agreement. One obvious condition is that there are significant opportunities for intradindustry specialization. This in turn means that economies of product specialization should far exceed product complementarities (economies of producing a full line of products). Another condition is that the costs of moving toward a more rationalized production structure should be well below the potential benefits.

The experience under the auto pact also suggests that Canadian negotiators will be quite concerned about the nature as well as the magnitude of the domestic employment that would be realized under any sectoral agreement. Specifically, Canadian negotiators would presumably want some assurances (either explicit or implicit) that Canada would retain a "fair" share of skilled jobs and employment related to research and development. The Van Roggen committee, among others, has suggested that it is unlikely that the United States would agree again to specific production safeguards in any sectoral agreement. Clearly, given sufficient incentives, such as access to long-term supplies of Canadian natural gas at attractive prices, the United States could be encouraged to agree to certain production safeguards in a sectoral agreement. However, it is probably that any such trade-offs would perforce take place across sectors rather than within sectors.

An implication of the foregoing evaluation is that, absent any broader cross-sectoral bargaining, future sectoral agreements should provide realistic prospects for an "equitable" sharing of skilled, technology-oriented employment without formal provisions being required to guarantee a satisfactory sharing. This suggests, among other things, that it would be difficult to implement a bilateral sectoral agreement in industries marked by extensive economies of scale and scope in R&D. That is, where clear advantages would accrue from conducting R&D for a wide variety of an industry's products in one central laboratory, Canadian concerns about suffering a relative reduction in R&D and related activities would, in the present political environment, likely preclude any significant sectoral rationalization of production activity. However, where R&D specialization is appropriate for at least a significant subset of an industry's output, prospects for successful bilateral negotiation are more realistic.

Another consideration apropos sectoral agreements worth bearing in mind is that to proceed outside the multilateral trade negotiations on a purely preferential basis would involve a GATT waiver, which is a difficult position to take. Preferential agreements are easier with respect to nontariff barriers, since the executive branch retains the authority to proceed with congressional approval. This suggests that potential candidates for bilateral sectoral agreements should be characterized by nontrivial nontariff barriers. Still another relevant factor is the anticipated growth rate of the industry. For a variety of reasons it would be easier to accommodate a movement toward increased specialization in a rapidly growing industry than in a slowly growing industry.

No clear-cut conclusion can be drawn from the operation of the Canada–U.S. Automotive Agreement of 1965[38] as to the distribution of the net benefits of potential sectoral agreements between Canada and the United States. Throughout the sixteen-year history of the auto pact there has been controversy as to the net benefits to the respective parties to the agreement. Numerous critics in both countries have maintained that the pact has produced negative results for their respective countries. The relatively old issues, such as developing a set of appropriate criteria by which to assess benefits and costs, the question of "equitable market sharing," the distribution of "efficiency gains," the use of "safeguards," all of which demonstrate how difficult it is to establish and retain a *limited* sectoral free trade agreement that satisfies each partner, have now been joined by the question of the very survival of the industry in North America and all that this implies in terms of the location of substantial new investment and R&D, the distribution of skilled employment in the industry, and the interventionist practices of states and provinces to tip the scales in decisions on plant locations.

Defenders of the auto pact argue that the benefits to Canada include increased value added in the assembly and automobile parts sector of the industry, the creation of large numbers of new jobs, increased wages in the industry to close the gap with the United States, increased specialization and productivity, and a decrease in automobile price differentials between the Canadian and U.S. markets. Critics of the Automotive Agreement argue that it has led to an unsustainable deficit in the original parts sector and that the specialization that has emerged in the industry results in Canadian companies doing little research and development and employing relatively few highly skilled workers. More moderate critics suggest that the auto pact had limited initial purposes and should not have been expected to solve all of the industry's problems. Nor should it have sought to achieve trade balance within sectors at all points in time. They also point out that part of Canada's problems with the pact may be due to Canadian requirements that have had the result of encouraging the production of less popular large cars in Canada. Thus while acknowledging that the auto pact has intrinsic economic benefits, more moderate critics suggest the need for a more flexible framework.

Other sectoral agreements have not received as much attention as has the Automotive Agreement, and given what is known the results are mixed. The sectoral agreement in farm machinery has been criticized along much the same grounds as the auto pact, while free trade arrangements in newsprint and the Defense Production Sharing Agreement have brought net benefits to the two economies. Thus, although a number of sectors have been suggested as candidates for arrangements of the auto pact type, there is no clear basis upon which such arrangements could proceed that would be satisfactory to all parties. Nor is it likely that the United States would be interested in sectoral arrangements that incorporated specific production safeguards.

INDUSTRIAL POLICY

U.S. and Canadian industrial policy objectives represent a serious long-term bilateral conflict area.[39] This conflict will stem from the basic fact that the industrial structures of the two countries and the aspirations for the future evolution of these structures are similar, except in size.

Because the two countries have such similar industrial structures, the problems they experience in third-country trade are not very significant in their bilateral trade. There is, for example, no serious bilateral conflict in agriculture or in such industries as textiles and shoes where both countries are facing similar problems in terms of adjusting to low-wage imports. Furthermore, both countries are experiencing a persistent shift toward a greater percentage of workers in service industries, most of which do not involve much trade. In fact, the areas of conflict are confined mainly to those industrial sectors where economies of scale and specialization are important—primarily consumer durables, a few nondurables, and industrial equipment.

The Canadian market is too small to permit economies of scale and specialization to be realized in a number of important industries. In only two ways has Canada been able to offset the handicap of limited market size. First, it has provided government support for manufacturing activities ranging from tariff protection to production subsidies. Second, it has worked out sectoral trade agreements with the United States to gain access to the entire North American market (in automobiles, farm machinery, and defense equipment). A third option, to require domestic rationalization (concentration of production of a specific good in the hands of fewer firms) has not been tried very extensively, although it is a course that a number of Canadians have begun to consider seriously.

We come, then, to a basic point of future bilateral economic conflict. If Canada is to pursue a policy of greater economic independence from the United States, it must do so in ways that will involve increased government intervention to offset the costs of operating within a limited domestic market. Furthermore, because of the basic similarity of the two economies despite difference of size, government intervention to increase the competitiveness of Canadian manufactured products in foreign markets will almost certainly be regarded as hostile by a U.S. government trying to achieve the same basic objectives, but from the base of a much larger domestic market and with a government that will not intervene as much to retain international cost competitiveness.

SOME CONCLUDING COMMENTS

With particular regard to both nations' support of domestic industry as well as other areas of contention mentioned here, perhaps the easiest way to avoid generating conflicts or to prevent them from developing to the point where they became public issues would be to make systematic and frequent use of consultative mechanisms so that neither nation is surprised and caught off guard by actions undertaken by the other. Such a mechanism could have proved beneficial, for example, in the decision by the United States to take countervailing action in the Michelin tire case. This does not mean that either government would be forced to change any action it has contemplated undertaking. However, with both governments becoming more actively involved in policy formulation that directly or indirectly affects the bilateral relationship, a better method is needed by which each nation can understand the ends and means of the other's policy thinking at an early stage. Such a process would no doubt point up certain mutually inconsistent plans contemplated by both nations; however, it would do so before positions on both sides of the border had a chance to harden and would offer both nations the possibility of reaching some compromise solution. At the very least this approach would notify both governments that they had embarked on a collision course.

NOTES TO CHAPTER 5

1. After the mid-1920s, with Britain's position as the leading trading and creditor nation weakened and America's influence as an economic and financial power strengthened, the United States had replaced the United Kingdom as the leading external influence on the Canadian economy. Canada's shifting orientation away from the United Kingdom and toward the United States continued throughout the interwar period, and in the aftermath of World War I the range and intensity of Canadian–American ties were changed in many respects.

2. The broad outlines of the transition toward the new relationship were discussed in *The New Environment for Canadian–American Relations*, a Statement by the Canadian–American Committee (Washington, D.C.: National Planning Association, and Montreal: Private Planning Association of Canada, 1972).

3. The sense of urgency over competition from newly industrialized countries has increased as the composition of exports from such countries has changed from more traditional labor-intensive manufactured goods and resource processing toward high technology and capital-intensive output. Industrialized countries are thus concerned with the effect of such competition not only on their traditional industries but potentially on their more advanced industries.

4. The cyclical ties between the two economies remain elusive. There appears to be a fundamental cyclical "empathy" in the North American economic system that affects both economies, although not in a fashion that precipitates a synchronous cyclical patterns or one of equivalent dimensions or common patterns.

5. The prospects for mitigating bilateral trade conflicts emanating from government redirection of economic decisions were probably better when Canada was led by Progressive Conservative Joe Clark, in the sense that the Clark government had a national economic development strategy more in tune with current U.S. developments.

6. Canadians appear to have developed a set of inflationary expectations that inhibit downward price movements. The resulting costs, along with the costs incurred from the National Energy Program (NEP) and the desire for "Canadianization" of the economy, may force the Trudeau government to impose temporary wage and price controls in the near term.

7. A good illustration can be found in the state of Canada-U.S. relations in the early 1970s. At that time perceptions in both countries of the bilateral relationship were undergoing a significant transformation. In Canada separateness from the United States remained a basic principle of Canadian nationalism, and anxiety over the implications of closer ties with the United States placed additional stress on the need to remain distinct from yet in broad harmony with that country. Indeed, Canadian public debate focused on the question of whether and how bilateral interdependence could be reduced or at least prevented from increasing substantially. Restrictive balance-of-payments measures taken unilaterally by the United States in August 1971 were seen by Canadians as demonstrating some of the risks involved in closer continental ties. U.S. attitudes toward Canada were also changing as part of an overall reassessment of the U.S. position in the world economy as well as in response to changing Canadian national attitudes and policies. For example, whereas the United States had previously been willing to exempt Canada, sooner or later, from restrictive economic measures imposed from time to time (like the Interest Equalization Tax and other U.S. capital restraint programs), its import surcharge and other measures taken in August 1971 to cope with balance-of-payments problems were applied equally to Canada and the rest of the world.

8. U.S. Department of State, "U.S. Relations with Canada," March 3, 1981.

9. During the president's visit, bilateral agreements were signed renewing the North American Aerospace Defense Command (NORAD) and ensuring citizens of both countries full social security benefits if they have lived or worked in the other country at some period. There was little if any progress, however, toward resolving a host of arguably more significant bilateral issues discussed during the visit.

10. Noting that Canada is one of "the most restrictive of industrialized nations with respect to foreign investment policy, Constable also stated: "[the

United States is] troubled by the investment policy implications of Canada's new NEP which establishes discriminatory measures against foreign-controlled investment in the Canadian energy sector. We have already expressed our concerns to the Canadians as well as [to] the investment committee of the Organization for Economic Cooperation and Development that this program represents a massive exception to the principle of national treatment." See Hy Solomon's article in *The Financial Post*, March 7, 1981, p. 1.

11.   The opposite was the case in the mid–1970s, with the decline in the "Cold War" confrontation.

12.   On the other hand, Canada is unlikely for some time to soften its position on the NEP with respect to Canadianization, procurement, and exploration grants, arguably the prime U.S. concern at present. And energy policy, generally speaking, affects commercial policy (subsidies, tariff and nontariff barriers, and various institutional arrangements affecting international trade) and raises questions about the role of government in influencing industrial structures. The decision to "buy back" Canadian energy resources increases the role of government and reduces the role of market forces in determining developments in Canada's energy sector, which, in turn, increases the likelihood of bilateral trade and other conflicts.

13.   Canadian economic development will also be affected by actions of the various provinces through investment in certain industries deemed significant for provincial economic growth and through economic regulatory methods that set the parameters for business conducted within the provinces.

14.   During the late 1970s perhaps a better spirit of intergovernmental consultation and cooperation existed than exists today. Yet the number of bilateral conflict areas was probably as great then as it is now. It is also interesting to note that one "cost" of greater Canadian and American awareness of the bilateral relationship is the increase in the number of actors or "voices" affecting the state of the relationship, such as the U.S. Congress, the U.S. executive branch, and Canadian provincial actors. More voices make agreement on resolving bilateral irritants more difficult.

15.   In terms of ratios of exports and imports to the production of goods (87 percent and 83 percent, respectively), Canada ranks first by far among the major industrial countries. Comparable figures for the United States are 25 percent and 31 percent, respectively. Production is defined here as all goods originating in the various sectors of the economy, that is, the sum of national accounts industry components on a value-added basis, excluding certain services and government enterprises.

16.   From 1970 to 1979, for example, each country's share of non–Communist exports declined as follows: United States, from 18.0 to 14.1 percent; Canada, from 5.9 to 3.9 percent. Over the same period, their shares of

non–Communist manufactured goods exports declined as follows: United States, from 18.4 to 15.5 percent; Canada, from 1.8 to 1.0 percent. (For U.S. shares, the percentages include exports of other countries to America.) See U.S. Department of Commerce, *International Economic Indicators*, March 1981.

17.   Data will differ to some extent, depending upon whether Canadian or American data sources are used.

18.   The statistical references mentioned in this section are presented as evidence of both the process and the state of Canadian–U.S. interdependence in trade. Although changes in trade patterns are normally regarded as the major indicator of economic integration or interdependence, there really are no reliable statistical indicators to show progress in integration or interdependence. Though widely used, ratios of each nation's trade with the other as a percentage of its total trade with all nations and the concentration of trade in several product categories as well as other relationships, such as changes in the ratio of each nation's trade with the other over a period of years or changing regional trade patterns in relation to GNP, lack theoretical support from which inferences on the progress of interdependence or integration can be drawn. For an extended discussion of this point, see Fritz Machlup, *A History of Thought on Economic Integration* (New York: Columbia University Press, 1977), chap. 3.

19.   One often overlooked yet important point about Canada–U.S. trade is that a significant amount of trade occurs in intermediate products—those products that are semifabricated and whose further fabrication or assembly are necessary to serve the needs of users. Intermediate goods trade links the production processes of the two economies and provides further evidence of the importance of each nation's trade to the economic well-being of the other. See Peter Morici, *Canada–United States Trade and Economic Interdependence*, Canada–U.S. Prospects Series (Washington, D.C.: National Planning Association, and Montreal: C.D. Howe Research Institute, 1980).

20.   One study suggests that Canada will retain a comparative advantage in trade determined directly or indirectly by its natural resource abundance until the year 2000. However, it is expected that a shift will occur away from nonrenewable natural resources and toward renewable resources. See Harry H. Postner, *Canada and the Future of the International Economy: A Global Modeling Analysis*, Economic Council of Canada, Discussion Paper No. 129, March 1979.

21.   This point is developed in B.W. Wilkinson, *Canada in the Changing World Economy*, Canada–U.S. Prospects Series (Washington, D.C.: National Planning Association, and Montreal: C.D. Howe Research Institute, 1980).

22.   Foreign ownership of Canada's oil and gas industry is mainly American. Mobil and Amoco have 100 percent ownership shares, Texaco 90 percent,

Shell 79 percent, Exxon 70 percent, and Gulf 60 percent. It is difficult to determine how a transfer of ownership will take place under the NEP, although the Canadian government promises that a fair market price will be offered.

23. In June 1976 the OECD adopted "Guidelines for Multinational Enterprises," one element of the Declaration on National Treatment, which stated the following: "that Member countries should, consistent with their needs to maintain public order, to protect their essential security interests and to fulfill commitments relating to international peace and security, accord to enterprises operating in their territories and owned or controlled directly or indirectly by nationals of another Member country . . . treatment under their laws, regulations, and administrative practices, consistent with international law and no less favorable than that accorded in like situations to domestic enterprises."

24. Discussion based on U.S. government sources.

25. "A blended oil price regime will produce a made-in-Canada oil price that will rise gradually and predictably. The price will remain well below world prices, and never more than 85 percent of the lower of the price of imported oil or of oil in the U.S. so as to preserve a competitive advantage for Canadian industry." *Canada Weekly*, November 1980.

26. Lower oil prices for Canadian manufacturers are consistent with the federal government's strategy to promote the growth of high-technology industries while at the same time dealing with the problem of regional income inequality.

27. Direct investment data reveal widespread American ownership and control of Canadian industry, which continues to have a significant impact on the transfer of technology and managerial and entrepreneural skills from U.S. parent companies to their Canadian subsidiaries and on each country's trade performance, capital formation rates, and balance-of-payments position. U.S. direct investment in Canada, about 22 percent of all U.S. investment abroad, tends to be concentrated in manufacturing, mainly paper and allied products, wood products, transportation equipment, chemicals and machinery, with the remainder largely in petroleum and in mining and smelting.

28. Some of these concerns can be summed up in one recent case history. A U.S. based company with an operation in Canada was acquired by a company based in another country (not Canada). FIRA required an extensive review of the Canadian operation even though the U.S. based company remained a corporate entity in the United States and ownership of the Canadian operation did not change. This review resulted in several directives from FIRA, which in turn resulted in additional government requirements to be implemented by this business, even though there were no fundamental changes in the character of this particular Canadian based business. The point is that a company investing in a country under the

terms of bilateral and multilateral norms should be able to expect that no further requirement would be unilaterally imposed, especially when there is no change in the underlying circumstances.

29. Discussion based on U.S. government sources.

30. Telecommunications, aerospace, and other high-technology industries have been identified as requiring a strong Canadian presence (see Cline Commission report), and commitments by the Canadian government to achieve and maintain that presence run counter to the view of allowing comparative advantage and world competition to determine a nation's industrial structure.

31. For an excellent discussion of the numerous issues raised over U.S. direct investment in Canada, see Steven Globerman, *U.S. Ownership of Firms in Canada*, Canada–U.S. Prospects Series (Washington, D.C.: the National Planning Association, and Montreal: C.D. Howe Research Institute, 1979).

32. In 1981, Commerce Secretary Malcolm Baldridge mentioned problems that have arisen with Canada over U.S. investment in that country but gave no indication of potential U.S. retaliation.

33. On the other hand, there are three reasons why foreign ownership need not be a serious bilateral conflict area. First, Canada's foreign ownership policy is likely to continue to be less restrictive than the policies faced by U.S. corporations in many other countries. In fact, Canadian legislation can be interpreted as making implicit policies explicit and subject to public review. Second, the attractiveness of Canada to U.S. investors has diminished in recent years, with production in the United States to supply the Canadian market becoming a more desirable option. And third, because Canada will continue to be concerned with keeping what it has, it is unlikely (except possibly in fuel production) that Canada's foreign ownership policy will evolve to the point where outflows of payments to foreign parents will be restricted. Nor is it expected that market shares of subsidiaries in Canada will be jeopardized by limiting reinvestment of earnings in established lines of activity.

34. Some of the material in the tariff and nontariff barrier sections is excerpted from Steven Globerman and will be contained in Steven Globerman and John Volpe, *Trade Liberalization in the North American Context: Problems and Prospects*, International Division, Chamber of Commerce of the United States (forthcoming).

35. There are numerous studies of the effect of the tariff on the Canadian economy. See D. Daly and S. Globerman, *Tariff and Science Policies: Applications of a Model of Nationalism*, Ontario Economic Council, Research Study No. 4 (Toronto: University of Toronto Press, 1976); Ronald J. Wonnacott, *Canada's Trade Options*, Economic Council of Canada (Ottawa: Information Canada, 1975); James Williams, *The Canadian–United States Tariff and Canadian Industry: A Multisectoral Analysis*

(Toronto: University of Toronto Press, 1978); and Wilkinson, *Canada in the Changing World Economy.*

36.   The literature on approaches to North American trade liberalization is voluminous. See, for example, Ronald J. Wonnacott and Paul Wonnacott, *Free Trade between the United States and Canada* (Cambridge, Mass.: Harvard University Press, 1967); Theodore Geiger, John Volpe, and Ernest H. Preeg, *North American Integration and Economic Blocs*, Thames Essay No. 7 (London: Trade Policy Research Centre, May 1975); Economic Council of Canada, *Looking Outward* (Ottawa: 1976); Jim Williams, *The Canadian–United States Tariff and Canadian Industry* (Toronto: University of Toronto Press, 1978); Wilkinson, *Canada in the Changing World Economy*; and the Standing Senate Committee on Foreign Affairs, *Canada–United States Relations*, vol. 2, *Canada's Trade Relations with the United States* (Ottawa: Queen's Printer, 1978).

37.   In a recent meeting between members of Senator Van Roggen's committee and prominent U.S. businessmen whose companies are heavily involved in the Canadian economy, U.S. businessmen persisted in discussing specific nontariff-barrier trade irritants (such as the transborder broadcasting issue), while the Canadian senators were only interested in U.S. proposals for trade liberalization. These discussions show that existing NTBs, in the absence of trade liberalization attempts, are becoming more intractable; and that trade liberalization can proceed perhaps in untraditional ways, for example, granting greater access to the U.S. market for certain segments of Canadian industry in return for some liberalization in Canadian nontariff barriers of concern to U.S. business.

38.   For a complete review of the origins, objectives, and earlier effects of the Automotive Agreement, see Carl E. Beigie, *The Canada–U.S. Automotive Agreement: An Evaluation* (Washington, C.C.: National Planning Association, and Montreal: Private Planning Association of Canada, 1970); see also general discussions found in *A Time of Difficult Transitions: Canada–U.S. Relations in 1976*, a staff report (Washington, D.C.: National Planning Association, and Montreal: C.D. Howe Research Institute, 1976); *Bilateral Relations in an Uncertain World Context: Canada–U.S. Relations in 1978*, a staff report (Washington, D.C.: National Planning Association, and Montreal: C.D. Howe Research Institute, 1978); and David Emerson, *Production, Location and the Automotive Agreement* (Ottawa: Information Canada, 1975).

39.   See Sperry Lea and John Volpe, "Conflict over Industrial Incentive Policies," in H. Edward English, ed., *Canada–United States Relations*, Academy of Political Science, vol. 32, no. 2 (1976); and John Volpe, *Industrial Incentive Policies and Programs in the Canadian–American Context*, Canadian–American Committee (Washington, D.C.: National Planning Association, and Montreal: C.D. Howe Research Institute, 1976).

6 ENVIRONMENTAL ISSUES
Canada and the United States

Annette Baker Fox

Are future political and economic developments in Canada likely to exacerbate environmental controversies between the United States and Canada? What American actions may add to such conflicts? How can contention be minimized? This chapter deals with issues arising from existing or threatened damage to the quality of air, water, and land in either country that call for remedial or preventive action involving the other country. The threat may originate in one country and adversely affect the other, or the problem may be one that cannot be dealt with except on a cooperative basis, calling for joint action and sharing of the responsibilities. The threat is usually posed by some economic development the expected adverse environmental consequences of which pit the promoters against those more concerned about unwanted side effects, and a choice has to be made by the appropriate governments on where to draw the line between "growth" that is desirable and the environmental costs of such development.

Especially since the early 1970s such issues have become more and more common on both sides of the border, but the existence of the border can accentuate the controversies involved and the border's significance has thus increased. In the history of the relationship between Canada and the United States many conflicts were the more acrimonious because developments in one country were out of phase with those in the other. The longer the lag between disturbing event and effort to reduce its ill effects the more bitter the controversy and difficulty in resolving it. Environmental issues arising between Canada and the United States are usually marked by a lag in consciousness that a problem exists until a crisis occurs, by a lag in technical capacity or knowledge to solve them, and by a lag in recognition that there is a bilateral interest in resolving them. (Not all these lags appear only on one side; some groups on each side may see the problem and desire some resolution earlier than others on their own side of the border.) Identifying the problem as a problem is only the first step, and the long time it takes to negotiate and agree on what to do about it, then to put the agreement into effect, is likely to exacerbate the situation. For these reasons efforts to anticipate future problems should be useful in reducing such lags.

Leaving aside specific controversies we can be fairly certain of the following general developments in Canada that may affect environmental relations with the United States: Further intense efforts to industrialize (and to "catch up") are likely to involve projects to produce energy, the most politically exciting economic problem of the last decade. Canadians will become at the same time increasingly concerned with environmental impacts of development, especially those from American sources. There will be more pressure on the United States for a joint approach to common problems that Canada cannot solve alone. This interest in cooperation will be accompanied by a continued ambivalence regarding modalities, due to increased concern in Canada for maintaining its sovereignty. Canada will also continue to be among leading states in seeking international action to reduce pollution in the oceans. And the two traditional problems in Canadian policymaking will continue and probably be accentuated: (1) constitutional controversies about the division of power between the federal government and the provinces and (2) harmonious but independent coexistence next to a neighbor ten times its size in population and economy.

We can also be sure of some general environmental trends affecting both countries. The environmental boundary shared by the two countries will widen increasingly, with more and more people further away from the actual border becoming involved. Additional sources of dangerous pollution will continue to be uncovered, and dangers will be revealed from practices whose hazards were earlier disregarded. Population growth will result in increased use of boundary waters, and more people will become involved in particular developments related to them. There will be more cases in which those on one side of the border will gain from a development at the expense of the other, in contrast to environmental issues where the resolution will benefit both fairly equally.

PROBLEMS OF A SHARED ENVIRONMENT

Regardless of future changes, certain underlying problems make transborder environmental issues inevitable. One of them was noted long ago by U.S. Secretary of State Elihu Root at the time the Boundary Waters Treaty was being negotiated. The weaker negotiating partner is much more attentive than the stronger to events across the border.[1] The inattentiveness of the latter thus tends to aggravate environmental tensions. Furthermore, most of Canada's population lives relatively close to the American border, thus making Canadians much more alert than many Americans to border problems. A brief sketch of other underlying problems illustrated by specific issues follows.

Canadians have long regarded themselves as downstream environmentally from the United States. Prevailing winds in the summer, for example, move to eastern Canada from south of the border, carrying with them many undesirable pollutants. A large part of the Canadian population lives downstream in the flow of waters in the Great Lakes, where a significant concentration of American population and industry will have used or misused common waters earlier. In the case of both air pollution and Great Lakes water quality it was the Canadians who first pressed for some remedial action. So far as air pollution is concerned, however, the largest single source of sulfur dioxide emissions in North America is financially troubled INCO's nickel smelter in Sudbury, Ontario, and some of this pollutant flows across parts of the eastern United States. As western Canada becomes more industrialized, larger and larger proportions of the United States will become downstream of the polluting effects of this change.

Where there is uneven and asymmetrical development of industry on the two sides of the border there has often been environmental concern on the less developed side. Thus as Canada catches up industrially, the initiatives to take environmental action are likely to be coming more from south of the border, where lengthier experience with industrial pollution produced a stronger environmental movement earlier than in Canada. Just as parts of the United States that feel economically deprived are deaf to environmental claims, so some portions of Canada are likely to come down firmly on the side of industrial development regardless of ecological damage, especially if employment is at stake. Claims against the newcomer are likened by one understanding American environmental official to the fifteenth shipwreck victim trying to climb aboard a boat already holding its capacity of fourteen. One may ask fairly whether it is the prior misusers of the environment or the newest entrant whose actions push pollution beyond the acceptable limit.[2]

The discrepancy in rate of industrialization has produced, among other controversies, widely divergent views of the two national governments on remedies, which relate in essence to the future "right to pollute." These divergences surface not only in matters of Great Lakes water quality but also in long-distance transport of air pollutants. Canadians argue for standards based on "assimilative capacity," while Americans would stop the pollution at the source regardless of cost, a cost Canadians say is unnecessary or too difficult to be borne. As a sympathetic American member of the International Joint Commission (IJC) once put it, Canadians feel "Now *you* can afford it, but we can't."[3] The later industrialization of parts of Canada also makes those regions reluctant to press prospective businesses too hard with environmental requirements for fear they will go elsewhere. Furthermore, different degrees of environmental regulation may be viewed as "unfair competition" by those subjected to the more intensive control. "Developing" provinces like Saskatchewan, especially, object to higher standards being imposed on new enterprises than those applied to existing industry.[4]

In the industrialization of some less-developed Canadian regions, newer uses of the land differ from those across the border. No longer is it an unspoiled Canadian environment that is threatened, a last wild frontier. Instead, as with the Saskatchewan coal-fired power development at Poplar River and projected coal mining and processing at Cabin Creek, British Columbia, threatening Montana rivers, American wilderness areas may be adversely affected by Canadian development. The issues become zero-sum forms of conflict, unlike those where both sides of the border are similarly used, as is the case with Lake Erie and Lake Ontario.

Related to these considerations is another underlying condition for conflict: differing appraisals of how much damage to the environment is tolerable. Some of these differences of attitude flow from the fact that Canada's population is spread thinly across a vast territory. Hence Canadians hold views about standards of water quality and how to achieve them that differ from those of Americans living close to one another and with a richer government treasury. Environmental standards in the United States are often more exacting than those in Canada, and efforts to make them applicable continentwide appear to some Canadians to be environmental imperialism. The absence of Canadian requirements for "scrubbers" for power plants using coal indicates different views about what amount of pollution is acceptable. Controversy over the Atikokan coal-fired generator in western Ontario and its threat to wilderness areas in the United States arises partly from this difference in perception. Some of this difference can be traced to the importance of a particular industry in the Canadian economy: Pulp and paper mills, which have long been major economic activity in Canada, are notorious polluters of air and water. If very expensive pollution controls are to be imposed on this industry, whose major market is in the United States, will American purchasers be happy to pay a higher price to achieve a more salubrious environment in Canada?[5] And will comparable standards be enforced on Canada's world market competitors in northern Europe?

On the other hand, Canadian sensitivity to the danger of oil spills from tankers moving along the coast is demonstrably much greater than that of Americans, who worry far more about energy scarcity on the U.S. side. (Provision in the Trans–Alaska oil pipeline law that Canadian citizens injured by a possible tanker oil spill were to be compensated in the same way as American citizens has not been much of a pacifier.) Canadians are more apt to become disturbed when the source of marine pollution is foreign (especially American) than when their own enterprise is responsible. Thus Canadian exploration for oil in the Beaufort Sea has aroused much less concern for possible ecological damage than the famous voyage of the *Manhattan* through arctic waters in 1969.[6] Depending on the circumstances, local commercial interests will sometimes oppose each other on environmental issues. The Canadian fisheries industry objected to the proposal by the Pittston Company for a supertanker oil refinery at Eastport, Maine, whereas the depressed Maine town initially supported the project for economic reasons. Of course, strongly held

views on how much environmental change is tolerable in the light of
energy needs also divide groups and agencies inside the two countries; transnational contacts between likeminded organizations may
alleviate or aggravate such conflicts. Canadian and American environmental protection groups have learned to work together to enhance
their influence.

Differences in economic or technical capacity to deal with environmental threats also help to explain continuing controversy. Canadians do not wish to pay a cost higher than absolutely necessary to
achieve a satisfying result. They are unconvinced that "the best available technology" is necessarily the best solution, and they dragged
their feet in accepting the idea that to clean up the Great Lakes requires cleaning up its tributaries.[7] The current Canadian pressure for
Americans to do something about long-range air pollutants concen-
trates on "acid rain." Other air pollutants with sources in both countries may be even harder to control. The range and intensity of U.S.
research efforts on acid rain, which were documented by the Environmental Protection Agency (EPA) in a research summary submitted during hearings held by the House of Representatives subcommittee on oversight and investigations would probably be very hard
to duplicate on the Canadian side.[8] Nevertheless the Canadian government intends to spend C$41 million by 1984 on a comprehensive
study of acid rain, one of the objectives being to secure additional
data to support its efforts in seeking U.S. cooperation.[9]

Whether or not there are differences in technical and economic
capacity, people concerned about environmental impacts of economic development on both sides of the border are faced frequently
with the inherent difficulties of regulation, including inadequate
knowledge upon which to base effective measures. Much effort must
still be expended to provide the data even for negotiation. Controversy is frequently engendered because many Canadians, like the managers of many American utilities, for example, demand irrefutable
proof that damage has already occurred before having to incur expense to stop the polluting practice. They are even less willing to
agree to prevent damage that has not yet been fully shown to have
taken place. Furthermore, some alternatives, like washing coal prior
to using it in power plants, may turn out to have undesirable side
effects. Other alternatives that earlier were depended upon to ameliorate pollution have since been shown to be decidedly counterproductive. "Tall stacks" to spread fumes far afield, where they presum-

ably would dissipate without harm, are now seen as simply adding to existing problems by injuring plant, animal, and human life far away from the source after the emissions are converted into even more harmful substances in the atmosphere.

One underlying condition that explains much controversy between Canada and the United States is the difference in political organization for dealing with environmental problems on the two sides of the border. Although the two federal governments set up environmental departments at about the same time, in the early 1970s, and both provinces and states also have environmental agencies, the distribution of political power in Canada makes its federal agency far weaker in this area.[10] It has even more difficulty in getting adequate funding than the EPA. Although the line between Canadian provincial and federal authority on environmental matters is not distinct, clearly the provinces have the greater constitutional powers, and they are watchful to protect them. Consequently it is not easy for the Canadian federal government to agree with the United States on national standards which, without provincial support, it may lack legal power to implement. To meet this problem with respect to acid rain, a December 1981 House of Commons act specifically authorized the federal government to regulate such air pollution in Canada if it threatened another country. Nevertheless there is a certain lack of complementarity in negotiations across the border. Who constitutes the opposite number? Because of the very touchy constitutional questions facing Canada, the federal government has long been cautious about exerting what powers it has over environment issues for fear of antagonizing provinces whose consent is desired for constitutional changes.[11] Meanwhile, although provincial officials lobby in Washington, U.S. federal officials feel inhibited about dealing directly with provinces for fear that Ottawa will take this amiss. Some of the provinces compete with each other for industry by offering lower environmental regulatory standards.

These differences help to explain some of the controversy over a number of specific environmental issues. The Poplar River coal-fired electric power plant is a project largely owned by a Saskatchewan crown corporation, and extensive negotiations between Ottawa and the province have been required to achieve pollution controls desired by the Americans.[12] Similar negotiations have been undertaken with respect to the Cabin Creek coal mining development in British Columbia, and the Great Lakes Water Quality Agreement could not be

concluded until the federal government in Ottawa had first negotiated an agreement with the province of Ontario regarding funds to
implement it. (It was not a question of Ontario having to be persuaded; the province in fact pushed the federal government into pursuing the agreement in the first place.[13]

Some features of the Canadian system surmount the obstacle of
jurisdictional conflict and permit government action to protect the
environment. The federal government can justify certain actions on
the basis of the requirements of the Boundary Waters Treaty. It can
offer financial inducements for provincial cooperation. Opposition
parties in the House of Commons can exert pressure on the federal
government to act, as was done in the early 1970s. And there are
various ways in which provinces can negotiate agreements among
themselves and with the federal government to bring about some
environmental improvement. Environmental officers at the two levels of government habitually cooperate with each other. Even Quebec has become active in pursuing environmental objectives, including those involving the United States, such as reducing acid rain. In
Spring 1980 the province of Ontario, backed by the federal government, imposed stringent new air pollution requirements on the
INCO smelter in Sudbury, which the company resisted with claims
that to conform would seriously injure its productive capacity.[14] But
the federal government has been unwilling to refer the controversy
over the Atikokan power plant pollution to the International Joint
Commission. The plant is an enterprise of the politically powerful
Ontario Hydro, and the federal government has maintained that the
plant would meet all Ontario environmental standards.

The functional counterpart in the United States to Canada's jurisdictional problems is the role Congress plays in the American system.
Executive promises notwithstanding, efforts to respond to Canadian
environmental concerns may be frustrated by lack of necessary Congressional action, or Congress may legislate without regard for Canadian interest. Relatively few congressmen are sensitive to the potential impact of American laws on Canadian concerns, although their
numbers are increasing.[15] What may appear to be of purely local or
regional interest in the United States often proves to be of intense
national concern in Canada.

During the U.S. electoral campaign in Summer 1980 the complex
relationships within the U.S. government worried the Canadian gov-

ernment, anxious to reduce the amount of acid precipitation flowing across the border to Canada. President Carter's energy plans included a large-scale scheme to require oil-generated power plants to convert to coal. Many environmentalists on both sides of the border thought the development of this program failed to provide adequate pollution controls. But the areas in which many of the plants were located and the regions from which the coal was to come were represented by some very influential congressmen impatient with stringent emission requirements.

Transborder relations are further complicated by another underlying condition in the American governmental system, the ability of some government agencies to ignore the role of others, such as the Environmental Protection Agency (EPA). The variety and semiautonomy of the agencies in the executive branch make environmental cooperation with Canada more difficult. It is hard for Canadians, whose parliamentary form of government makes policy easier to be determined upon and implemented, to understand the more complicated internal decisionmaking process in the United States. How this difference in political systems can affect environmental relations could be seen when the 1978 revision to the Great Lakes Water Quality Agreement was held up for several months after preliminary signature because the U.S. Office of Budget and Management had to assure itself that there were no open-ended financial commitments.[16] The lengthy conflict between Canada and the United States over pursuing the Garrison diversion plans in North Dakota, which probably would seriously damage Canadian waters, was characterized by intense conflict within the United States executive branch. The Bureau of Reclamation in the Department of the Interior was pressing hard to continue the project (as were senators and representatives from North Dakota), while other agencies were opposed.[17]

In domestic as in bilateral environmental matters, decisionmaking is simpler in Canada than in the United States, where, for example, the construction of a port for oil delivery requires permits from four levels of government and numerous agencies at each level. As two Canadian environmental specialists commented: "The road to American energy-facilities siting and energy-transmission decisions runs through a very considerable although not impenetrable thicket."[18] In the particular Canadian case they cited, all that was eventually decisive in turning down an application for an oil delivery port at

Kitimat, British Columbia, was the prime minister's determination that such a terminal was not needed for Canadian purposes, and the hearings preceding the decision were then recessed.

Another underlying difference in political systems between the two countries lies in the preferred modes of protecting the environment. In general the Americans rely on courts to enforce legislative and administrative regulations. The Canadians prefer to set objectives and then negotiate with individual industries toward reaching them or to establish guidelines and then persuade specific enterprises to adopt them.[19] Canadians claim this system is more realistic and flexible. The class actions permitted in U.S. courts are not part of the Canadian court procedures. Attitudes toward using courts to enforce standards may reflect a cultural difference: Americans are known to be litigious. However, as an attorney for the Natural Resources Defense Council in the United States observed in 1980, "Litigation may be more dramatic and have established the permanency of the environmental interest in politics and policy, but it is limited in importance today as other forums grow in importance."[20] He was referring especially to administrative proceedings setting regulations.

Although some Canadian agencies like the National Energy Board are required, like their U.S. counterparts, to make environmental assessments of proposed projects in their respective jurisdictions, their bite is less sharp and the degree of public participation in these processes is much smaller in Canada than in the United States.[21] In general, the Canadian political system is much less open to the influence of pressure groups than are U.S. administrative agencies. A major exception was the famous Berger hearings and report on a proposed gas pipeline to run up the Mackenzie River valley through the Northwest Territories. These highly publicized meetings were the livelier because the project involved bringing American gas to the United States through a Canadian region recognized to be ecologically delicate and socially fragile.

"Access" to administrative hearings and proceedings is in fact another touchy point. The United States has provided rights of access for Canadians as well as Americans in various kinds of environmental hearings and enforcement of the rules. American officials would like this right to be reciprocal. The Canadian government has held back, partly for fear of encroachment on its sovereign responsibility to protect its own citizens without their having to seek redress in a foreign forum.[22]

Regardless of the far more numerous agencies involved in environmental matters on the American side, within the U.S. Department of State there is one environmental specialist in the Office of Canadian Affairs, while the Canadian Department of External Affairs has five such experts in its Bureau of United States Affairs. This is probably a reflection of concern not so much over environment generally as over a major issue in relations with the most important country with which Canada must deal. Thus the Canadian government is especially well equipped to watch for and express views on environmental issues with the United States. Even so, it is common practice for the Canadian government to let American agencies and groups fight out an issue arising in the United States, only joining in seriously when the decision appears likely to go against the Canadian interest.

If in revising the Clean Air Act in mid-1981 Congress greatly weakens its provisions, the difference between Canadian and American national regulation to protect the environment will be reduced. However, if Congress eventually follows the recommendations of the five-year survey made by the Commission to Review the Clean Air Act, which reported early in March 1981, the United States will remain in the forefront of countries protecting the environment through national legislation.[23]

The differences in governmental attention to environmental matters, less in Canada domestically but more internationally, showed up in the campaign to arouse U.S. officials to control the rising levels of acid rain. Despite the much more elaborate administrative machinery for protecting the environment on the U.S. side, the Canadian environment minister pointed out in June 1980 that one impediment to progress was that the EPA appeared to lack the authority" to bring about rapid and major reductions in sulphur dioxide and nitrogen oxide emissions."[24] Some environmental groups on the American side would dispute this statement. EPA officials, whose authority applies only to new power plants, maintain they are doing the best they can under the provisions of the Clean Air Act as it stands.[25]

The Canadian complaint points up another underlying condition that can be found on both sides of the border, slippage between legislation, administrative rulemaking, and eventual application. The implementing of American obligations, under the Great Lakes Water Quality Agreement, to reduce pollution from municipal sewage flows fell far behind schedule for various reasons, as the Canadians frequently pointed out. One cause was President Nixon's impounding of the federal funds necessary for carrying out some of the projects. Another was the elaborate administrative procedures under the U.S. Clean Water Act. The very number of agencies involved on the American side slows up keeping a promise made to the Canadian government. Still another factor has been that so long as politicians were concerned with energy scarcity, the EPA was no match for the Department of Energy.[26] The EPA's own procedures stress a state-by-state approach; and some politically weighty states, such as Ohio, have been recalcitrant in pushing controls over air-polluting industry.[27] Slippage occurs on the Canadian side as well and is regularly noted by concerned American officials.

Some of the slippage is caused by the inevitable tensions among competing domestic special interest groups and various government agencies. Transnational coalitions of environmental groups may moderate the tension or may aggravate it but in either case will prolong the bargaining for an acceptable solution. Politicizing an issue, as occurred in the Garrison Diversion case, may bring matters to a head but in an atmosphere of greater acrimony. From an environmentalist point of view, the longer the delay in proceeding on a contested project the better, because, as in some instances to be noted, the reasons for the proposal may disappear in the meantime. This is more likely to be the case on the American side, as the Canadian government has recognized in the past when it pursued a tactic of watchful waiting. Another kind of slippage seems to Canadians likely to occur as a result of the presidency of Ronald Reagan. President Reagan's lack of interest in environmental protection has been widely cited in Canada; his concern to reduce regulations on industrial activities, especially the production of energy, has been well publicized; and his appointees for leading posts dealing with environmental matters are regarded by critics, rightly or wrongly, as generally hostile to protective measures.

Finally, conflict inevitably arises, when shared resources are involved, over how to share the costs of maintaining or reviving a salubrious environment for those resources. Although the Great Lakes Water Quality Agreement and its revision are landmarks in bilateral or international cooperation for environmental purposes, their negotiation and implementation were attended by intense disagreement on myriad points.

Specific Current Issues

In view of all these underlying conditions aggravating environmental conflicts between Canada and the United States and considering developments already taking place in Canada, it may seem strange that controversies do eventually get pared down to manageable proportions. As the Great Lakes Water Quality Agreement indicates, these issues are seldom completely resolved but continue to require attention and negotiation. A brief examination of some that have continued into the 1980s will show how they have been handled and how changing conditions keep them alive even if somewhat subdued.

A number of specific current environmental issues that are likely to continue for some time are related to the expansion of energy sources. Two specific projects for thermal-power generating plants on the Canadian side have brought protests from Americans fearing pollution of air and water. The Atikokan coal-fired thermal electric power plant is close to the Boundary Waters Canoe Area of Minnesota and the Voyageurs National Park. The less stringent air quality controls exercised by the Ontario government make this project feared not only by American wilderness enthusiasts but also by local Canadian environmentalists, since it is near Quetico Provincial Park. Members of the Minnesota congressional delegation sought the aid of the EPA; the Minnesota Pollution Control Agency conducted hearings; and the U.S. State Department was alerted to take up the matter. Conservationists from both countries have formed an international coalition to protect the region from this source of air pollution.

Unlike this controversy, that over the Saskatchewan Power Corporation's Poplar River coal-fired power project was submitted to the International Joint Commission for assessment of its potential impact on water quality and apportionment of waters of the river that flow into Montana. (Potential damage to air quality has been differently handled.) The province recognized the federal government's role under the Boundary Waters Agreement and participated with the Canadian government in its negotiations with the United States government and that of the state of Montana to find a modus operandi for resolving the problems this lignite mining and power project presented for irrigation uses of the water in Montana, including that on the Fort Peck Indian Reservation.

Water apportionment proved a difficult sticking point but was largely settled through IJC procedures. The air pollution problems were reduced after a report of the IJC's International Air Pollution Advisory Board in 1975, following which the Saskatchewan Power Corporation agreed to install improvements to remove most of the particulates for at least the initial installation. Without waiting for the final IJC report on water quality the company proceeded with the second half of the installation in 1980. The IJC later did find that some adverse effects were likely to occur, suggested monitoring, and indicated a method for determining appropriate compensation for the damage downstream.[28]

The Cabin Creek, British Columbia, coal mining project of British owned Rio Algom presents serious threats to nearby Glacier National Park and the Flathead National Wild and Scenic River Area, which have aroused not only Montana citizens but also the state government and congressional delegation and have caused the U.S. State Department to take up the issue. A decline in the Japanese market for the intended coal output at least temporarily suspended the Rio Algom development, which was not one referred to the IJC. Instead the Canadian government had tried to reassure concerned American officials that the British Columbia guidelines would be adequate to handle the problems envisaged.[29]

The shoe is on the other foot in the Pittston Company's proposed supertanker port and oil refinery in the economically depressed town of Eastport, Maine. Tankers would have to come through the narrow Head Harbor Passage, whose waters are treacherous and claimed by Canada to be under its jurisdiction. Tanker traffic would threaten the delicate ecological balance in that area. Complicated state and national administrative moves to assess environmental effects on the American side and gradually ascending Canadian protests, have prolonged consideration to the point where controversy over that particular project may become moot. Meanwhile alternative energy solutions become more attractive, and the town has not renewed the company's options. On the other side of the continent Seattle City Light has sought to implement a long-standing agreement permitting the Ross Dam in the Skagit River to be raised and thereby to flood a British Columbia valley used for recreation. Changing social values have caused the Canadians to oppose rights granted earlier and to seek ways to assure Seattle the increased power it desires in some less environmentally harmful way. Ironically, the original right to raise the dam was accorded after a favorable report by the IJC in 1942 and after agreement on compensation was reached in 1967. Like the other projects just mentioned, the conflict between industrial development and adverse environmental effects has since sharpened.

The altering of water courses in boundary areas not only for power generating but also for flood control and irrigation is a recurring issue in which the IJC has often become involved. Earlier successes in resolving specific controversies do not prevent the rise of other issues elsewhere as agricultural development proceeds on both sides of the border. The Garrison Diversion unit is part of a vast land-reclamation scheme for North Dakota, the planning for which began in 1944. Only in the last decade did the Canadians become alarmed over the consequences for the Souris River and Red River as they continued their flows into Canada, and this concern increased as different kinds of potential damage to their waters and their livelihoods became better realized. The eventual investigation by the IJC and its report confirming the dangers to Canadian waters have so far merely helped to slow up and diminish the size of the undertaking so as to restrict the ill effects for Canada. So also have two law suits instigated by the National Audubon Society. The Canadian government and the province of Manitoba have been very strongly opposed to the project, and a coalition of environmental groups on the two sides of the border has fought it. Nevertheless, the ultimate disposition of the controversy is more likely to be determined by the opposition within the region on the American side, conflicts among interested federal agencies in Washington, political rivalries at the state and national level, congressional maneuvers, and shifts in presidential favor.[30]

Far to the east, a Canadian flood-control project has aroused concern on the American side, though the scale of the project, the intensity of animosity, and the national irritation attending the Garrison Diversion are absent. The IJC's investigation of the effects on the waters of Lake Champlain of flood control works on the Richelieu River in Quebec has raised local doubts as to the validity of its findings on how to ameliorate the unfavorable ecological consequences.[31] This type of approach, to find a balance between conflicting interests, is one often employed by the IJC.

Sharing common waters always produces controversy over their use and abuse, and Canada will be the more likely plaintiff. After three earlier attempts by the IJC to help to resolve pollution prob-

lems in the Great Lakes, its report of 1970 finally resulted in negotiations for the Great Lakes Water Quality Agreement signed in 1972
and revised in 1978. Many issues could not be settled the first time
nor included even in the revision. The implementation of the agreement or lack thereof, desirable measures to be undertaken, and division of costs will be continuing sources of dispute, yet this agreement
remains a remarkable international achievement. It also marks the
first time that the IJC was given a mandate for continuing to monitor
and report on progress and was charged with making recommendations for further controls on pollution. Standards were set and schedules laid down for meeting them, both of which were tightened up in
the 1978 revision, while the area of involvement was expanded with
respect to waters covered and types of pollution to be controlled.
Not only industrial and municipal waste were included but also pollution from agriculture, forestry, and other land use.[32] Although
controversy about some of the issues involved will continue long into
the future, so will further agreements.

Expansion of the area of agreement seemed to lie in store for another shared water, the seriously polluted St. John River, running
between Maine and New Brunswick. However, despite a bilateral inquiry under NATO's Committee on the Challenges of Modern Society and an IJC recommendation that a similar water quality agreement be devised for this region, none has materialized. Apparently
the necessary widespread concern and support for such a formal contract are lacking.

Although coastal waters are to some extent shared, agreement on
the regulation of tanker traffic through them to avoid oil spills has
divided the two countries. Although the United States did not respond favorably to a Canadian suggestion that the IJC investigate the
problem as it related to the Strait of Juan de Fuca and tankers carrying Alaskan oil to refineries in the state of Washington, the two countries did eventually agree on an alternative method of avoiding some
of the risks involved. A Canadian system, vessel traffic management,
devised to control navigation somewhat as air traffic at major airports is controlled, has found favor with the U.S. government. The
coast guards of the two countries would be involved in what is a necessarily integrated system for Puget Sound. By statute and administrative action also the two countries are cooperating to regulate
movements of vessels in order to minimize accidents, determine responsibility if one happens, ensure compensation, and plan clean-up

measures if oil spills occur.[33] This agreement regarding Puget Sound does not quell Canadian concern over other tanker movements from Alaska along the Canadian coast on the way to the western ports of the United States, a question always related to the location of pipelines that might be an alternative method of transport of oil from the north.

In the Arctic itself Canada which seems to be posing a threat as it pursues the search for oil in the ecologically delicate Beaufort Sea. Despite the danger of blow-out, drilling on the continental shelf is likely to continue and unlikely to be halted by Canada's National Energy Board. (Canada's Arctic Waters Pollution Act applies only to vessels.)

The air pollution shared by the Detroit–Windsor and Port Huron–Sarnia localities eventually moved the governments of Michigan and Ontario to come to a formal understanding, along with the two national governments, to refer the matter to the IJC for some solution. The result was a system of monitoring by the IJC over persisting emissions from both sides of the border to work toward achieving particular air quality objectives.

On the currently most contentious environmental issue, acid rain, Canada has taken the offensive in pressing for action on a problem common to both countries. A number of the controversial projects already mentioned involve emissions that combine to cause serious deterioration of the air over long distances, and the 1978 revision of the Great Lakes Water Quality Agreement provides for identifying airborne pollutants entering these lakes. But the pressure now is for a general air quality agreement. By a series of statements starting in July 1979, the two governments have indicated their intention to negotiate a formal commitment. Although the IJC is not involved in the inquiries leading to the anticipated compact, in carrying out its general watch over air quality all along the border as well as its Great Lakes monitoring tasks, it spurred the move toward the agreement.

The problem entails far more than border pollution. Like the eastern states on the American side, Canada appears to be receiving more air pollutants from far away in the interior of the United States than it is exporting. Although Canada produces half the sulfur dioxide that falls as acid rain in that country, the other half is said to come from the United States, which generates five times as much air-polluting sulfur emissions as Canada. Nevertheless, substantial amounts coming from Canadian sources could have a crucial impact on some American localities. While working toward a general agreement, the Canadian government will continue to press the U.S. government to take adequate account of the risks of increased air pollution in its drive to convert oil-generated power plants to coal. On the Canadian side this is not a party issue; the drive comes from leaders of all three leading parties, and Quebec and Ontario as well as the federal government have been exerting pressure on the United States.[34] Their task may be helped somewhat by the shared concern of numerous groups in the United States that have criticized the adequacy of controls over air pollutants as the plants convert.

At least some of the Canadian complaints may be alleviated by the interim agreement signed August 5, 1980. It contains promises to enforce existing rules to help meet the air pollution problems while new domestic controls are being developed and to give advance notice and consult when there are changes in policy or practice affecting transboundary flows of pollutants. Meanwhile the great need for more adequate knowledge to deal with the problem is to be met by increased cooperation in pursuing scientific studies, monitoring the air, and conducting research on techniques to control air pollution. The bilateral Research Consultation Group on Long Range Transport of Air Pollutants, which issued its first report in November 15, 1979, and second one year later, is conducting further joint studies of air pollutants as they move from the United States into Canada, monitoring pollution levels, and otherwise adding to the information necessary for effective measures to be framed. Meanwhile five task forces dealing with different aspects* have been preparing for the projected air quality agreement negotiations scheduled for late 1981.

While this particularly disturbing environmental issue is being confronted, others lurk in the background that have not yet become bilateral sources of controversy but could do so in the foreseeable future. Some of them already have been called to public attention by environmentalists, although not in such a way as to divide the two countries or reflect changes coming from the Canadian side.

---

*Rapporteur's note: Coincident with the announcement of its National Energy Program and with mounting U.S. concern over investment relations with Canada, the Canadian government has sharply escalated its acid rain complaints against the United States, asking for immediate action, apparently overlooking the fundamental need for much more scientific knowledge as to sources, causes, effects, and preventive measures. Prime Minister Trudeau took up the matter with President Reagan in July 1981, receiving assurances that the United States regarded the acid rain issue seriously and had no intention to export pollution.

They include safer disposal of toxic wastes already buried but now presenting dangers to the environment. The transborder movement of polychlorinated biphenyls (PCBs) has induced the two countries to start negotiating an agreement controlling such transport. Dangerous pollutants in the lower Niagara River discovered to be coming from old dumps of harmful wastes on the American side already had brought forth protests from the Canadian government in late 1980.[35]

Some hazardous waste might better be classified as nuclear, where the dangers include possible radiation from the production of nuclear energy or other nuclear activities. These can cause other injury to the environment, including thermal pollution such as the rise in water temperature in the Great Lakes caused by the many nuclear power plants in the basin.[36] The Great Lakes Water Quality Agreement of 1978 includes provision for limiting radioactivity in that region as well as for seeking solutions to the handling of hazardous wastes.

Certain military practices, including military waste disposal, can damage the environment, but such activities are usually overlooked or exempt from requirements imposed on others.[37] High-voltage transmission lines for exportable surplus electricity have aroused concern among those whose lands they traverse. Extensive use of some kinds of agricultural pesticides and chemical fertilizers has been shown to endanger life and health, but sensitivity to such risks has not yet become an international problem.[38] New or expanded exploitation of certain natural resources on one side of the border is more likely to raise questions on the other. For example, potential harm to the environment from prospective mining, drilling further for gas in the Great Lakes, and "excessive" clearing of timber, all of which are foreseeable on the Canadian side, could become issues. Proposals to make winter navigation of the Great Lakes possible, requiring measures that would seriously alter the ecological balance of the waterways, have begun to cause alarm in certain circles, including some in Canada. Future uses and misuses of the Yukon River and its surroundings may divide opinion in Canada and neighboring Alaska. Harmful emissions from automobiles have not caused international friction, partly because American standards are automatically applied to an automobile industry "integrated" on a continental basis. On the other hand, differences in the toleration of noise pollution might be a far-off source of concern dividing neighboring peoples. Not so far off are transnational worries over the protection of cross-border movements of the caribou in the far north and protection of native peoples from the impact of economic development activities in which both countries are involved.

RESOLVING AND PREVENTING CONFLICT

Whether these issues are only on the horizon or are immediately facing the two countries, Canada and the United States have evolved a large number of instrumentalities for managing them. Some have already been mentioned in the course of discussing specific controversies. In actual practice a number are mingled, used seriatim, or used simultaneously. The least publicized but probably most important is the daily transnational cooperation by administrative agencies most directly concerned. These include Environment Canada and the U.S. Environmental Protection Agency, as well as state and provincial environmental offices; but they are by no means confined to environmental agencies. It is their contacts, often spurred by expressions of concern from private groups, that usually set in motion consideration of a problem and of ways to resolve it by a presentation of facts and different perceptions of the problem. Often such contacts are sufficient to defuse a potential issue.

In the absence of such contacts, problems may arise if an agency on one side proceeds on its own without consideration for the possible impact on the other country, a common occurrence within the U.S. government. Yet the Canadian government has sometimes been sensitive to measures of the United States government designed to take Canadian interests into account. Thus the requirement in the U.S. Environmental Policy Act of 1969 that an environmental impact study include sections of a project that would cross another country's territory aroused the Canadian government's concern over whose documents would be used.[39]

If the facts are lacking or are differently interpreted, negotiation may be the next step; the U.S. Department of State or Canada's Department of External Affairs or both may enter the scene to perform their diplomatic role. For example, prior to any action by the International Joint Commission, the governments must negotiate a reference to it, including the terms and framework for its investigations.

Even after the facts and their significance have been determined, the "political masters" of those who have accomplished this task may choose to ignore them or to proceed without regard to them. Such may also be the fate of a report and recommendation of the IJC. Nevertheless, at least on the American side, there are ways that the other country's interests can be expressed, as when Canadians lobby in congressional circles or testify before appropriate congressional committees. As in the February 1980 hearings of the U.S. House of Representatives subcommittee on oversight and investigations, regarding acid rain, the Canadian government's views may even be invited. If strategically located congressmen or a sympathetic administrative leader become favorably involved in some environmental negotiations, their support may be the key to success for an agreement between the two countries.

If the issue is a general one, such as the water quality of the Great Lakes or long-range transfer of air pollutants, diplomatic negotiation is obviously necessary to produce a formal agreement. Although Canadians earlier toyed with the idea of pressing for a treaty, they have since been satisfied that a formal agreement will satisfy their concerns that a continuing commitment has been made by the U.S. government. Unhappy experience with the U.S. Senate's procrastination on the fisheries treaty signed in 1979 may confirm the wisdom of accepting a formal executive agreement on environmental matters.

As seemed to have occurred in the Garrison Diversion controversy, one difficulty in relying upon diplomatic representation is that both the U.S. State Department and the Canada's Department of External Affairs have often exhibited great caution in standing up to other agencies that would proceed contrary to the expressed interests of the other country. The foreign ministries have also been slow to proceed against the wishes of politicians with a special concern for a project the other country opposes. These politicians may be either federal or state and provincial. The traditional diplomatic route, central government to central government, is customarily relied upon by the federal government in Canada, as in the Eastport refinery controversy, rather than contact with the government of the state most involved, whereas the U.S. State Department has taken the position in this case that the government of Maine should act first prior to the State Department's dealing with the Canadian government.[40]

Federal, state, and provincial officials all get engaged when the IJC is given the task of fact-finding, for which it is ideally suited and for which it has earned over long years a reputation for reliable neutrality. On its investigatory boards are administrative officials who would ultimately be responsible for carrying out recommendations the governments accepted. They bring to their task the expertness needed by a commission that traditionally has been an uninstructed international commission operating by consensus. Each country having three commissioners, equality of membership makes the IJC an especially attractive instrumentality to the Canadian government. This is one reason why the Canadian section, though not very large, has been better financed (at least up to 1980) and has had a larger staff than the American section, perennially constrained by lack of funds and staff.[41] Service on the boards provides a direct line of communication between opposite numbers on the two sides of the border, often valued by their agencies for this reason. Where IJC boards of control are established, their membership becomes a source of personnel when new inquiries are set up.

At least two sets of public hearings are held in affected localities, one at the time of the investigation, the other preparatory to the commission's report. At least in principle these hearings give all interests a fair chance to express themselves. Private citizens also serve on some of the advisory boards. Among the new duties acquired by the Commission in the Great Lakes Water Quality Agreement is to report to the public on the progress made by governments in carrying out their agreed upon schedules, a task performed independently of the governments concerned. Yet strangely enough, no counterpart exists on the American side to testimony on the work of the IJC before the Canadian House of Commons standing committee on external affairs and defence. Only at appropriations hearings does the American section come before a congressional committee. The newly found voice of Canadian environmentalist groups may enliven the proceedings of the IJC as it carries out its own new duties, for which a regional office has been established in Windsor, Ontario.

Nevertheless, the work of the IJC is only one link in a negotiating process between the two federal governments leading to their eventual decision on an issue. The commission cannot initiate investigations on its own but must wait for a reference from the two governments. The governments have already come to some preliminary meeting of the minds on a solution and look to the IJC to provide objective information and recommendations, from which the governments can then choose. As a former member of the Canadian section has described the functioning of the IJC, detailed proposals to implement the results of negotiations already conducted can help the governments elicit political support and calm domestic opposition. The terms of reference are carefully bargained beforehand, and a framework is laid down that will ensure that the IJC will make proposals within the range of alternatives believed to be acceptable.[42] The suggestion that the IJC be given enforcement powers is quite unrealistic for many reasons. Nevertheless it can alert a responsible agency, such as the EPA, to an infringement of an agreement. When the Georgia Pacific Company failed to take agreed upon antipollution measures to protect the St. Croix River, the IJC followed this course.[43]

Sometimes the two governments refer an issue to the commission in order to delay a decision until a time more propitious for choice. Delay is in fact one basis for criticism of the way the IJC functions. Its procedures require much time, during which those immediately interested in investing in a project are left in doubt as to the outcome. There is delay also in getting a problem to the IJC, which then may not have a chance to investigate it until the environmental damage has become very serious.

The IJC cannot meet all the needs for reconciling environmental conflicts between Canada and the United States, and other restrictions prevent it from serving as the general vehicle for dealing with bilateral environmental concerns. Its work will necessarily remain ad hoc, at least as it is presently constituted, and it cannot provide an overview of problems dealing with the environment. It can neither decide policy by choosing between the alternatives it presents nor lay down priorities. Both governments will carefully preserve their powers in this regard. The IJC has "a built-in predisposition to constructive problem-solving," according to one expert opinion, but many of the new environmental issues are in the nature of a zero-sum game, and it is very difficult for the commission to find something for everyone to take home.[44]

Arbitration, one IJC function provided for in the Boundary Waters Treaty has never been employed. The reasons are many, including that the U.S. Senate would have to be engaged in the procedure. Arbitration or judicial decision by some other international tribunal. while theoretically possible for settling environmental issues, have not in fact been employed.

Some rules or guidelines that might apply to the settlement of Canada–U.S. environmental issues could also be laid down by multilateral agencies such as the UN's environmental program, the Intergovernmental Maritime Consultative Organization, the OECD, or NATO's Committee on the Challenges of Modern Society. So far, however, these groups have confined themselves to studies, general recommendations, environmental advice, and exchange of technical information. These are useful in themselves, and both Canada and the United States have actively participated in these activities.[45] The principle was accepted fifty years ago in the famous Trail Smelter case, that one country should not act in such a way as to damage the environment of another. This rule has since been elaborated in multilateral organizations dealing with environmental problems. (In essence, it is also part of the 1909 Boundary Waters Treaty.)

Either Canada or the United States could take by itself some legislative or administrative action that would satisfy the claims of the other. It is here that access to U.S. tribunals and especially to congressional committees for the presentation of some Canadians' interests may produce a satisfactory outcome without joint action.

Then there are possibilities that private organizations can settle an environmental dispute without government action. Not only environmental groups but labor unions and business groups might see their interests served by pressing for protective measures to be employed by particular industries, especially where competition might be the stimulus. They might further their ends through transnational contacts with likeminded groups on the other side of the border. The big question remains: Who is to pay for the environmental decision, whether made by government or by private enterprise?

CONCLUSIONS AND RECOMMENDATIONS

There is no quick institutional fix for minimizing environmental conflicts arising from changes taking place in Canada, nor can there usually be a permanent solution to any specific problem ending it once and for all. The underlying causes for friction enumerated earlier will remain, especially those stemming from the differences in size of the two countries and the difference in stage of economic development both inside Canada and between Canada and the United States.

Perhaps one basic controversy flowing from these disparities, whether to deal with pollution by stressing "assimilative capacity," as the Canadians wish, or to shut all polluting off at the source, the American preference, could be managed by combining the two approaches on an ad hoc basis. Whatever the capacity, each should be obliged to restrict its pollution and not to overload that capacity, nor take advantage of improved conditions resulting from the other's antipollution actions. Negotiations could proceed on the method of sharing this burden. In this context Anthony Scott's elaboration of the idea of buying and selling "pollution rights" could be seriously considered.[46]

The United States will always be the greater polluter, and in the past the Americans have been less demanding of the Canadians to take environmental measures than have the Canadians with respect to the United States. This tolerance is beginning to change with further industrial development in Canada, and the shift may make the Americans more sensitive than they have often been in the past to environmental claims from the Canadian side. The incongruity of interests will remain a thorny problem: how to convince decisionmakers that prevention of an as-yet-unproved danger must be attempted and how equitably to deal with the anticipated "new" pollution as against that of the polluters already existing. The control of long-range transfer of air pollutants presents an especially difficult problem since the costs of prevention will fall on areas far from those that will most benefit.

Many of the specific environmental issues can be better managed in the future by heeding the promises already made in the August 1980 interim agreement looking toward an air quality compact. For example, more serious, more energetic, and better funded efforts to enforce existing laws, prior consultation, more scientific research—all these will help to reduce the lag between appearance of a problem and a satisfying answer to it. The perpetual demand for better coordination between agencies could also be heeded.

Sometimes when a development project on the American side is slowed down by environmentalist' actions, the delay turns out to be economically advantageous to the project's proponents, though that fact is seldom so recognized. Given the recent reduction in the market for new energy supplies, environmental pressure to halt or modify new production has proved to be an economic boon.[47] Energy hysteria periodically grip leaders in both countries, but especially Americans, and presents special challenges to those who would protect the environment. Delays in carrying out such projects are not the same as delays in recognizing promptly the environmental risks they involve. At the moment this stricture applies particularly to a too hasty conversion to coal from oil-fired plants before proper environmental measures can be taken. Canadian worry about this is the greatest source of friction with Americans over environmental questions.

Reducing the lags between problem and resolution may sometimes be possible if both federal governments are readier to engage the states and provinces facing each other across the border in dealing with problems that are often quite local. Pressures for greater access by the public to environmental decisionmaking could reasonably be acceded to. This is a delicate subject for Canadians, who are less trustful of public participation in policymaking. The expansion of transnational coalitions of environmental groups may alter Canadian attitudes and raise general levels of information in the field. However, environmental groups on both sides, though earnest in their efforts to cooperate, are severely limited by lack of funds and personnel in attending to joint problems. At the parliamentary level, increased knowledge and sensitivity to the other country's concerns can result from the activities of the Canada–U.S. Interparliamentary Group, which regularly has environmental issues on its agenda. On the U.S. side more regular Congressional review of progress in implementing of bilateral agreements would be desirable.

The involvement of both provincial and state officials and of the public in ways to improve sensitivity and reduce lags in appreciation of environmental problems has been shown to be helpful by the way the IJC functions. Its usefulness could be more generally recognized and more resort made to its services, though one must always recognize its limitations and the danger of overloading it.

Ideally, environmental conflicts between Canada and the United States could diminish if the whole ecological system derived from the uses of land, air, and water were the focus of some joint activities. Among others, a former Canadian member of the IJC, Maxwell Cohen, has proposed such an approach.[48] Whether a special bilateral environment agency to perform this function would further this aim is not clear. What is clear is that unrelated issues between Canada and the United States should never be consciously linked, a practice

which officials of both countries shun anyway, despite some un-
sophisticated pressure to do so. Meanwhile the general rules of neighborly comity which apply across the border on different issues arising
between the two countries should continue to serve as the foundation for minimizing the environmental impact of changes in Canada.

In summary, whatever the future holds for constitutional changes
in Canada, friction between the two North American countries over
environmental questions will continue. However, the adverse effects
could be reduced if the following were to occur:

1. For reasons of international goodwill if for no others, the new
   government should become increasingly sensitive to environmental hazards that concern our northern neighbor.

2. Congress and others should continue to expect the Environmental Protection Agency to carry out its appointed tasks and should
   strongly support its efforts to control air pollution.

3. Electric power generating plants that convert to coal from oil
   should at the same time take prescribed measures to reduce the
   air pollutants that would otherwise greatly aggravate the current dangers of acid precipitation affecting both Canadians and
   Americans.

4. The working groups preparing for the projected Canada–U.S.
   air quality agreement and the promises made in the August
   1980 interim agreement need to be closely monitored.

5. Policymakers ought to become more aware of the International
   Joint Commission's usefulness in dealing with transboundary
   environmental problems.

6. Where provincial jurisdiction is clear, direct contacts between
   U.S. federal officials and Canadian provincial officials on environmental matters should not be avoided in the expectation that
   Canadian federal officials would similarly treat with American
   state officials where appropriate.

NOTES TO CHAPTER 6

1. Noted by Charles R. Ross in "National Sovereignty in International Environmental Decisions," p. 268 of P.P; Dwivedi (ed.) *Protecting the Envi-*

ronment: Issues and Choices—Canadian Perspectives (Toronto: Copp Clark, 1974).

2. Karl K. Jonietz, "U.S.-Canadian Environmental Relations," in John E. Carroll (ed.) *Proceedings of the Canada–United States Natural Resources and Environmental Symposium* (Durham, N.H.: Institute of Natural and Environmental Resources, University of New Hampshire, 1978), p. 9.

3. Charles R. Ross, "The IJC: A U.S. View," in Allen P. Splete (ed.) *Toward A Better Understanding: Canadian–American Relations* (Canton, N.Y.: St. Lawrence University, 1974), p. 73.

4. Grant C. Mitchell, "The Transboundary Environment: A Provincial Perspective," in Carroll, *Canada–United States Natural Resources and Environmental Symposium*, p. 14.

5. Robert Forster, "Canadian–American Forest Policy: A Potential for Conflict or Cooperation," in John E. Carroll (ed.) *Canadian–American Natural Resource Papers, 1975–1976* (Durham, N.H.: Institute of Natural and Environmental Resources, University of New Hampshire, 1976), p. 3.

6. Edgar J. Dosman, "Arctic Seas: Environmental Policy and Natural Resource Development," in O.P. Dwivedi (ed.) *Resources and the Environment: Policy Perspectives for Canada* (Toronto: McClelland and Stewart, 1980), pp. 198 and 200.

7. Don Munton, "Great Lakes Water Quality in Environmental Politics and Diplomacy," in Dwivedi, *Resources and the Environment*, p. 170; William R. Willoughby, *The Joint Organizations of Canada and the United States* (Toronto: University of Toronto Press, 1979), p. 491.

8. U.S. House of Representatives, Committee on Interstate and Foreign Commerce, Subcommittee on Oversight and Investigations, *Hearings, Acid Rain*, 96th Cong., 2d sess (1980), pp. 205–229.

9. *Canada Weekly*, November 19, 1980, p. 6.

10. John R. Sharpe, "Canada–USA Environmental Relations," in Carroll, *Canada–United States Natural Resources and Environmental Symposium*, p. 10, discusses this division. See also W. Brian Woodrow, "Resources and Environmental Policy-Making at the National Level: The Search for Focus," in Dwivedi, *Resources and the Environment*, pp. 32–33; Dale Gibson, "The Environment and the Constitution: New Wine in Old Bottles," in Dwivedi, *Protecting the Environment*, pp. 106–119; and Stanley B. Stein, "Environmental Control and Different Levels of Government," *Canadian Public Administration* 14 (no. 1, Spring 1971): 141–143.

11. O.P. Dwivedi, "The Canadian Government Response to Environmental Concern," in Dwivedi, *Protecting the Environment*, pp. 173–175.

12. *Canada Weekly*, August 17, 1977, p. 5; November 16, 1977, p. 3; November 5, 1980, p. 3.

13. Munton, "Great Lakes Water Quality," p. 161.

14. *Wall Street Journal*, May 2, 1980; Jon R. Luoma, "Troubled Skies, Troubled Waters," *Audubon* (November 1980): 100–101.

15. Developments in the Garrison Diversion controversy well illustrate this proposition, as noted in Kim R. Nossal, "The Unmaking of Garrison: United States Politics and the Management of Canadian–American Boundary Waters," *Behind the Headlines* 37 (no. 1, 1978), esp. pp. 21–22.

16. Munton, "Great Lakes Water Quality," p. 173; Willoughby, *The Joint Organizations of Canada and the United States*, p. 49.

17. Nossal, "The Unmaking of Garrison," pp. 4–6, 8, 12–13, 15, 25; John E. Carroll and Roderick M. Logan, *The Garrison Diversion Unit* (Montreal: C.D. Howe Research Institute, 1980), chap. 5.

18. W.R.D. Sewell and N.A. Swainson, "West Coast Oil Pollution Policies: Canadian Responses to Risk Assessment," in Dwivedi, *Resources and the Environment*, p. 229.

19. Bruce Mitchell, "The Provincial Domain in Environment Management and Resource Development," in Dwivedi, *Resources and the Environment*, pp. 52–53; David Estrin, "Tokenism and Environmental Protection," in Dwivedi, *Protecting the Environment*, pp. 123–124, 126.

20. Ross Sandler, "Equal Time in the Courts," *Amicus* (Winter 1980): 4 (later renamed *The Amicus Journal*).

21. Estrin, "Tokenism and Environmental Protection," pp. 135–137; Paul Wilkinson, "The Role of the Public in Environmental Decision-Making," in Dwivedi, *Protecting the Environment*, pp. 246–247.

22. Ross, "National Sovereignty," p. 276; David G. Le Marquand and Anthony Scott, "Canada's International Environmental Relations," in Dwivedi, *Resources and the Environment*, p. 85.

23. "The Fight over Clean Air Begins," *Science* (March 20, 1981): 1325–30, discusses the commission's report and some reactions.

24. *Canada Weekly*, July 9, 1980, p. 2.

25. "EPA's Acid Test," *Amicus* (Summer 1980): 2–3. A major problem was the more lenient treatment of "old" coal-fired generating plants than "new" ones.

26. Illustrative is testimony in *Hearings, Acid Rain*, especially pp. 277, and 296–298.

27. Ibid., pp. 324 and 719.

28. International Joint Commission, *International Poplar River Water Quality Study: Main Report, 1979*, and *Water Quality in the Poplar River Basin*, January 1981; and *Canada Weekly*, August 17, 1977, p. 5; November 16, 1977; and November 5, 1980.

29. Hans J. Peterson, "The Cabin Creek Coal Project: An Environmental Problem and Recommendations," *Social Science Journal* (January 1977): 33–38.

30. For example, the project was among those in President Carter's 1977 "hit list" to be reviewed for probable elimination from among congressionally approved water projects. On the Garrison Diversion see Nossal, "The Unmaking of Garrison," and Carroll and Logan, *The Garrison Diversion Unit*.

31.   International Joint Commission, *Regulation of the Richelieu River and Lake Champlain: An IJC Report to the Governments of Canada and the United States*, January 1981.

32.   Munton, "Great Lakes Water Quality," passim; Willoughby, *The Joint Organizations of Canada and the United States*, pp. 43–48; U.S. Department of State, "Great Lakes Water Quality Agreement, 1978," *Bulletin* (January 1979): 23–24.

33.   Sewell and Swainson, "West Coast Oil Pollution Policies," pp. 222, 239–240; U.S. Department of State, "Energy: Crude Oil Transportation Arrangements," *Bulletin* (December 1979): 39; "Exchange of Notes between Canada and the United States: Constituting an Agreement on Traffic Management for the Juan de Fuca Straits," *International Perspectives* (March–April 1980).

34.   See, for example, the studied presentation of the Ontario Ministry of the Environment, *The Case against the Rain: A Report on Acidic Precipitation and Ontario Programs for Remedial Action*, October 1980.

35.   *Canada Weekly*, December 24, 1980, and December 31, 1980, p. 3.

36.   Ted Schrecker, "Canada's Nuclear Commitment: A Challenge in Technological Assessment," in Dwivedi, *Resources and the Environment*, esp. p. 291.

37.   Patrick Kyba, "Problems of International Environmental Regulation," in Dwivedi, *Protecting the Environment*, p. 294.

38.   For example, aerial spraying to control spruce budworm in forests on the two sides of the boundary is now feared to be environmentally harmful.

39.   Joel J. Sokolsky, "The Canada–U.S. Alaska Highway Pipeline: A Study in Environmental Decision-Making," *American Review of Canadian Studies* (Autumn 1979): 89.

40.   Allen L Springer, "Licensing the Eastport Refinery: Adequate Recognition of Canadian Environmental Interests?" mimeographed paper for 5th biennial meeting of the Association for Canadian Studies in the United States, Washington, D.C., September 29, 1979, p. 10.

41.   Willoughby, *The Joint Organizations of Canada and the United States*, pp. 54–55, 59; International Joint Commission, *Annual Report—1977*, p. 38.

42.   Le Marquand and Scott, "Canada's International Environmental Relations," pp. 81–82.

43.   Willoughby, *The Joint Organizations of Canada and the United States*, p. 50.

44.   The words were those of Peter Wilson of the Canada Department of Fisheries and Environment at the New Hampshire symposium, 1978, in Carroll, *Canada–United States Natural Resources and Environmental Symposium*, p. 12. The zero-sum game aspect is particularly acute in the controversy over acid rain, since the region from which the emissions mainly come

is relatively invulnerable to the harmful effects but would have to bear the main burden for any curbs imposed. See Don Munton, "Dependence and Interdependence in Transboundary Environmental Relations," *International Journal* (Winter 1980–81): 174.

45.　For example, under the aegis of the Economic Commission for Europe, they joined thirty-two European countries in November 1979 in a declaration of some principles that should govern protection from long-range transboundary air pollutants (Munton, "Dependence and Interdependence," pp. 170–171).

46.　Anthony Scott, "Can the IJC Concept be Strengthened to Deal with Future Western Border Issues?" mimeographed, May 3, 1980, revised version of paper delivered to Western Social Science Association, Albuquerque, N.M., April 1980, pp. 27–28.

47.　Note, for example, Anthony J. Parisi, "Utilities Have Cause to Thank Their Critics," *New York Times*, September 7, 1980.

48.　Maxwell Cohen, "The International Joint Commission—Yesterday, Today, and Tomorrow," in Carroll, *Canada–United States Natural Resources and Environmental Symposium*, pp. 32–33.

7 U.S.-CANADIAN DEFENSE RELATIONS
An Assessment for the 1980s

Douglas J. Murray

As we enter this decade, defense continues to be one of the least contentious aspects of U.S.-Canada relations.[1] Indeed, as Richard J. Smith, former director of the U.S. State Department's Office of Canadian Affairs, pointed out in early 1980 to the first meeting of the U.S.-Canada working group, "the [defense] relationship is one of unparalleled intimacy." The reason is fundamental. The truly unique defense association between the United States and Canada, which evolved over forty years, serves both parties' most basic national objective, the security of the North American continent. Today the relationship is so interwoven into both nations' defense policies that it is difficult to contemplate any disagreement serious enough to lead to its dissolution.

The North American defense cooperative relationship rests on two pillars: joint physical defense of the continent, as manifested in the North American Aerospace Defense Command (NORAD) and some 200 other bilateral defense agreements; and cooperation in weapons research and manufacture, as manifested in the Defense Production Sharing Agreement (DPSA) and the Defense Development Sharing Agreement (DDSA). Both pillars rise from the same foundation: a

---

The views expressed herein are those of the author, a lieutenant colonel in the U.S. Air Force, and do not necessarily reflect the views of the U.S. Air Force or the U.S. Department of Defense.

221

mutual perception of the threat to the national security of the North American continent. Inevitably, ongoing changes in the threat, in the context of the growing economic interdependence of the two partners and the desire for greater autonomy in Canada—as reflected in the earlier Trudeau effort to implement the foreign policy of "the third option"[2]—are creating both stresses and changes in the relationship. In the words of a former secretary of state, the "unique" relationship between the United States and Canada has been replaced by a "special" relationship, the precise nature of which the partners have not quite decided on, particularly with respect to defense.

This chapter analyzes this relationship, its past, present, and future, in order to define a course of action that the United States should adopt *with* Canada during the next decade to reaffirm the association and in so doing enhance North American security. The chapter is divided into three parts: a review of the nature of the relationship (its past), a discussion of the current issues with which it must deal (its present), and the development of a proposal that will not simply resolve these contemporary issues but revitalize the association (its future).

THE NATURE OF THE RELATIONSHIP

To understand how the U.S.-Canadian defense relationship developed, one should examine three factors that have forged the metal that holds the association together: geography, a forty-year tradition of cooperation, and cross-border (transnational) decision dynamics.

Geography

Geography has impelled—indeed, compelled—the United States and Canada to cooperate in the defense of the North American continent and, in this effort, to become involved in the political process of how best to provide for its security. In terms of physical defense, geographic contiguity has made the two nations that share the North American continent an inseparable defensible unit to be studied as a single defineable issue area. John Diefenbaker, prime minister of Canada, in the House of Commons on February 20, 1959, stated it best: "Under the irresistible dictates of geography, the defence of

North America has become a joint enterprise of both Canada and the United States."

As a general rule, technology reduces the significance of geographic contiguity in the creation of geopolitical defense units. Not so in the case of the United States and Canada, however, for nuclear weapons that can be intercontinentally delivered have reduced the two nations to a single target area. Unlike America's other allies, Canada's physical location between the two superpowers has guaranteed its involvement in any conflict between them. Accordingly, attack warning installations in Canada's vast northern expanses are a major asset in keeping credible the response of a significant portion of the U.S. strategic forces, which is vital to the maintenance of a strategy of deterrence. At the same time, falling along the flight of Soviet missiles, Canadian aerospace becomes the battleground for the defense of these forces should deterrence fail.

The defense of North America also inseparably links Canada and the United States to the nations of Western Europe. The European link is manifested in three ways. First, the Western European nations are considered integral parts of the Western sphere of influence and, through the North Atlantic Treaty of 1949 are linked to the defense of the North American continent. An attack on any North Atlantic Treaty Organization (NATO) member nation is by mutual agreement of the NATO partners the same as an attack on the North American continent.

In fact, the operative threat scenario to North American security postulates thermonuclear war beginning with a Warsaw Pact attack on Western Europe. As then Canadian Minister of Defence Leo Cadieux, speaking in the House of Commons in December 1968, pointed out, "the forum where the superpowers' interests most clearly impinge on each other is Europe and, hence, Europe is the geographic region where Canada's security is most in jeopardy."[3] On the one hand, Western Europe has become the first line of defense for the North American continent. On the other, the ability to defend the North American continent enhances the credibility of allied forces to deter attack in Europe.

A second manifestation of the European link is that both the United States and Canada, as NATO members, have committed sizable forces to the defense of Western Europe. Thus the politics of North American defense has a NATO input. Bilateral decisions on the nature of the North American defense effort are at least indirectly influenced by the views of the individual NATO nations and the alliance as a whole. This was most graphically portrayed in the recent debate within Canada over the purchase of a new fighter aircraft, during which NATO requirements for such an aircraft had to be weighed along with the needs of NORAD.

Cooperative Tradition

The success of the U.S.–Canadian defense relationship is also the result of a history of cooperation that dates back to the outbreak of World War II. It was through that cataclysmic struggle that Americans and Canadians alike first perceived that the security of their hemisphere was a mutual problem that had become relevant for joint public policy.

That perception gained its first official expression in the Ogdensburg Declaration of August 18, 1940. One notes with interest that the declaration itself was no more than an unsigned press release on a meeting between Canadian Prime Minister Mackenzie King and President Franklin Roosevelt held at Ogdensburg, New York, the previous day. It has since become "the spirit under which virtually all other security treaties, executive agreements, various understandings, and cooperation relative to or affecting North American security are authorized."[4]

Eight months later, on April 21, 1941, after another meeting, this one at Hyde Park, King and Roosevelt issued a corresponding statement on defense–economic cooperation. The product of these two informal meetings and the accompanying, equally informal, announcements that followed is the cooperative relationship that now exists.

The history of that evolving relationship is an amalgam of three policy histories: American defense policy, Canadian defense policy, and North American air defense policy. In the evolution of North American security since 1939, this seamless web of three policy chronologies displays two distinct historical patterns.

The first of these patterns is the tendency for Canadian defense policy objectives to accommodate, with some lag, those of the United States. For example in 1958 Canadian defense policy stressed manned aircraft interceptors (at that point, the Canadians very much wanted to sell their projected interceptor, the AVRO Arrow, to the

United States). During this period Washington's policy, which had been similarly directed earlier in the decade, was moving away from highly sophisticated aircraft toward more intricate detection systems. Instead of manned interceptors, the United States began discussing a semiautomatic ground environment (SAGE) system, gap filler radars and unmanned interceptors, such as the Bomarc missile. Yet after Washington persuaded Ottawa that this was the way to go, and just as Canada had established two squadrons of Bomarcs, the United States again switched signals. On March 25, 1960, defense officials in Washington announced that they had decided to develop a less elaborate automated defense system against manned aircraft, one that could be brought on line earlier, and to utilize the consequent savings to develop a sophisticated missile and space defense system. Thus, at a time when Canadian defense forces were continuing to prepare for active defense against a manned bomber attack on the North American continent, U.S. defense policy planners were arguing that the threat from missiles was overriding and that the immediate priority was passive defense through new missile and space defense warning systems. But when the Canadians finally agreed that passive defense was the way to go, the United States began talking about the need for an active defense system (the antiballistic missile (ABM) system). Thus Canada consistently found its policy one step behind that of the United States.

The second and more significant pattern is a product of the first. Based upon the level of consensus (or the lack thereof) between the defense policies of the United States and Canada, we can identify three periods in the history of the politics of North American defense: convergence (1940–1964), divergence (1964–1975), and reassessment and uncertainty (1975–present).

Convergence. The first historical period was marked by the initiation and enhancement of defense cooperation between the two nations. This is the period that Melvin Conant has called the "time of the great compact." It begins with the Ogdensburg and Hyde Park declarations of 1940 and 1941, respectively, and includes the establishment of a joint defense plan for North America during World War II, the creation of the North Atlantic Treaty Organization, the establishment of the North American Air Defense Command and the creation and expansion of a defense economic relationship that some have called the North American common defense market.

The U.S.–Canadian contributions of 1940–1945 were vital for the successful prosecution of the war and laid the foundation for joint defense planning and implementation that would continue in the years following. Even more important to establishing a North American defense unit, the war had created within the publics of both the Untited States and Canada the realization that in matters of defense, the common border joined rather than separated their two nations; never again could either nation pursue entirely independent defense policies.

As Soviet political ambitions and "menace" arising from them became clearer (highlighted for the Canadian public by the revelation of a Soviet espionage operation in Ottawa), and the realities of a new type of warfare were assimilated (highlighted for the publics of both nations by the Soviet detonation of an atomic device in 1949 and its development of a sophisticated long-range delivery system a year earlier), the joint defense planning effort shifted to arrangements in the far north. The realization of this new Soviet threat, reinforced by events in Korea in 1950, resulted in the creation of what Samuel Huntington has called "a continental defense system." This system was composed of the early warning radar nets (Distant Early Warning Line (DEW), Mid–Canada Line, and the Pinetree Line), constructed between 1952 and 1958, the North American Air Defense Command (established 1957), the defense production and development sharing agreements (a defense economic arrangement that evolved between 1958 and 1963), and nearly 200 other bilateral defense agreements.

In sum, the first twenty-five years of the defense relationship were a remarkably fruitful period. By the beginning of 1964 the U.S.–Canadian defense alliance had grown to a size and complexity unimagined at its inception in 1940. However, this growth would not continue into the latter years of the decade. The concept of a continental defense system would not be challenged, but the orientation would change. This resulted essentially from the fact that the high degree of convergence between the U.S. and the Canadian defense policies found during the first period began to break down. Divergence was the result of the evident inability of the Canadian government to accommodate the changes in the North American defense relationship demanded by the new American strategy of flexible response, a strategy designed to meet a new type of Soviet threat.

Divergence.   By 1964 the nature of the Soviet strategic threat had changed from bombers to missiles. The Soviet bomber threat projected for the 1950s never materialized, as the Kremlin elected to develop intercontinental missiles as its primary strategic offensive force. In the 1960 U.S. presidential election, in fact, the issue was an alleged missile gap. At the same time the wholesale creation from former European colonies of newly independent nations, to become known collectively as the Third World, set the stage for a type of warfare in which a nuclear arsenal had no rational place. The possibility of guerrilla warfare and of conventional forces fighting limited wars with nonnuclear weaponry began to dominate U.S. defense thinking. The realization that the North American continental defense system developed in the 1950s was irrelevant against a threat of Soviet missiles and equally irrelevant when the values and institutions of the North American continent were to be defended, not in the aerospace over the continent but in "wars of national liberation" somewhere in the developing world, resulted in the development of the new American defense strategy called flexible response. Although not opposed to the strategy, the Canadians objected to being directed by Washington to change their defense policy to meet that strategy, particularly when such changes resulted in altering Canada's national priorities. Critics argued that Washington, not Ottawa, was making Canadian policy.

The era of divergence (1964–1975) can be subdivided into two distinct periods, each beginning with a Canadian defense white paper, those of 1964 and 1971, and a Liberal Canadian administration, those of Lester Pearson and Pierre Elliott Trudeau. During the first period Canada stressed international interdependence built upon peacekeeping missions for the United Nations. During the second period Canada focused on national independence built upon Canadian national sovereignty missions.[6] The net result of the quest for a defense policy made in Ottawa, however, was a marked reduction in the military capability of the Canadian forces. There was, for instance, a significant reduction in manpower. A Canadian peak force of 123,000 in 1963 had by 1975 dropped to 78,000.

The 1964 defense white paper was strongly influenced by Prime Minister Pearson, who in 1965 had been the architect of the UN peacekeeping force in the Middle East. Pearson asserted that, since the most likely threat to Canadian and North American security would not come from an all-out thermonuclear war in Europe but from low-level conflict within the developing world, Canada must develop a conventional, mobile, flexible force capable of responding to such conflicts as part of UN peacekeeping forces. Ironically, however, the 1964 white paper did not reduce Canada's commitment to NORAD nor to NATO. It did produce ambivalence. On the one hand, it suggested the need for a new, more independent policy for Canada directed toward the UN peacekeeping mission and called for the creation of flexible forces to meet this requirement. However, at the same time, it advocated the maintenance of the existing commitments to both NORAD and NATO, all this at lowered levels of real expenditure.

The ambivalence was short-lived. As early as 1965, the perceptions of the Pearson administration concerning NATO were changing in light of the French military withdrawal from the organization. Changing also was the attitude toward peacekeeping as a result of the Congo operation. The Pearson administration was faced with a dilemma. On the one hand, the defense systems acquired at great expense during the period of convergence were becoming obsolete. On the other, the kinds of forces required to fulfill the requirements to the UN set down in the 1964 white paper were essentially non-existent.

The dilemma was compounded by the sagging defense budget. During the five years of the Pearson administration, as the result of extensive social programs and inflation, defense appropriations fell from 23.7 to 16.8 percent of the budget and from 4.5 to 2.8 percent of the gross national product as the projected savings from the 1968 reorganization of the Canadian forces failed to materialize. The result was gradual decay in the Canadian ability to support its NORAD and NATO missions. In this sense the defense white paper resulted in a defense role for Canada that was neither new nor independent. On the contrary Canada's role in the defense of North America began to lose credibility if not viability. Pearson's successor would attempt to remedy that by reducing overseas commitments and by giving Canadian foreign and defense policies a uniquely "Made in Canada" label. These efforts, however, would disrupt the defense consensus between the United States and Canada.

When Pierre Trudeau became prime minister in 1968, few doubted that there would be a significant change in the government's orientation to foreign and defense policies, but no one envisioned the extent of that change. Earlier, drawing a lesson from the expulsion of the United Nations Emergency Force (UNEF) from Egyptian territory in Spring 1967, Trudeau had rejected the thrust of the 1964 white paper toward peacekeeping and embraced the view that the concern of Canada's defense and foreign policies should be first and foremost Canada and Canadian sovereignty. As a result, the new administration's first act was to order a major review of those policies.

That review, the conclusions of which were reported in the defense white paper of 1971, established a new priority for Canada's defense efforts. Peacekeeping was deemphasized, and first priority was again given to the national sovereignty mission. Above all, Trudeau wanted to assure that defense priorities were responsive to Canadian national interests and international developments affecting Canada, not necessarily to the dictates of Washington. The white paper identified four major roles for the Canadian forces:

- The surveillance of Canadian territory and coastlines;
- The defense of North America in cooperation with U.S. forces;
- The fulfillment of agreed upon NATO commitments; and
- The performance of such international peacekeeping roles as would be found significant.

Although Canada thus remained committed to the continuance of the North American defense system and to its modernization, that commitment would not include Canadian involvement in any active missile defense system. The area in which Trudeau's defense policy diverged the most from the stated U.S. defense policy of flexible response, however, was NATO.

On April 3, 1969, Pierre Trudeau exploded an alliance bombshell by announcing that, although Canada was not withdrawing from the organization and in fact wanted to reaffirm its commitment, it would begin a phased reduction of its NATO forces. Plans were announced for reducing the NATO contingent by 50 percent and identifying a nonnuclear role for the remainder. The defense budget was frozen for three years at C$1.8 billion.

The net result of these reductions was a decrease in the defense capability of Canada—manpower, equipment, money—to support both the NATO and the NORAD mission.

Reassessment and Uncertainty.   The third period in the evolution of North American defense begins with a speech in Ottawa by Canadian Minister of Defence James Richardson on January 17, 1975. By suggesting a possible convergence of Canadian policy with U.S. policy toward NATO, the speech indicated a shift from the 1971 white paper. For example, there was a clear indication that the downward trend in defense spending would be reversed and that major new pieces of equipment would be purchased, including a new fleet of long-range patrol aircraft (LPRA) and a new fighter aircraft (NFA).

The 1975 statement signaled a reevaluation of Canadian defense policy was underway, a reevaluation that would be mirrored in Washington, particularly with respect to air defense, once the Carter administration took office two years later. As those reevaluations are still not completed, their impact on the future of the North American defense system remains uncertain. Admittedly, in a series of policy statements from both countries in the years that have followed, some of the specifics have been clarified; however, the overall philosophy and orientation, particularly with respect to the future of the U.S.–Canadian defense relationship, is not clear. For these reasons, the current period in the history of North American defense is one of reevaluation and uncertainty.

Two factors precipitated the 1975 policy change. The first was considerable criticism of Trudeau's defense policy in the Canadian press and within NATO. The second was a suggestion by then Secretary of Defense James Schlesinger, in a press conference on September 16, 1975, that Canada should assign NATO greater priority than NORAD. Schlesinger stated that he preferred Canada continue a mix of land and air forces in Europe. The diminished bomber threat meant that we needed not new interceptor aircraft, but rather tanks to help NATO meet the formidable Warsaw Pact tank threat to West Germany.

The last catalyst for the 1975 policy change was the Defence Structure Review (DSR) by the Canadian Ministry of Defence begun in November 1974 combined with the U.S. Department of Defense's decision, in the same year, to structure its North American air defense force primarily for peacetime surveillance and control and consequently to reduce the role of manned interceptors and active air defense. These three factors have produced a current Canadian orientation toward defense that suggests agreement with the United States that Canada's contribution to NATO is a vital part of the Western deterrent, that it must be increased, and further, that the time has come to restore to the Canadian armed forces a capability to fight.

Decisional Dynamics

A third factor that has enabled the cooperative defense arrangement to endure is the presence of a well-developed, sophisticated, and decentralized defense decisionmaking structure and process in which the United States and Canada are able, either formally or informally, to identify, discuss, and resolve interalliance issues before they endanger the association's existence. A significant part of this structure is what Roger Swanson has called the "U.S.–Canadian constellation"—a group of inter- and intragovernmental bureaucratic actors.[7]

Within the national security area two key components are the Permanent Joint Board on Defense (PJBD) and the defense production and development sharing steering committees. The PJBD, created by the Ogdensburg declaration on August 18, 1940, played a significant role in the planning and execution of the North American defense program during the war. Following the war the PJBD initiated the various air defense radar lines, formulated the requirements and oversaw the creation of NORAD in 1958, and was instrumental in the creation of the defense production sharing program that same year.

Including on the U.S. side representatives from most of the components of the "Canadian constellation,"[8] the board normally meets three times a year. Business is conducted without formality and the agenda in recent years has included all of the important bilateral defense issues, significant economic questions such as the utilization of the St. Lawrence Seaway, military procurement issues, and NATO standardization. The agenda items are generally considered and discussed until a consensus is reached. There is no formal voting procedure and only unanimous recommendations are forwarded. Issues formally introduced by members of the board may originate in agencies of either government. Similarly, decisions or recommendations, when and if subsequently approved by both governments, become the executive directives to the particular government agencies concerned.

The major utility of the PJBD and its most meaningful influence on the defense decision process, however, exist in the informal, off-the-record contacts and discussions among its members and their staffs. As one Canadian embassy official has observed: "The PJBD provides a forum that would otherwise be impossible.... It transcends department bickering between the two countries.... Formal contacts do not count as much as the informal discussions outside of the meetings. . . . Letters, reports, telephone calls, etc., from one member to another . . . get action."[9]

The board thus provides an established formal channel for military, diplomatic, defense, and other civilian officials to discuss issues and ultimately develop an consensus position that can be referred back to the respective governments for implementation. In addition the PJBD enables officals to establish back-channel, unofficial contacts.

These contacts have enabled the PJBD to mesh the military requirements of North American defense with political, economic, and other societal considerations in order to facilitate the continuation and expansion of the continental defense system begun in 1940. The complexity of U.S.–Canadian interdependence in the 1970s has meant that defense arrangements have ramifications in the domestic, economic, and political spheres of both countries. The prestige and experience acquired through the nearly forty years of its existence, the mixed membership of civilian and military agencies, and the informality and flexibility of its procedures, have enabled the PJBD to handle the sensitive issues more effectively than any single national or governmental actor.

The DPSA steering committee is the counterpart of the PJBD in the defense economic area and has been responsible for overseeing this arrangement. As discussed below, it played a major role in resolving the trade imbalance dispute of the early 1970s. Within these two corporate bodies the most pervasive if not always the most influential grouping has been made up of members of the military organizations of the two nations. Indeed, the genesis of U.S.–Canadian military linkage dates back to the interwar period when the Canadian military elite developed ties with their British counterparts under Commonwealth aegis, although it was not until the Cold War era that the corresponding linkage with the American military became prominent. Today these ties are kept active through the numerous joint planning, operations, and training exercises in which the two nations' military services participate.

The relationship between the Canadian command and its American counterpart has sometimes proven to be closer even than relations among the different services of the same nation. For example, one commentator relates the story of the U.S. Navy's desire for information that the U.S. Air Force would not release to it. The U.S.

Navy therefore had the Canadian navy (Maritime Command) request that the Canadian Air Command obtain the information from the U.S. Air Force and pass it on to them.[10]

The two major loci for intermilitary linkage have been NORAD and the Military Cooperation Committee (MCC). As Mc Lin points out, the military of the two nations jointly provided the real impetus behind the creation of NORAD, bringing it into existence, de facto, ten months before the Canadian Parliament began debate on its creation.

Headquartered in Colorado Springs and staffed by military officers of both countries, NORAD serves as a forum in which the daily business of North American defense, as well as military perspectives and positions on various U.S.–Canadian issues, can be shared and discussed. Currently there are more than 8,700 Canadians assigned to NORAD in the United States and Canada who interact daily with their American counterparts. The significance of this relationship and its place in decisionmaking regarding North American defense is best demonstrated in the Canadian military response to the Cuban missile crisis of 1962. As reported by Ghent, while the Diefenbaker government was slow to respond to the crisis, the Canadian military was not.[11] When the American components of NORAD went into an advanced defense readiness condition, the Canadian deputy to NORAD (through Minister of Defence Harkness) put the Canadian forces on alert two days before formal cabinet approval of the act. Similarly, although not even formally included in NORAD, the Canadian army and navy responded. The army activated its communications systems and declared itself ready to go. Meanwhile the chief of the Canadian naval staff, under the cover of repeating a major naval exercise to correct errors, authorized—on his own and hours before even the defense minister approved it—the order for the Atlantic based fleet in Halifax to prepare for sea. The subsequent timely deployment of the Canadian navy to the North Atlantic to track Soviet submarines and keep an eye on the Russian "fishing" fleet enabled the American navy to move south into the blockade zone.

The result of this response was that, while its government was publicly ostracized for apparent nonsupport of the American president, Canada was in actuality the only American ally to provide active military support during the Cuban crisis, a fact that explains, perhaps, why Kennedy was so restrained in his criticism of Diefenbaker.

In short, as Jocelyn Ghent has observed: "The Canadian military perceived and acted on a threat that was defined not by their own government, but by the trans-governmental group to which they felt much closer, the Canadian–American military."[12]

The MCC, the other principal organization for U.S.-Canadian military interaction, came into existence in February 1946 as a section of the PJBD. In 1949 the MCC was separated from the PJBD. Currently the MCC consists of a Canadian and an American section, with each section composed of a chairman, a secretary, and six members drawn from the country's uniformed services. The United States is represented by two members each from the army, navy, and air force, and Canada has similar representation drawn from the country's mobile, maritime, and air commands. The MCC is jointly responsible to the Canadian chief of defense staff and U.S. joint chiefs of staff.

In recent years, the MCC has emerged as a significant actor. As one participant has pointed out: "The MCC is not a lobby for a particular force structure but provides a good and reliable place for staff level military unofficial discussions that go on. The working group meetings are valuable discussion groups. The meaningful discussions are off the record." Similarly, another MCC member has commented: "The MCC meets formally only twice a year, but between these meetings the process of coordination continues. Each service meets and talks frequently, especially by telephone and not on only agenda items. If I have a problem, I call my MCC counterpart. It is a way to go around the embassy and attache system. A direct authorized contact. It is quite effective."[13]

One U.S. defense official summarized the cross-border defense interaction roughly as follows: "At the Assistant Secretary and assistant defense ministerial level, there is frequent contact; but in regard to military contact, there is an extremely close relationship, particularly within NORAD."[14]

CURRENT ISSUES

Geography, a forty-year history of defense cooperation, and a unique decisionmaking structure form the context in which policy decisions on the future of U.S.-Canadian defense relations will necessarily be made. The direction that these decisions should take will be discussed in the next section. Here the issues that those decisions must address are reviewed. These issues can be categorized into two sets, corresponding to the two elements of the North American cooperative defense relationship: physical defense and economic cooperation in defense production.

Defense–Strategic Issues

The most critical if not pervasive issue that defense decisionmakers on both sides of the border must resolve in this decade concerns the future course of the defense relationship. As underscored in the preceding section, the association came into existence as a result of a common threat and a consensus on how that threat should be met. The current problem is that, as the threat has changed, the consensus has broken down, at least at the national executive and legislative levels of government.

The early warning radar lines, NORAD, most of the 200 bilateral agreements, and, in fact, much of what Canada contributes to North American security, were created in the 1950s, in response to the Soviet bomber threat. In the last twenty years, the character of that threat has shifted from the bomber to the intercontinental ballistic missile (ICBM). As that threat changed so did the mission of NORAD, reflecting a reduced role for much of the air defense network created during the 1950s. Two of the most recent examples of this realignment are the decision in the fall of 1977 to deactivate the U.S. Air Force Air Defense Command (ADCOM), the Air Force Major Command (MAJCOM) managing the assets of the American component of NORAD, and the decision in 1980 to establish a Space Defense Operations Center at the NORAD Cheyenne mountain complex. If the first decision acknowledged the downgrading of the anti-bomber defense mission by fragmenting management of U.S. assets controlled by NORAD between two commands,[15] the second signaled an enhancement of the space mission by establishing an agency to provide command, control, and communications to manage the space defense operations. The current mission of NORAD was summarized by Secretary of Defense Harold Brown in his budget report for fiscal year 1982. He stated:

> Our surveillance sensors are designed to provide tactical warning and to assess the size and objective of a missile attack on North America. . . . *Together with*

Canada, we are developing an air defense system to provide tactical warning and characterization of bomber and cruise missile attacks, to provide a limited air defense in war, and to control access to North American airspace in peacetime and crises. Furthermore, we are improving surveillance systems to warn of attack on *U.S. space systems*, and we are continuing R&D on anti-satellite techniques as the basis for future space defense. [Emphasis added.] [16]

The problem, as this statement suggests, is that while the NORAD mission has changed to include space, the basis for the Canadian contribution has not. It is still predominantly air defense with the result that as the perception of the bomber threat to this continent has decreased so also has the Canadian contribution. The reduced Canadian contribution results in part from a not infrequent view within Canada that any Canadian contribution to North America security is superfluous since the United States must defend Canada regardless of the level of Canada's participation.

Some analysts take issue with the position that Canada's role is insignificant. They offer three compelling reasons for maintaining an air defense system with Canadian participation. The first is to deter a Soviet bomber attack that might otherwise be launched if the Soviets felt that North American air defenses were so degraded that they could penetrate them successfully. A second rationale is to defend against a small-scale air attack upon the United States from a Third World nation, such as Cuba. A final reason concerns the intended mission of the Soviet Backfire Bomber [17] and the Soviet potential to develop a long-range, air-launched cruise missile, either of which increases the airborne threat to the continent and the need to continue an air defense network.

The inability of the two countries to define the joint air defense mission and to specify Canada's role in it is reflected in the agenda of U.S.–Canadian defense issues over the last ten years. [18] The challenge for U.S. and Canadian policymakers in this decade, therefore, is to delineate the air defense requirement and Canada's role in meeting it. Fortunately, the effort has already begun.

In 1979 realizing that disagreement (both between and within the two nations) over the importance or necessity for an air defense mission [19] had resulted in nearly twenty years of reduced funding, resulting in a predominantly obsolete, uneconomic, and marginally effective system, the Canadian minister of defense and his American counterpart established an ad hoc air defense steering group. The jointly manned group was charged with doing a zero-base, in-depth study of the atmospheric defense problem. It reported its findings in 1979 in a classified document, *Joint United States/Canada Air Defense Study (JUSCADS)*. Based upon an assessment of the threat through the end of this century and an evaluation of current and projected capabilities, the study concluded that the North American air defense requirements and mission were ambiguous and recommended that each nation undertake an independent evaluation to determine policy recommendations to guide future plans and programs, with the hope of resolving the ambiguity. As the first step in this evaluation, in August 1980, the secretary of defense and his Canadian counterpart approved a *Joint Policy Statement on the Air Defense of North America*.

After reaffirming the existence of the airborne threat to the continent and the need to continue to cooperate within the NATO framework in the air defense of that continent, the joint communiqué established the following objectives for this air defense mission:

> Canada and the United States will maintain jointly an air defense system capable of providing tactical warning and attack characterization (i.e., threat assessment and analysis), of limiting damage to strategic retaliatory forces and C^3 (Command Control Communication) nodes and of exercising control of peacetime access to continental airspace. The system will be capable of providing timely, reliable and unambiguous attack warning to a level sufficient to support the survival of strategic forces located in North America. . . . The system will provide a hedge against future enhancement of Soviet long-range bomber capability and long-range cruise missile development and deployment.

The statement concluded by reestablishing the need for a continuing air defense system.

> In order to contribute to the deterrence of an attack on North America, there will be a continuing requirement to maintain a prudent minimum level of air defense capability within a system structured to be adaptable to changes in the threat and to advances in technology. Canada and the United States believe that their joint air defense objectives must be attained and joint planning goals fulfilled in order to assure the required level of air defense capability. That level should be attained as soon as practicable and maintained for as long as is needed.

Concurrent with this policy statement, the U.S. Air Force, in response to a congressional request for an integrated air defense modernization plan, developed an *Air Defense Master Plan* that is currently undergoing review and evaluation within the Department of

Defense. The plan reportedly concludes that North America's present air defenses are inadequate to meet a significantly increased Soviet bomber threat composed of the Backfire bomber and expected deployment of a Soviet long-range, air-launched cruise missile on other existing bombers. To meet this threat the document outlines an extensive modernization plan to update radars, develop new systems, expand the AWACS fleet and increase the F-15 interceptor force.[20]

It is expected that once the U.S. Air Force study has been assessed by the Department of Defense (DOD), it will become the basis for a DOD air defense Master Plan. Once that plan has been coordinated within the Canadian Ministry of National Defence, it will serve as the basic blueprint not only for air defense modernization but also for the future direction of the U.S.–Canadian strategic defense association.

A related issue this master plan will affect is NORAD (and NATO) cost sharing. Presently, Canada contributes approximately 10 percent of the cost of NORAD (a figure derived from the fact that the Canadian population is approximately 10 percent the population of the United States) and ranks near the bottom of the list of members in terms of its contributions to NATO. The United States maintains that the Canadian contributions, particularly those to NORAD, should be increased. Canada, on the other hand, argues that it is paying its fair share and that what it lacks in quantity it provides in quality. There is merit in both positions.

The Canadian Defense Effort.   Canada, a nation of nearly 24 million, has an all-volunteer armed force of 78,646. Approximately 1.5 percent of the male population between eighteen and forty-five is in the military. (Statistical data in this section is drawn from *The Military Balance 1980/81.*) Since 1968 the army, navy, and air force have been unified into a single service composed of three commands, air, maritime, and mobile.

In many significant ways the military of Canada and the United States are more similar than they are different. Both are modern and dedicated forces with a professional and well-educated officer corps. To be sure, there are differences in size and organization, but those have not inhibited the development of the very close working relationship between the two military organizations discussed in the first section of this chapter.

The Canadian military can be viewed as in search of an identity, existing among a people whom Richard Preston described as harboring "an unmilitary psyche."[21] Canadian society has never appreciated the contribution of its armed forces, and this has had a psychological effect on their evolution. Lack of public appreciation as well as diminished budget support has created a morale problem within the military that impacts on recruitment and the capability of the reserves. Colin Gray believes that the Canadian military is faced with a crisis of relevance.[22]

Existence in an unmilitary society[23] under a government whose leader has been described as antimilitary[24] has profoundly affected the development of the Canadian profession of arms.[25] The Canadian military, unlike its American counterpart, lacks an appreciation of the military role in the political process. One student of Canadian defense has highlighted the lack of any tradition of higher politico-military staff work in the Canadian forces in a quote from a senior privy council official:

> Our officers stop their development at the lieutenant-colonel level. They don't want to consider the articulation of political and military policy. When chided about this, they reply that the Services are *fighting* forces—"tell us what to do, and we'll do it." They advise going to External Affairs for foreign policy advice and studies. But when you do that you find that there is no one in EXTAFF who really understands military affairs.[26]

One manifestation of this apolitical perspective is the absence of intense interservice rivalry and bureaucratic political infighting so prominent in the American services. The Canadian armed forces are consensus-oriented. This is not to say that individual commanders of one or more of the three major commands within the unified forces might not disagree among themselves and have strong opinions on a particular issue. It does mean, however, that these differences are not relayed to civilian leaders and are not institutionalized into bureaucratic service rivalries. This interservice relationship results in part from unification and in part from the limited size of the forces. Primarily, however, it is the product of close personal relationships among the leadership cadre of the three major commands, whose origins lie in their common backgrounds at the three unified service academies of Canada, whose unification predates by decades the unification of the forces in 1968.

Perhaps the most significant result of interservice collegiality, at least among the decisional elite in Canada, has been to facilitate a process in which the military has been largely immune from the national debates over Quebec separation. The Canadian armed forces thus serve as a unifying factor within Canadian society.

In terms of gross national product (GNP), Canada's defense expenditures are among the smallest in NATO. In 1980–81 they totaled U.S. $4.24 billion, which is less than 10 percent of the federal budget and 1.8 percent of the GNP. However, this snapshot does not reflect the current trend of Canadian financial commitment to defense for, as discussed in section one, there has been an upward trend in defense outlays since 1975. Thus, while prior to 1980 Canada had never met the NATO goal of a 3 percent increase in real spending per year, it now appears that this goal will be met during each of the next five years. Furthermore, during the past four years Canada has embarked on a capital reequipment and modernization program. This program includes the acquisition of new long-range patrol aircraft, Leopard tanks, armed personnel carriers, and F–18 fighter aircraft. Canada also is about to initiate a major shipbuilding program, has already become a major supporter of the U.S.–NATO AWACS program, and has committed aircraft to the NATO airlift augmentation program. Canadian maritime forces also make a significant contribution to the antisubmarine mission in the North Atlantic.

Canada currently has 5,000 troops stationed in Europe. The contingent is composed of one mechanized brigade group (3,000 troops) and one air group (three squadrons of CF–104 aircraft). In addition, one mechanized infantry battalion (2,500) stationed in Canada is trained and earmarked for NATO deployment.

To NORAD Canada provides four main and seventeen auxiliary Distant Early Warning sites, one Baker–Nunn camera for satellite tracking, twenty-four long-range radar identification sites of the Pinetree line, and three all weather interceptor squadrons of thirty-six CF–101 Voodoo aircraft. In addition, in return for Canada's support of the NATO AWACS, Canada will co-man U.S. AWACS aircraft assigned to NORAD. (An issue yet to be resolved is who will pay for training the Canadian crew members.) Canada also has agreed to pay, in effect, for the two regional operations control centers (ROCC) that are part of the seven ROCC NORAD surveillance system.

At present the increase in Canadian defense spending to meet the NATO 3 percent goal and their decision to modernize the NATO forces have allowed attention to shift to the cost sharing issue on the Canadian contribution to NORAD. For the moment the issue's resolution awaits the release of the DOD air defense master plan, which will define future systems' requirements. Ultimately, however, if the cost sharing question is to be resolved, a formula will have to be developed that takes into account the entire spectrum of the Canadian contribution to North American defense, including its role in the Defense Production and Development Sharing Agreements.

Defense Economics Issues

Integral to the North American defense system is the unique cooperative defense economic association, embodied for the most part in the U.S.-Canadian Defense Production and Sharing Agreements and the Defense Development Sharing Agreement. These agreements, which the reader will recall were originally signed in the late 1950s, were designed to achieve greater integration of U.S.-Canadian military production, greater standardization of military equipment, wider dispersal of production facilities, establishment of supplemental sources of supplies, and greater flow of defense supplies and equipment between the United States and Canada. The stated purpose of the association was to promote more effective coordination of the economic resources of the United States and Canada for the common defense. On the more pragmatic side, however, the agreements of 1958–59 were designed to sustain the continuing participation by Canadian industry in the defense business by providing it more effective access to the U.S. defense market. That objective has been achieved. By agreement to eliminate tariff duties, "Buy American" requirements and "gold flow" differentials[27] that are applicable to other nations' bids, Canadian firms have been placed on a relatively equal footing with U.S. firms in competing for U.S. defense contracts.

In the early 1970s the future of this arrangement became a critical issue in defense relations between the United States and Canada. At issue was the flow of military trade between the two nations, which, as a result of the large amounts of Canadian materials bought by the United States to prosecute the Vietnam War, was tilted heavily in Canada's favor.

Today, the trade balance is a nonissue from the U.S. view, in part because it has swung back in favor of the United States by at least $300 million; but, more important, because the two nations, working through the DPSA steering committee, have been able to develop a formula for calculating the balance that considers a variety of factors in the trade relationship, most significantly "offset" agreements.[28]

This formula has not resolved the basic offset issue, however, which resolves around the Canadian demand for large economic offsets on proposed Canadian purchases of military equipment from the United States. The question of offsets, along with a series of continuing trade restrictions on both sides of the border, form the major defense–economic issues in U.S.–Canadian defense relations today.

The Offset Issue.   There is concern in the United States that the Canadian policy of requesting specific offsets and the waiver of recoupment charges,[29] as exemplified in the purchase of the long-range patrol aircraft (CP–140) and the F–28, could undermine the spirit of the defense sharing agreements. In the two cases mentioned previously, Canadian industry receives between 65 and 130 percent of the costs of those systems as offsets for purchasing the aircraft from U.S. manufacturers. Canada also has been exempted from significant portions of the recoupment charges.

In response, the Canadian government has stated that, in accordance with a growing international practice of requiring industrial benefits when purchasing offshore major weapon systems, the government's policy is to require such compensation, both in the military and civilian sectors of the economy, from the company or country obtaining the contract. The Canadian position is that offsets are necessary for the development of an internationally competitive Canadian industry. Further, they have argued that domestic political necessity requires some type of offsetting arrangement to make such military purchases acceptable to the Canadian Parliament. The Canadians have recognized, however, that the existence of the sharing agreements and the long-standing defense–economic relationship have modified these requirements, making them less direct, longer term, and not necessarily appropriate except for cases involving major acquisitions.

Economic Barriers.   The second area of contention between the United States and Canada in the defense economic area is a variety of barriers erected by each nation to the free flow of defense goods between the two nations. Each of these constraints affects a specific aspect of the trade equation. Some constraints are the product of a strong nationalistic or—more frankly, protectionist—domestic political orientation. Others result from domestic programs that have unintended side effects on the defense trade with the neighboring country.

On the Canadian side, there are three major restrictions. These include the 10 percent "Buy Canadian" preferential (not always applied by the Department of Supply and Services (DSS)); the imposition of tariff duties on goods imported under all prime contracts valued at less than $250,000 (and on all subcontracts); and various administrative provisions that exclude U.S. bidders from certain areas, such as shipbuilding.

More extensive is the list of U.S. restrictions that are irritants to the Canadians, most of which originate as U.S. congressional responses to domestic protectionist pressures. One official with the Canadian Department of Industry, Trade, and Commerce explained the nature of the restraints well when he said:

> As you are well aware, funds required by the U.S. Military Departments for operation and procurement of material is voted each year by Congress, and money is provided by enactment of the Defense Appropriations Act. Over a period of years, special conditions have been introduced into this Act, which restrict the freedom of the Military Departments to spend the authorized funds. These legislative restrictions, although not specifically directed at Canada, have tended to become perpetuated in Defence Appropriation Acts, and they restrict the scope of Canadian participation in United States Defence programs.[30]

The U.S. constraints can be discussed in four categories. In the first are limitations resulting from amendments to appropriation bills and other U.S. laws. The most extensive of these was designed to protect the U.S. food, clothing, and textile industries from extremely low import prices. The Berry amendment to the Annual Appropriations Act, implemented by the Armed Services Procurement Regulations (ASPR, para. 6–302), prohibits the procurement of any article of food, clothing, cotton, woven silk and woven silk blends, spun silk yarn, cartridge cloth, synthetic fabrics or coated synthetic fabrics, or wool not grown, reprocessed, reused, or produced in the United States. Further, the common interpretation of the amendment is that not only must the material be of U.S. origin, but also the product incorporating the material must be purchased from domestic U.S. suppliers. This restriction prevents Canadian firms from supplying the United States with such items as uniforms, parachutes, and life rafts.

The restriction contained in the specialty metals rider to the Berry amendment also inhibits defense trade. First introduced as part of the Defense Appropriations Act for fiscal year 1973 and defined in ASPR 6–305, it prohibits U.S. military purchase of certain articles containing any of a number of specialty metals unless they were smelted in steel manufacturing facilities within the United States or its possessions. The category of articles includes aircraft, missiles, and space systems, ships, tanks, automotive systems, weapons, and munitions.

The Burns–Tollefson amendment prohibits U.S. procurement of naval vessels from foreign sources and the subcontracting of major components of hulls or superstructures of naval vessels from such sources.

The Bayh amendment, first added to the 1973 DOD Appropriation Act, prohibits funding research and development from a foreign source unless there is no U.S. source "equally competent" to carry out such research and development at an equal cost. This restriction directly affects defense development sharing because it means that before DOD can buy from Canada, it must completely and formally canvass the U.S. industry to ensure that no U.S. company is competitive.

In addition to these three amendments, a number of conditions tend to limit cross-border trade: small business (10 USC 2301, 15 USC 631, and the Annual DOD Appropriation Act 15 USG 644, 15 USC 637), which specifies that certain types of procurement are restricted to U.S. small businesses; labor surplus (Defense Manpower Policy No. 4), which restricts procurement for performance by labor surplus areas; minority groups (ASPR 1–332); depressed industries (ASPR 1–806); and prison-made goods (18 USC 4124) and blind-made goods (41 USC 48), which require that federal departments purchase from federal prison industries and agencies for the blind any of their products that meet specifications.

In addition ASPR 1–315 requires that all government and contractor purchases of jewel bearings be made from the William Langer Jewel Bearing Plant, Rolla, North Dakota; ASPR Section VI, Part 1, adds an additional differential to that required by the Buy American Act to foreign bids or quotes on materials and supplies for use overseas that means offshore Canadian firms receive no Buy American exemption; and ASPR 6–700 specifies that foreign content in items procured by the United States in implementing its Military Assistance Program (MAP) cannot exceed 50 percent of the value of the end item, which means that Canadian contractors' eligibility to bid on MAP procurement prime contracts is limited, and that, on subcontracts, Canadian firms can only supply up to 50 percent of the value of the end item.

A second category of restrictions is primarily administrative. These restrictions include: (1) the foreign military sales administrative charges—the Arms Export Control Act of 1976 (PL 94–329) requires that DOD add an administrative charge of approximately 3 percent to all foreign military orders (prior to the implementation of this act a waiver had existed exempting Canada from paying such administrative charges); (2) differences in cost accounting standards; (3) problems in auditing and inspecting records, arising from the fact that the original 1951 agreement creating the arrangements for reciprocal audit of contracts has disappeared (!); (4) the numerous legal reviews of international agreements that require a number of legal experts at the individual contracting service, at DOD and at the State Department to review and approve agreements, a process that results in excessive delays and backlogging of contracts; and (5) inadequacy of the communications channels to make American decisionmakers and manufacturers aware of the DPSA program and its benefits. A third category of constraints results from national security considerations. Specifically, Canadian access to contract information and participation in the development and production of defense equipment is inhibited by the NOFORN (no foreign), COMSEC (communications security), and nuclear hardening restrictions.

These restrictions have been particularly prohibitive to recent Canadian efforts to participate in the joint development and production of space-related systems. Canadian industry believes that unless it can get into the field of space development early, Canada will never be able to develop the technology to compete effectively. Canada argues that it can make a major contribution in the field of space communications, but existing U.S. regulations deny Canadian contractors access to the kinds of information they need to compete for such contracts.

A final category would have to be called psychological. It relates to the U.S. belief that when it comes to the development and production of defense equipment, "Nobody does it better" than the United States. U.S. military technology is viewed as superior to that of any other nation. The result of this attitude is the Canadian complaint that the really important development projects go to the United States and the ones that Canada receives have very little potential for ever going into the production stage. In addition, Canadians complain of a hesitancy in the U.S. military services to cooperate fully in the Defense Development Sharing Agreement or to seriously consider Canadian equipment.

Today Canada wants to participate in more technologically sophisticated development programs but cannot because of these various constraints. Further, Canadians are concerned that recent U.S. efforts to achieve standardization within NATO by signing a series of reciprocal defense procurement memoranda of understanding will result in a relative diminution of current U.S.-Canadian links. Canada is worried that the U.S.-European "two-way street" will bypass the existing well-traveled road between Ottawa and Washington, D.C.

The real problem is that there is little official recognition in Washington, particularly within the Congress, of the benefits (or even the existence) of the defense-economic dimension of the U.S.-Canadian defense association. The need for a major education effort on both sides of the border at the highest levels of government is evident. Until this is done, the issues discussed in this chapter will not be resolved, and the trade restrictions will continue. Both nations should agree to work toward eliminating the various barriers affecting the defense trade between them. Intransigeance on this issue ultimately will destroy the economic benefits of the defense relationship.

POLICY RECOMMENDATIONS

The evolution of U.S.-Canadian defense relations and the current status of these relations having been reviewed, a U.S. policy strategy to address the current issues in order to ensure the continuation of the relationship can be suggested. If that relationship is to endure, both nations must realize that their security is inextricably linked historically, geographically, and economically. Likewise each nation must recognize and be responsive to the political realities of the other that might affect their respective level of participation. Thus, for example, the Canadian government, responding to domestic pressure, argues that it would be politically impossible to purchase a major weapon system without certain offset arrangements. At the same time, however, the Canadian government is not responsive to U.S. domestic political pressure, primarily exhibited in the Congress, that is activated by the effects of these offsets on the U.S. labor market or the balance of trade and payments.

Similarly, there is a tendency in the United States to see offset arrangements as inconsistent with the DPSA. But the U.S. government is also frequently oblivious to the domestic forces within Canada that see these offsets as the means to maintain the viable defense industry that is necessary for the cooperative effort to function.

As each nation attempts to resolve the issues discussed previously, its focus must include the benefits as well as the costs of the relationship. The ultimate benefit, of course, is security. But both nations gain from the association in numerous other ways. In no area is this more clearly demonstrated, yet less understood or appreciated, than in the defense–economic sphere. For example, on the Canadian side of the border, the association has brought numerous and far-reaching benefits to Canada's defense industry. At the most basic level, it has enabled that industry to survive and even to prosper through a unique form of specialization.

The general director of the office of international special projects in the Canadian Department of Industry, Trade, and Commerce, in speaking of the benefits accrued to Canadian industry, has written:

> Canadian defence industry has specialized in relatively narrowly defined areas of transportation, communications and navigation. . . . Our successes in other world markets have usually followed as a result of being successful in the U.S. market. Our most successful sales have generally been in subsystems and components.[31]

In testimony before the Senate of Canada in 1976, the same official, in response to a question on the number of people employed in the industry, commented:

> We deem them to be in the range of 10,000 to 12,000 directly employed on the manufactured items being sold to the U.S. However, you have this flow-down effect back in Canada as well. The chap who produces the aircraft engine castings buys bits and pieces from other Canadian firms. By the time this has flowed through the system, you have in the neighborhood of 100,000 to 115,000 people involved. This is not full time, of course. You have in any one of these different years, however, 10,000 to 12,000 people employed directly in these areas in sales vis-à-vis the U.S. and 100,000 to 115,000 on a supplier basis in Canada. . . . Over the years there have been approximately

500 individual firms involved. . . . However, at any one time there will be in the range of 150 to 170 firms directly engaged in selling to the U.S. at the prime or subcontract level in the defence industrial sector.[32]

In addition to these benefits received by Canadian industry, the Defence Industrial Productivity Program, instituted by the Department of Industry, Trade, and Commerce (DOITC) to enhance Canadian competitiveness and thus participation in the DPSA program, has had a profound impact on the domestic industry of Canada. The expenditure of $362,563,995 in industrial assistance for a total of 419 projects completed from 1959 to 1975, for example, has resulted in accumulated sales, mostly for export, of $5,672,248,820 — a ratio of 15.6 to 1. Detailed analysis of the results indicates that 83.3 percent of the 419 projects resulted in actual sales for Canadian firms and that benefits were received by as many as 206 companies. Similarly, during the period 1963–1980, the Defense Development Sharing Agreement resulted in a total of 75 projects with a total value of US$1.07 billion.[33]

These gains to the defense sector of the economy have also affected other sectors. One Canadian embassy trade official has estimated that every dollar involved in defense export sales to the U.S. military results in a total of about nine dollars in other exports or a corresponding reduction in imports. This has a significant effect on lessening the balance of payments pressure on Canada. These gains result from the sale of defense materiel to countries other than the United States, export sales of related commercial equipment to the United States and other nations, reduction of imports of defense materiel and the reduction of imports of high-technology commercial equipment. Furthermore, production sharing activities have provided Canadian industry access to advanced technology techniques. It provides the only means by which a number of Canadian industries have been able to be kept informed about technological advances in electronics and aerospace engineering. The 1971 defense white paper summed up quite well the benefits gained by the civilian economic sectors when it stated:

Defence expenditure forms an important component of Federal Government expenditures and one which has considerable impact on Canada's economy. This expenditure, largely taking the form of salaries paid to military and civilian employees and or payments for goods and services, clearly has yielded important incidental benefits to economic growth.[34]

The program also has benefited the Canadian Department of National Defence and the Canadian armed forces by enabling them to acquire sophisticated military equipment on the most economical terms. This benefit results from either longer production runs in a specialized Canadian industry, itself a benefactor of the relationship, or direct purchases from the United States. The agreements have assured the Canadian military forces a logistical and defense industrial base in Canada that has helped these forces meet the equipment requirements necessary for participation in the defense of North America (NORAD) and Western Europe (NATO).

The Canadian government and the various agencies of the executive branch of that government have also gained through the relationship, which gives these agencies access to the Washington decisionmaking circles not only on matters of national security but on economic and social issues as well. This access and whatever political leverage may come from it enhance the place of Canada in its relations with other world powers. Few other nations of the world with the power capability of Canada—a middle power—are so frequently consulted by a major power, and few other nations have the potential to play a greater role in the maintenance of world peace by serving as an intermediary. The relationship provides the Canadian government a voice not only in daily decisions concerning North American defense but also in the more vital, long-range, strategic decisions on issues of war and peace, such as arms and conflict control negotiations.

Across the border, the relationship has proven beneficial to the U.S. Department of Defense. Canadian industry is a cost-effective and reliable alternative source of military supplies in time of emergency. In World War II Canadian firms supplied certain kinds of aircraft. During the Vietnam War, Canada filled requirements for many important items without any major political repercussions and with the highest quality of materiel delivered on schedule and at competitive prices. In addition, by enabling Canada to purchase its major defense equipment from the United States, the relationship has encouraged standardization even though, as the critics point out, this is standardization based on U.S. products. "Canadianization," that is, the modification of this equipment to meet Canadian requirements (as in the CP–140 case), does not appear to be a major obstacle to these gains.

But these benefits to the American armed forces are not limited to wartime. In time of peace, the competitive environment created by introducing Canadian producers into the North American market-place has given the U.S. military and DOD a broader base from which to draw goods and has provided, in a number of cases, less costly products and, in a few cases, a reliable source for products which are not available in the United States. (For a more detailed discussion, see note 35.)

The existence of the defense development sharing program has been of significant benefit to the research and development (R&D) efforts of the DOD. In the first place, since Canada pays up to 50 percent of the R&D costs of joint projects, it has reduced by half the cost of R&D programs that would otherwise be funded solely by DOD. Second, by enhancing competition among bidders for proposals, development-sharing results in lower R&D costs, even lower production costs. Third, it enables the military services to participate in advanced development projects in Canada, thus giving them access to high-technology developments to which they might not have been previously exposed. The program has stretched the DOD R&D dollar and reduced "gold plating," encouraged competitive prototyping, and provided additional opportunities to investigate potentially significant breakthroughs in defense technology. For example, in the areas of communication and Short Takeoff and Landing (STOL) aircraft technology, Canada has enhanced U.S. development. In brief, since DOD has and continues to benefit from the program, its original objectives have been largely realized. However, other segments of the American economy and society have benefited also.

One such class of benefactors has been American industry in general and certain multinational corporations in particular. As already suggested, the program has created more work for Canadian defense firms, which has meant enhanced profits to U.S. multinationals, since more than 50 percent of the prime and subcontracts placed in Canada are with Canadian corporations at least 70 percent U.S. owned. In addition, U.S. Department of Labor statistics suggest that as many as 10,000 jobs in the United States are created or are dependent on the relationship with Canada. More specifically, for the years 1973, 1974, and 1975, there were 13,734, 15,820, and 12,046 jobs created, respectively. Also little doubt exists, at least among Lockheed executives interviewed, that the Canadian purchase of the long-range patrol aircraft (LRPA) from Lockheed helped to stabilize the corporate health of that firm, one of the major DOD contractors in the United States and one particularly dependent on defense contracts.

As in Canada, there are also political benefits to the U.S. government from participation in the defense economic relationship. It encourages Canadian cooperation in North American defense and participation in NORAD and NATO and Canada's continued purchase of major weapon systems from the United States. The cost sharing agreement for the Goose Bay, Labrador, air base is unique to the NATO alliance and is a product of this relationship. There is little doubt that the DPSA has assured the continuation of the 200 bilateral defense agreements between the two nations. For example, benefits of the defense–economic relationship were one consideration in the negotiations that resulted in Canadian participation in the AWACS program. Similarly, Canadian industries' desire for a share of future space development, in order to acquire the technology necessary for a competitive advantage in that market, provides the United States a way to encourage Canada to play a larger role in NORAD and NATO and pay a greater share of the costs.

Finally, because the defense–economic relationship has brought real benefits to various groups within each nation, it has created a stronger, more viable, defense cooperative effort. There are a number of indicators to support this observation. First, standardization and rationalization of the defense effort has occurred, and the combat capabilities of U.S. and Canadian forces are stronger because of it. Second, transnational (between U.S. and Canadian firms) and transgovernmental (between U.S. and Canadian governmental bureaucracies) coalitions generate powerful political forces to enhance North American defense. Third, the numerous cooperative mechanisms that have been created over the forty-year history of the relationship have established an enduring infrastructure upon which future problems can be resolved and cooperative efforts initiated. Fourth, the Canadian defense industry, which in 1959 was at the point of collapse, has survived and prospered because of the sharing agreements. Since then, there has been movement toward the integration of the defense industrial capabilities of the two countries such that "a Canadian firm can be providing literally nuts and bolts into a U.S. defense manufacturing plant and vice versa."[36] The result has been that the overall defense industrial base of North America has been enhanced and with it the offensive and defensive capabilities of the military forces of the two nations. Ultimately the credibility of the North American deterrent has been strengthened. In this regard it is particularly regrettable that, at a time when congressional studies are indicating the inadequacies in the U.S. industrial base,[37] we forget that Canada can help as it has three times before. Canada is, after all, an active participant in the U.S. industrial mobilization production planning program and, as such, shares with the United States the responsibility to ensure that the joint U.S.–Canadian industrial defense base is capable of producing adequate quantities of materials in a timely fashion. It is in the best interest of the United States to encourage the exchange or transfer of technology between the two nations in order to ensure the qualitative superiority that has characterized the weapon systems of the West.

The opportunity and the challenge for U.S. defense decisionmakers in this decade is to capitalize on these benefits in order to energize both partners to redefine and rejuvenate the relationship. The Reagan administration came to office speaking of "a new beginning" for America. It is more than coincidence that the new president initiated that "beginning" by visiting Canada. The recent renewal of the NORAD agreement and the forthcoming air defense master plan will support the effort further. However, a more dramatic step must now be taken.

It is time for a series of formal, high-level consultations to respecify the entire relationship. There is a compelling need for discussions to reeducate bureaucratic decisionmakers and educate new political appointees on both sides of the border about the various defense strategic and defense economic arrangements. One of the major shortcomings of the cooperative effort in the past has been the fact that the relationship has evolved through a series of press announcements and letters of understanding, primarily between members of the executive branches of the two nations. This fact has not only created legal difficulties but also resulted in an absence of official recognition in Congress. In fact, many of the constraints discussed earlier resulted from simple ignorance in Congress of many aspects of the special defense–economic relationship.

The need is to establish a dialogue between the various executive and legislative agencies of both nations to review and evaluate the current level of interactions. Such a dialogue and its product will do much to resolve the issues discussed here. The mechanisms to get this process underway already exist in the PJBD and the DPSA steering

committee. At the direction of each government these joint committees can lay the groundwork necessary for the review and the negotiations that would likely follow. However, once the preliminaries are
completed and agendas developed, the arena for the issue resolution
process ought to shift to the secretarial and ministerial levels and
ultimately to the chief executives of the two nations. Throughout,
the respective legislatures of the two nations must be involved in the
process. As discussed earlier, this type of review is already underway
in the area of air defense. The requirement now is to extend it to
every aspect of the relationship, particularly the defense–economic
one, and to incorporate the results into a formal proclamation or
joint defense white paper. Within this process, the United States
must seek the following objectives:

1. A rapid completion of the air defense review in order to reach
an early decision on (a) the future utility of the DEW line system;
(b) the development and deployment of alternative warning systems,
such as the OTH–B radar and AWACS; (c) the nature of the Soviet
airborne threat as a result of the introduction of the Backfire bomber
and development of air-launched cruise missiles; and (d) the employment and deployment of new interceptor aircraft. The United States,
by necessity, must take the lead in addressing these force modernization questions, but it must make Canada an integral part of the decision process.

2. A reappraisal of the NORAD cost sharing program. The
United States must take the lead in developing a comprehensive cost
sharing program that takes cognizance of quality as well as quantity
of contributions. Such factors as the role of Canadian industry in the
U.S. defense mobilization base and the benefits of the defense production and development sharing programs should be included in the
calculus.

3. Continued emphasis on the modernization of the Canadian
armed forces to ensure that the reequipment of these forces is consistent with their mission. First priority must continue to be given to
the Canadian contribution to NORAD and NATO. At a time when
the European nations, such as Great Britain and West Germany, are
talking of reducing their commitment to NATO, it is vital that Canada not follow a similar course. At the same time the United States
must recognize the efforts made by Canada since 1975 in modern-
izing its forces to include the purchase of new long-range patrol

planes, new fighter aircraft, and involvement in the NATO AWACS program. According to recent polls the Canadian electorate, particularly the young, are gaining an expanding awareness of the Soviet threat and need for a strong military. The United States must capitalize on this awareness.

4. A continued nurturing of the historically close relationship between the military forces of the two nations, recognizing that the Canadian forces are a highly dedicated and professional fighting force. Further, the United States should realize that these forces, which include French Canadians, contribute to the bonds of Canadian unity.

5. A renewed effort to encourage the Canadian government to enhance its civilian and military airlift fleet and its commitment to the NATO civil augmentation program. As the United States develops a viable program to modify passenger aircraft for cargo use in emergencies, Canadian participation should be solicited.

6. A continuous review with the Canadian authorities of the existing bilateral military arrangements (such as those dealing with overflight rights and the use of Goose Bay Air Base, Labrador) and defense plans, recognizing the sensitivity of the Canadian public to some of these arrangements and plans.

7. Close cooperation and consultation with Canada on U.S. arms control efforts, in terms both of strategic and theater nuclear forces. Sensitivity must be accorded to the Canadian view of nuclear weapons and to the fact that Canadian cities are as much Soviet targets as U.S. cities. Canadian defense authorities need be privy to U.S. strategic thinking and planning.

8. A high-level, all-encompassing evaluation of the defense production and development sharing agreements programs with all the players (military, political, and economic, governmental and nongovernmental) taking part.

9. The elimination, when possible, of existing barriers to defense economic cooperation.

10. Resolution of the offset issue, recognizing political and economic imperatives in both nations. The recent effort to include offsets in the calculations of the military trade balance under the DPSA is a significant step in the right direction.

11. Recognition of Canada's contribution to the defense industrial base and her inclusion in the plan to expand that base.

In summary, because defense relations between the United States and Canada have in recent years been among the least contentious, their true importance has not always been appreciated. In this decade, the major thrust of U.S. defense policy vis-à-vis Canada must be to reemphasize and nurture these relations. The realization of the foregoing recommendations will do much toward that end.

NOTES TO CHAPTER 7

1. This is not to suggest that U.S.–Canadian defense relations have always been harmonious. For example, inherent Canadian aversion to nuclear weaponry resulted in a major crisis between the United States and Canada in the early 1960s over the deployment of nuclear armed antiaircraft missiles in Canada. Since then the United States has been careful not to offend this sensitivity. Today no Canadian weapon system in NORAD or NATO is nuclear-equipped.

2. The third option called for an increase in Canadian economic relations with Europe to offset existing economic ties with the United States.

3. Quoted on p. 64 of Reginald H. Roy, "Canadian Defence Policy, 1945–1976," *Parameters*, 6 (no. 1, 1976).

4. Conant, 1974, p. 4.

5. Douglas J. Murray, The Relation between International Relations and Domestic Politics: The Politics of North American Defense, Ph.D. Dissertation, University of Texas, 1979.

6. R.B. Byers and Colin S. Gray, *Canadian Military Professionalism: The Search for Identity*, Canadian Institute of International Affairs, Wellesley Paper, February 2, 1973, p. 16.

7. Roger Swanson states, "In examining the formulation and implementation of United States policy toward Canada, it is tempting to conclude that the United States government, per se, does not exist. The United States policy process is heterogeneous, not homogeneous. . . . An understanding of this heterogeneous United States intra-action is essential in understanding the United States–Canadian interaction. The United States operates in the interaction, not as a unitary government but through a 'Canadian constellation'—a number of loosely allied organizational components, arbitrarily considered as a grouping, which have functional or geographical responsibilities in matters directly or indirectly affecting Canada." In Roger Frank Swanson, "The United States Canadian Constellation I, II" *International Journal*, 27 (no. 2, Spring 1972): 185–218, and 28 (no. 2, Spring 1973): 325–367.

8. The board is composed of two national sections. At the head of each section is a chairman appointed respectively by the president of the United States and the prime minister of Canada. These two political appointees report directly to their respective national chief executives, issuing a detailed report following each meeting. The military membership includes members and assistant members from each of the military services, a member from the office of the joint chiefs of staff, and a military secretary for each section. Defense is represented on the American side by the assistant secretary of defense for international security affairs and on the Canadian side by the associate assistant deputy minister for policy. The U.S. State Department is represented by the deputy assistant secretary of state for Canadian affairs and the deputy director of the Office of Canadian Affairs; the Canadian Ministry of External Affairs by the director general, Bureau of Defence and Arms Control, and the head of the North American section of the Defence Relations Division. In addition, Canada is represented by an official from the Defence Program Branch of the Department of Industry, Trade, and Commerce.

9. Interviews with defense and military officials in Ottawa and Washington, D.C.; and *Joint Policy Statement on the Air Defense of North America*, 1980; *NORAD Reveual Agreement 1981*.

10. Jon B. McLin, *Canada's Changing Defense Policy, 1957–1963: The Problems of a Middle Power in Alliance* (Baltimore: The Johns Hopkins Press, 1967), p. 39.

11. Jocelyn Maynard Ghent, *Canada, the United States and the Cuban Missile Crisis*, a paper presented at the Fourth Biennial Conference of the Association for Canadian Studies in the United States, October 7–8, 1977, Burlington.

12. Ibid., p. 23.

13. Interviews with defense and military officials.

14. Ibid.

15. The U.S. Air Force Tactical Air Command (TAC) now manages the interceptors and the Strategic Air Command (SAC) the atmosphere attack warning assets. Operational control of both remain with CINCNORAD, now a three- rather than a four-star position.

16. Harold Brown, U.S. Department of Defense Annual Report FY 1981, 1980, pp. 116–117.

17. "Backfire" is the NATO designation for the newest Soviet supersonic bomber (first noted in the early 1970s) that is similar to the U.S. Air Force's B–1 though smaller and with a lighter payload. Designated as a medium-range bomber (approximately 3,000 miles), it has the capability when northern based within the Soviet Union and with certain mission profiles to strike the continental United States. It is considered by defense analysts to have a significantly improved capability to penetrate U.S. air defense systems.

18. Three examples of such issues are NORAD renewal, the status of the early warning radar lines, and cost sharing. With respect to the NORAD issue, the gradual deemphasis on the air defense mission by the United States has led to Canada's reluctance to extend the agreement for more than five years at a time. For example, in 1973 the uncertainty about the feasibility of the over-the-horizon Backscatter (OTH–B) and the airborne warning and control aircraft (AWACS) deployment led the Canadian government to support only a two-year renewal until such time as the air force defined the future role of air defense. It is interesting that during the most recent renewal negotiations this past year, perhaps in anticipation of the soon to be published air defense master plan, there was little debate over NORAD's future. The Canadians agreed to the renaming of NORAD to *Aerospace* instead of *Air Command*, to recognizing officially the space surveillance functions of NORAD, and to removing the ABM caveat.

The second issue is the status of the Distant Early Warning (DEW) line. The Carter administration proposed to reduce the number of radar warning sites. The Canadians have objected to any reduction until completion of the air defense master plan. They are concerned with the adverse impact on the local communities surrounding the DEW line sites, since the closure would result in the loss of approximately 130 jobs and the elimination of health, fire, water, and sewer services provided by the sites. The Reagan administration provided funds in the fiscal year 1982 budget to operate all of the existing sites, while a study is carried out of means to improve early warning and aerospace surveillance. The cost sharing issue is discussed later in this section.

19. The air defense mission can be defined as (1) active when it entails damage limitation through the use of interceptor aircraft and ground or air control intercept radars or (2) passive when it entails simply attack warning, assessment, and surveillance through various warning radar systems such as the DEW line sites. AWACS can be used for either mission.

20. The plan as described in *Defense Daily.* "According to AF planners, the limited U.S. air defense capability would require the following: (1) Modernization of warning and surveillance systems to provide 'reliable, clear, and unambiguous indication' of a Soviet bomber/air-to-surface missile attack. Steps funded in the FY '82 budget are not adequate. (2) Development and deployment of two large Over-The-Horizon Backscatter (OTH–B) radars on the East and West Coasts. These radars can detect large aircraft with 'high certainty' at ranges of 1800–2000 nautical miles, and the AF believes they would prevent the Soviets from considering making a bomber attack by going around existing north-looking surveillance systems. As for replacing the north-looking radar, the AF says the OTH–B may not be technically feasible because of the frequency of ionospheric disturbances in northern Canada. Current funds are for development and possible deployment of the two OTH–B radar. (3) Improved north-

looking surveillance. In addition to the possible but not certain OTH–B option, the AF is considering the options of upgrading and gap-filling the the current Distant Early warning (DEW) Line and employing space-based radar. (4) Expansion of the currently planned force of E–3A AWACS assigned to the Continental United States. In addition, the Air Force wants to improve the alert capability of the available E–3A to generate aircraft on warning. (5) Expansion of the currently planned force of F–15's assigned to CONUS for air defense. If the circumstances warrant, these fighters could be assigned elsewhere." (*Defense Daily*, 114 (no. 29, February 13, 1981): 226–227.

21. Adrian Preston, "The Profession of Arms in Post–War Canada," *World Politics*, 23 (no. 2, January 1971): 189–214.

22. Colin Gray, *Canadian Defence Priorities: A Question of Relevance* (Toronto: Clarke Irwin, 1972), p. 50.

23. George J.G. Stanley, *Canada's Soldiers: The Military History of an Unmilitary People*. (Toronto: Macmillan of Canada, 1960).

24. See Luther J. Zink, "Why Trudeau Hates the Military," *Toronto Sun*, April 2, 1976.

25. Preston, "The Profession of Arms in Post–War Canada."

26. David P. Burke, The Unification of the Canadian Armed Forces: The Politics of Defense in the Pearson Administration, unpublished Ph.D. dissertation, Harvard University, Cambridge, Mass., 1975, p. 345.

27. These differentials operate in essentially the same way. A certain percentage of a foreign company's dollar bid on a U.S. contract is added on top of the amount of that bid, thus increasing its price and making the American contractor's bid more competitive. The differences exist to discourage the letting of defense contracts to foreign contractors. In the case of Canada, as a result of these agreements, these differentials are not applied.

28. Offset agreements involve the consent of the selling country or corporation to purchase goods or services from the buying country not necessarily directly related to the system or equipment being transacted. Coproduction, a type of offset, is the assignment by the seller (nation or corporation) to the buyer (nation) of authority and responsibility for production of all or part of a system. An example of coproduction of an entire system is the manufacturing under license (licensed coproduction) from France and West Germany of the Roland missile system. An example of coproduction of components is the agreement between the United States and a consortium of four European countries to produce the F–16 fighter aircraft. The objective of both offsets and coproduction agreements is that they return to the buyer some or all of his investment by way of creating jobs, etc., in the buying nation. Generally, the U.S. Defense Department is opposed to entering into such agreements unless (1) it is absolutely necessary for the completion of the transaction, which is viewed to be in the

best interest of the United States; (2) it is cost effective; and (3) it results in a mutual reduction in barriers to trade. In those cases an analytical framework is applied to determine if the transaction is in the best interest of the United States. Thus in practice the U.S. government has entered into such compensatory agreements when it has advanced the course of weapon standardization, particularly within NATO. (Drawn from DOD draft directive "Compensatory Offset and Coproduction Agreements with Other Nations.") In keeping with common usage, this chapter does not differentiate between these two types of compensatory agreements. Both are referred to as offsetting arrangements, offset packages, or industrial benefits programs.

29. Recoupment refers to the efforts of the nation that develops a weapon system to recoup some of the research and development costs by adding a percentage of those costs onto the sales price of the system.

30. Interviews with defense and military officials.

31. Frank Jackman, "The Canada–United States Defence Production Sharing Arrangement," mimeograph, 1976.

32. Canada Senate, 30th Parliament, 1st Session, Proceedings of the Standing Senate Committee on Foreign Affairs, April 6, 1976, pp. 30:14.

33. Interviews with defense and military officials.

34. Donald S. MacDonald, *Defence in the 70's*, A White Paper (Ottawa: Information Canada, 1971).

35. Douglas J. Murray, *An Evaluation of the U.S.-Canadian Defense Economic Relationship and the Applicability to NATO Standardization*. OASD/ISA International Economic Affairs, June 19, 1978.

36. Jackman, "The Canada–United States Defence Production Sharing Agreement," p. 12.

37. U.S. Congress, House of Representatives, 96th Congress, 2nd Session, Panel on Defense Industrial Base of the Committee on Armed Services, "The Ailing Defense Industrial Base: Unready for Crisis" (Washington, D.C.: U.S. Government Printing Office, 1980).

8 QUEBEC TRENDS vs. U.S. INTERESTS AND POLICIES*

*Alfred O. Hero, Jr.***

This chapter begins by tracing the evolution in French-speaking Canada of the concept of Quebec as the linguistic, cultural, and political base of francophones in North America. After a very brief consideration of the nonfrancophone Quebec minority, the nature of Quebec nationalism, and perceptions of it by many anglophone observers in Canada and the United States are examined. The response of the Canadian federal government to the aspirations of Quebec nationalism is summarized and the most likely scenario projected for Quebec

*The rapporteurs recognize that the issue of francophone Quebec and its relations with the rest of Canada is a highly sensitive matter charged with emotion. Probably no presentation on this subject would meet with universal approval for its objectivity. Some members of the working group have questioned the wisdom of including a special chapter on Quebec, and some have specifically asked to be noted as objecting to this one. The rapporteurs wish to emphasize that members of the working group are committed only to the support of the policy statement (Chapter 1) and not in any way to the conclusions of the subsequent chapters. This one is presented as a report on francophone Quebec by the American most knowledgeable on the subject, who is prepared to defend his conclusions. The rapporteurs believe that all interested Americans will benefit from reading it.

**Director, World Peace Foundation. This chapter is derived from parts of a broader study and forthcoming book on the implications of Quebec developments for the long-term interests and policies of the United States, by Louis Balthazar, Professor of Political Science at Laval University, and the author. Professor Balthazar provided major initial input for the first half of this chapter and constructive, detailed criticisms and suggestions on successive drafts of the chapter as a whole. The author alone is responsible for the analysis, tone, and judgments in this final version."

261

in relation to the rest of Canada, with implications of this scenario for the United States suggested. The chapter concludes with some recommendations for U.S. public policy and private action.

Particular emphasis is given in this chapter to the underlying perceptions, attitudes, and priorities of the Quebec francophone majority and its principal social and political groups and influential elites. Insofar as possible the analysis is derived from representative opinion surveys and other empirical indicators, from the considerable existing body of serious relevant research, from recent political developments, and from close observation over a number of years. Without any attempt to engage in an inevitably risky and probably disappointing effort to anticipate events over the next several years, longer term trends likely to impinge upon U.S. interests are identified. The purpose of the chapter is not to argue a point of view but to describe a situation that is too little known to most Americans.

QUEBEC INCREASINGLY SYNONYMOUS WITH FRENCH CANADA

By 1981 widespread consensus had developed among culturally, socially, and politically alert francophones living in Quebec that their society and its provincial institutions had become the only effective embodiment of their language and culture on the North American continent likely to endure over the long term. They had come to realize that francophones outside Quebec, except perhaps the approximately 200,000 Acadians in northeastern New Brunswick, would always remain minorities in essentially English-speaking societies into which most of them would integrate within a generation or two.

This consensus is to be found in the several major provincial political parties, among persons with diverse views on social and economic policy, and across the spectrum of professions, occupations, and levels and styles of life. It is far from limited to the 41 percent of the total electorate (47 percent of francophones) who voted for the Parti Québécois (PQ) in 1976, nearly the same proportion who voted "yes" in the 1980 referendum, or the 49 percent (57 percent of francophones) who voted PQ in 1981. It includes most of those francophones who would prefer that Quebec remain part of a renewed, more decentralized, but viable Canadian constitutional system, as well as social democrats and the very few francophones further to the political left.

Even those able francophone elites active in the national Liberal party, including many who have held important positions in the federal government and who work as much or more in English than in French in their careers, more often than not privately subscribe to this view of Quebec as the cultural–linguistic stronghold of francophone North America. They tend to prefer to live in and retire to a French-speaking milieu, to work in French rather in English, and to spend most of their leisure with other francophones with whom they feel more at home than in the predominant anglophone North American culture.[1] Those who are realistic about the survival of a small culture of 5 million francophones within an intimately interdependent economy of 240 million, dominated by a dynamic, generally attractive anglophone civilization, are understandably anxious about the future. But most feel the preservation and development of their language and culture to be worthwhile, though they may differ in the economic, constitutional, and political approaches which they would choose to achieve that end. Most francophone Quebeckers today thus accept the general idea of Canadian linguistic and cultural duality. This would constitute two factors: A French-speaking Quebec on the one hand, wherein ability to communicate in French is essential to the pursuit of a satisfying career and to participation in social, political, and economic affairs; and the rest of Canada, where English is a sine qua non, though minorities may use other languages among family, friends, and in institutions composed of people of like linguistic and cultural backgrounds.

During the "quiet revolution" of the 1960s, of which the main protagonist was initially the Liberal provincial government under Jean Lesage and thereafter Union Nationale governments under Premiers Daniel Johnson and Jean Jacques Bertrand, it became widely accepted in Quebec that French Canadian survival and development depended upon the existence of a modern, industrialized society where francophones were the majority. The Quebec government was and would remain the only social and political institution in North America where French Canadians were really in control, where they had or could develop the complex network of institutions, communications, and informal human relationships necessary for the consolidation of a modern French-speaking society and where a francophone society could become attractive enough to hold its more able talent and thus compete in the modern industrialized world. Only there, and, depending on Quebec's success, perhaps in adjoining Acadia, could one live, work, learn, and prosper in French with the essential infrastructure of educational and vocational institutions, libraries, media, and so on. Only if such a base existed in Quebec could francophones elsewhere in Canada hope to see their minority rights accorded serious attention by the omnipresent anglophone society and its supporting political system. In return for francophones accepting the necessity of communicating in English outside Quebec, nonfrancophones, including immigrant groups, should accept the necessity of learning French in order to pursue satisfying careers in Quebec.

Whereas other provinces and regions seek expanded jurisdiction from the central government over their natural resources, investment policies, taxation, foreign trade, and other economic interests, Quebec's struggle for wider provincial jurisdiction is qualitatively very different in ascribing priority to cultural and linguistic goals and in the political and economic powers necessary to achieve them.

It was natural that French-speaking Canadians should come to view the Quebec government as the only institution under their control able to achieve these goals. Jean Lesage argued that "Quebec is the political expression of French Canada" and that his government was the only legitimate spokesman for French Canadians.[2] In demanding that all political powers connected with the development of a distinctly francophone culture be returned to Quebec, Lesage reflected the desire of hundreds of politicians and civil servants to strengthen their impact on Quebec society and their authority to work more independently of Ottawa. But he also reflected the attitudes and feelings of most politically and socially alert Quebec francophones, for whom Quebec was not only their native province but also their unique cultural homeland, with a more conservative, less cosmopolitan political base in smaller communities and rural areas. Lesage counseled that Quebec must achieve either equality with anglophone Canada or independence from it. The next Liberal premier, Robert Bourassa, spoke of cultural sovereignty and was in frequent conflict with Ottawa over his Quebec government's claims to jurisdiction in such fields as language, communications, culture, and social security. The "beige paper" of Claude Ryan's Liberal party (PLQ), while arguing eloquently for a vote of "no" in the 1980 referendum on sovereignty-association, nonetheless maintained that "within the Canadian political family, Quebec society has all the characteristics of a distinct national community."[3]

Such views permeate the more serious modern French Canadian plays, novels, and poetry as well as the elite and popular press. They likewise are reflected in the two major federal study reports dealing with problems of Canadian unity—that of the Royal Commission on Bilingualism and Biculturalism (the "B and B" or Dunton–Laurendeau Commission), established by the Pearson government during the Lesage regime, and that of the Task Force on Canadian Unity (the Pépin–Robarts report) set up by the Trudeau government after the PQ unexpectedly won the November 1976 Quebec election. Both bodies enlisted the serious efforts and reflections of the best minds across the country, the vast majority of whom preferred that Quebec remain a part of Canada. As early as 1965 the B and B report elaborated the concept of two majorities,[4] while the Pépin–Robarts task force in 1979 described the underlying relationship between Quebec and the rest of Canada as one of duality.[5] According to the task force report Quebec must be recognized as the francophone cultural metropolis in North America. Whether or not it remained in the Canadian confederation, Quebec represented a specific society within Canada because of its peculiar history, language, civil law, common origins, of its population, perceptions, and politics.

For Quebec francophones, the Pépin–Robarts concept of a Canadian duality of language and culture corresponded with their new self-image. A generation or so earlier, many French Canadians would have thought of themselves as a people spread across Canada and would have accepted the designation "ethnic minority." Today they see themselves as Québécois, possessing a traditional homeland in North America and a status different from that understood by the term "ethnic group" as used in Canada and the United States.[6]

Statistics, opinion surveys, and other empirical evidence indicate that a trend toward the concentration of French-speaking society in the province of Quebec has been underway for some decades. During the last half-century, the proportion of francophones in the total Canadian population gradually declined. It is projected to decline further, from 27 percent in 1980 to 21-24 percent by the end of this century. This decline has been accompanied not only by the growing concentration of francophones in Quebec but also by a gradual increase in the proportion of francophones among Quebeckers—from 78 percent in 1960 to 81 percent in 1980, projected to reach 85 percent or more by the end of this century.[7]

The proportion of the French-speaking population outside Quebec has dwindled, according to decennial censuses, to 4.4 percent in 1976, and is projected to drop to 2.2 to 3.5 percent by the end of this century. Fewer francophones leave Quebec for English-speaking Canada, and their children are assimilated at accelerating rates.[8] The study of French in anglophone secondary schools and universities outside Quebec has actually fallen off since the promulgation of the Official Languages Act in the late 1960s,[9] despite federal bilingual programs costing well over $1 billion and the marked increase in the teaching of French to anglophone children in elementary schools, particularly in New Brunswick and Ontario. This dwindling number of French-speaking Canadians outside Quebec has on successive censuses been more and more concentrated in bordering New Brunswick, Ottawa, Sudbury, and other Ontario communities near Quebec.[10] If recent trends continue, it is estimated that by the year 2000 some 93–95 percent of all francophones in Canada will live in Quebec.[11]

Under an immigration policy worked out by the Quebec and federal governments, the trend in recent years has been for fewer non–French-speaking immigrants from abroad to settle in Quebec.[12] At the same time, under Law 101 enacted in 1977 (discussed below) an increasing number of nonfrancophone immigrants to Quebec are learning French and sending their children to French schools.[13] Moreover, the number of younger native anglophone Quebeckers who speak reasonably fluent French is sharply greater than among their parents, and growing numbers of their children are going to French schools or to French-immersion schools designed for anglophone youngsters. Although a number of younger anglophones, particularly the better educated, have left or will leave Quebec for career opportunities elsewhere, the degree to which linguistic versus economic opportunities has been responsible is unclear. It is clear, however, that most new immigrants, growing numbers of earlier immigrants, and native anglophones, without losing their native language and culture, are gradually accommodating themselves to a primarily French-speaking society.[14]

The Pépin–Robarts report, which recognized Quebec as representative of French-speaking Canada, was generally acclaimed among

Quebec elites, including supporters of the PQ as well as of the PLQ, as an able analysis of the basic problems and as a constructive basis for dealing with them.[15] In vain they encouraged the Trudeau government, which had set up the task force, to adopt its recommendations in negotiating a new federal constitutional arrangement with the provinces. Even a significant number of those who voted "yes" in the Quebec referendum shortly thereafter did so mainly to convince Ottawa and anglophone Canada to take Quebec's demands seriously in negotiating a new federal arrangement.

Opinion surveys indicate that not only the politically alert and articulate elite but also the majority of francophone Quebeckers favor changes in Quebec's relationship with the rest of Canada. Their views usually occur in an ideologically coherent pattern: a conception of Quebec as the seat of a qualitatively different culture requiring a significant transfer of power for its preservation and development; a personal identification with Quebec and its government more than with Canada and its government; and approval of French as the language of work and education for all except a small, truly anglophone minority. Majorities of both university-educated francophones and influential elites reflect this pattern of views.[16] Support for either independence or devolution short of it and for the provisions of Law 101 is especially widespread among younger professionals in the media, law, the arts, academia, and political life—groups apt to have a disproportionately strong influence on political thought and action in the next two decades.[17]

Since the mid-1960s growing majorities of those Quebec francophones who have expressed opinions have supported at a minimum significant changes in the Canadian federal system toward devolution of powers to the provinces, in Quebec's case especially in respect to language and culture. Forty-nine percent in May 1980 favored so changing the constitution, contrasted with only 29 percent who preferred the status quo. These proportions compared with 11 percent versus 64 percent, respectively, in the other provinces.[18] Another survey a year before found that 56 percent of francophone Quebeckers would increase provincial powers by constitutional change versus 36 percent who would not, contrasted with 27 percent versus 64 percent in other provinces.[19]

Three months after the 1980 referendum, 61 percent of francophones thought their PQ government was right in pressing Ottawa for change in the status of the province.[20] A series of surveys between

April 1979 and June 1980 sponsored by the federal government discovered that two-thirds of all Quebeckers (including nonfrancophones) favored major constitutional changes toward provincial autonomy. Short of such "in the next two years," 58 percent said they would be either "very" or "rather" dissatisfied. Eighty percent preferred that their provincial government should have more control over provincial economic development, 48 percent believed that Quebec should have its own seat in the United Nations, and 58 percent thought that a constitutional compromise toward more provincial powers could ultimately be achieved between sovereignty-association as proposed by the PQ government, and the current federal system.[21] In March 1979 47 percent of Quebec francophones, contrasted with only 25 percent of other Canadians, anticipated either no federated Canada or a considerably more decentralized one within ten years.[22] Just before the 1981 Quebec election, francophone expressed more confidence that a PQ rather than a PLQ government would achieve such a revised federation,[23] certainly an important reason for the PQ's victory.

Furthermore in 1979 48 percent of francophone Quebeckers considered the provincial government and only 30 percent the national government to be *their* government, contrasted with 13 percent versus 73 percent among Quebec nonfrancophones and 28 percent versus 62 percent, respectively, in the rest of Canada.[23] A much higher proportion of francophone Quebeckers than of Canadian anglophones expressed lack of confidence in the federal House of Commons to represent their interest in 1974.[24] At that time francophone Quebeckers and residents of the Atlantic provinces thought more highly of their respective provinces than did Ontarians and Canadians to the west. Quebec francophones entertained the least favorable opinion of the government of Canada and Ontario the most.[25] A federally financed survey shortly prior to the sovereignty-association referendum of May 20, 1980, again found Quebec francophones more attached to and identified with Quebec than with Canada.[26] Only in Newfoundland does such a large fraction of the electorate identify more with their province than with Canada.[27] A majority of francophone Quebeckers in 1980 thought their linguistic and cultural identities threatened by the present federal–provincial arrangement.[28]

Francophone Quebeckers favoring independence rose from 7–9 percent in 1962–1967 to 16 percent in 1970, 21 percent in 1973, and 24 percent in 1976 and have since remained between one-fifth and one-quarter of the Quebec francophone population.[29] Eighty-nine percent of these proindependence Quebeckers voted for the PQ in 1976, including a significant minority with more conservative, pro-free-enterprise, economic and political views than those endorsed by the PQ platform. Apparently independence was more important to them than economic issues. Those who favored either independence pure and simple or independence with a common market with Canada (the PQ sovereignty–association proposal) numbered 48 percent of Quebec francophones in March 1977,[30] a figure that remained a stable 47 percent as of shortly before the 1980 referendum.[31]

A majority of Quebec francophones also want national recognition of a special status for French over English in Quebec and the extension of francophone schools and other services across the country if Quebec is to remain part of Canada.[32] Seventy-seven percent in 1980 approved of the requirement of Law 101 that French be the language of work in all medium and large businesses in the province; only 6 percent were opposed.[33] Although 76 percent approved of providing English public schools (which would also require pupils to learn French) for children of parents whose language was English, a majority believed that children of immigrant parents whose native language was not English should attend French schools.[34] Mr. Ryan's and his PLQ's compromises with nonfrancophone preferences in regard to the language of schooling and work were a major factor in the PLQ's loss of its overwhelming majority of predominantly francophone ridings in 1981.[35]

Although majorities of the francophone Quebec public support federal bilingual programs and think that French schools should be provided wherever there are sufficient francophone parents who want them,[36] few francophones in Quebec are optimistic about the long-term effectiveness of federal programs to develop the use of French in federal agencies or to prevent the cultural and linguistic assimilation of children of francophone minorities living far from Quebec.[37] More important, relatively few think such programs will have more than marginal influence on the development of Quebec culture; indeed, most feel that only if there is a dynamic French culture in Quebec will these programs have much likelihood of success.

At the same time that most francophones agree that Quebec should increasingly become a society in which its members communicate in French, English will necessarily persist as the first language for an important minority, particularly around greater Montreal, and as the means of communication with the rest of North America, not only for Quebeckers whose careers require it but for the growing mass who journey outside Quebec for business or pleasure, who tune in to American TV and radio, read American publications, and deal with the many American and Canadian anglophones who come to their province.

THE NONFRANCOPHONE QUEBEC MINORITY

The 19 percent of the Quebec population whose native language is not French is composed approximately three-fifths of people whose native language is English and two-fifths of immigrants of other linguistic groups. They constitute both a central problem and an opportunity for the objectives of the francophone majority.

Until relatively recently in control not only of much of the Quebec but also of the Canadian economy, Quebec anglophones have traditionally considered themselves part of the anglophone Canadian majority rather than an influential Quebec minority. As recently as the 1960s they maintained their own extensive system of schools, McGill, Concordia, and Bishop's Universities, hospitals, media, services, and other community institutions. They have for generations regarded the francophone majority in rather condescending terms — as generally backward, resistant to change, ethnocentric, intolerant, lacking initiative, and inept in the technological and entrepreneurial world. Quebec anglophones managed to lead on the whole prosperous, satisfying careers and lives without learning French and with little contact on an equal basis with francophones. Their opposition to the growing demands of francophone nationalism has understandably been bitter, much more so than that of anglophone Canadians elsewhere.

Larger majorities of Quebec nonfrancophones than of citizens of the other nine provinces have opposed virtually all the aforementioned linguistic–cultural measures favored by francophone majorities. Thus, whereas francophones identify more with Quebec and its government than with Canada and the federal government, the reverse is overwhelmingly the case among nonfrancophones.[38] Whereas most of the former favor devolution of powers from the center, a large majority of the latter favors further centralization or at the least minimal federal compromise with francophone demands.[39] Paradoxically, Prime Minister Pierre Trudeau is more popular among Quebec anglophones and immigrants than among francophones. Among anglophones and immigrants 85–90 percent of those expressing opinions or voting have consistently opposed Quebec independence, with or without economic association, have voted against the PQ, and voted "no" in the referendum.[40]

Large nonfrancophone majorities oppose the major provisions of Law 101 that are supported by francophone majorities.[41] Even in respect of the considerably milder Language Law 22 of the Bourassa government (for which government the vast majority of nonfrancophones voted), only 7 percent in 1974 approved, while 19 percent wanted it made less restrictive and 53 percent wanted it abolished.[42] Younger, university-educated nonfrancophones are significantly less hostile to francophone objectives than their seniors. Nevertheless, considerable numbers—more well-educated anglophone young people than those of immigrant background—are seeking careers outside Quebec.[43]

The problems of long-term accommodation on the francophone side are also significant. Although francophones have considerably less negative impressions of their anglophone compatriots than the latter do of them,[44] francophones hold more negative, stereotypical views about most nonfrancophone immigrant groups than do anglophones in Quebec or elsewhere in Canada.[45] Most immigrants who have not spoken French on arrival in Quebec have typically aspired to economic and social mobility into the anglophone middle and upper classes in Montreal and in North America generally. They have learned little or no French and have strongly opposed the demands of francophone nationalism, in particular the requirement that their children go to French schools.[46] Some have been arrogant toward francophones. Thus francophones hold somewhat more negative views of Jews[47] and most other nonfrancophone ethnic groups than either Protestant or Catholic anglophones across Canada.[48] Language and culture have much more bearing on francophone intergroup attitudes than does religion.

However, such ethnocentric prejudices decline with education, as they do among anglophones.[49] Interestingly enough, francophones who support the provisions of Law 101 and independence, with or without association, for Quebec are more tolerant about minorities than are the fewer who favor the federal status quo.[50]

Quebec Jews have become the most bilingual group in Canada after native francophones. The younger generation in particular has learned French and complied with Law 101 in growing numbers.[51] Jewish controlled Steinberg Food Stores was the first major chain to become bilingual in advertising, price posting, and consumer relations. Understandably anxious from their experience with other nationalisms, particularly in Central Europe, a number of Jews feared shortly after the 1976 provincial election that Quebec nationalism might also include anti-Semitism. Apparent sympathy for Palestinian claims against Israel among young, university-educated francophones tended to fuel that concern. A number of Jews moved assets out of Quebec after the 1976 election, and a significant number, especially among the young, left to pursue careers and live elsewhere.[52] Most impartial observers, including Jews, have since concluded that francophones, regardless of their prejudices, are no more and perhaps are less inclined to anti-Semitic behavior than anglophone Canadians.[53]

Since the 1976 elections, there have been indications of gradual progress toward accommodation by both francophone and non-francophone Quebeckers. In the 1981 election the PQ elected two anglophone deputies and gained a larger minority of anglophone and, especially, immigrant votes than ever before. In the heavily non-francophone district of former Premier Bourassa, a sufficiently large minority of Greeks voted for PQ candidate Godin to assure his victory. No official connected with the PQ government has manifested any anti-Semitic attitudes. In the spring of 1980 former Liberal deputy in the National Assembly and pediatrician, Victor Goldbloom—at the time president of the Canadian Council of Christians and Jews—congratulated the Lévesque government on doing more to meet the concerns of Quebec Jews than had the preceding government of which he was minister of environment and urban affairs.

The more that Quebec francophones develop confidence about the viability of a French-speaking society in their province, and about anglophone acceptance of this francophone objective as a legitimate one, the more inclined they are to deal constructively with the pluralist nature of their society. As more children of immigrants attend schools with francophones and are integrated into French-speaking society, that society should become less provincial and more cosmopolitan in its outlook.[54]

QUEBEC NATIONALISM: SOME AMERICAN PERCEPTIONS VS. REALITIES

The essence of Quebec nationalism is the belief that Quebec is a distinct, French-speaking society, which for its preservation and development in an overwhelmingly anglophone North American environment requires francophone control of its cultural, political, and economic institutions and systematic orchestration by its provincial government. Unfortunately, most Americans, including the foreign-policymaking elite, as a consequence of their own history, predominantly anglophone language and culture and "melting pot" tradition, and their much greater familiarity with English-speaking Canada, tend to react with more suspicion and anxiety to Quebec nationalism than the facts would warrant. This section deals with certain American apprehensions as to the nature of Quebec nationalism.

Contrary to the suspicions of some Americans, the Quebec nationalist movement is neither more left-wing radical or Marxist, nor right-wing conservative,[55] no more imprudent, or anti-American, than anglophone Canadian nationalism. Whereas the latter is directed primarily against the United States, Quebec nationalism is mainly concerned about the anglophone provinces, especially Ontario, about a federal government apt to be controlled increasingly by anglophones little sensitive to francophone priorities, and about domination by the Quebec anglophone minority, which, at least until very recently, neither integrated into Quebec life nor learned the majority language.

In respect to most political and economic issues of potential concern to the United States, the attitudes of francophone Quebeckers are congruent with overall patterns among the Canadian English-speaking majority or diverge from them only marginally. Indeed, francophone political and economic thinking, tastes, and life-styles, at least at the mass level, are much more like those of other North Americans than those of francophone Europeans. Trends since the Second World War have generally been toward a narrowing of earlier differences between Quebec francophones and other Canadians and Americans in many respects. A sharp decline in the Quebec birthrate to a level below the national average and the collapse of clericalism in Quebec—doubtless interrelated phenomena—have eliminated two major differences.

Until after the Second World War the uniqueness of French Canada was maintained by the pervading social role of a traditional Catholic Church in a homogeneous, largely agrarian, rural, and small-town society. Being francophone was virtually synonymous with regular religious practice, large families, and Church-encouraged defensiveness toward and social isolation from anglophone, largely Protestant North America, which controlled the American and Canadian economies, including Quebec's. But, within a generation following the war, rapid industrialization, urbanization, mass communications, and the greater integration of francophones into the North American economy were accompanied by a major decline in the influence of the Church. Quebec francophones changed from one of the most practicing religious groups on the continent to the least so among predominantly Roman Catholic ethnic and national groups—to approximately 25 percent regular Mass attenders in the province as a whole and much lower averages among younger francophones in Greater Montreal. By the mid–1970s francophones were hardly replacing themselves, and the Church had at most only a marginal role in the phenomenon of Quebec nationalism dealt with in this chapter. The principal remaining exceptions are linked with the cultural and linguistic issues noted previously. One characteristic of Quebec francophone nationalism is its emphasis on collective rights and on an active role for the provincial government in advancing collective cultural and linguistic objectives. Like most groups who think themselves little understood and believe their identities to be threatened by much more populous and influential groups surrounding them, the protection of individual rights seems hardly sufficient to guarantee group rights and cultural survival. This emphasis on group rights by Quebeckers is as true of conservatives as of centrists and francophones left of center. Constitutional guarantees, judicial and quasi-judicial mechanisms, and the values of most elites apt to exert political power make it unlikely that the emphasis on collective rights will be allowed to erode those of individuals. For example, the Quebec Charter of Human Rights, combined with the extensive powers and disproportionately nonfrancophone composition of the Quebec Human Rights Commission, provides one of the most effective provincial safeguards in Canada.

Recent anxiety in the United States in this regard seems traceable mainly to Law 101 passed by the PQ majority in 1977, its predecessor, Law 22, enacted under the Liberal Bourassa government, and to the closely related opposition of most Quebec elites to the inclusion of a bill of rights that would apply to language in any new Canadian constitution. Law 101 made French the official language, required that all public services be in French, that most dealings with the provincial government be conducted in French, and that companies other than family businesses and other small enterprises with primarily anglophone employees and clients operate in French except in their dealings with English-speaking individuals and institutions from outside the province. To prevent francophones from sending their children to English schools and to influence the pattern of integration of immigrants away from the English-speaking minority toward the French majority, only children of parents who had themselves attended English schools in Quebec and those Quebeckers with one or more of their children already in English schools could henceforth attend English primary and secondary schools. Apart from its linguistic goals, Law 101's central economic goals are to open opportunities to francophones in upper corporate echelons, to change Quebec's economic image to accord with its cultural environment, and to remove traditional francophone reservations about entrepreneurial, managerial, and technical careers.

Americans influenced by nonfrancophone Canadians, particularly from Montreal, have criticized Law 101 as infringing on the individual's right to public schooling in a minority language, a right that exists in few other societies, and of conducting business in that language. However, as the opinion surveys noted earlier suggest, most francophones support the objectives of Law 101. A provision of the law allows temporary residents, like Americans assigned to U.S. corporate subsidiaries, to send their children to English public schools for three years, renewable for an additional three. It seems reasonable to most francophones that Americans living in the province for more than six years should wish to have their children learn the majority language by attending French schools. The law does not apply to private schools or to postsecondary education.

Americans who fear a "Cuba of the North" point to the violence of the PLQ in 1970 and to the handful of articulate radicals among intellectuals, professors, and university students. In fact, there are very few traces of radical ideologies to be found in opinion surveys, in the francophone media, in political life, literature, drama, or the arts. Indeed, national opinion surveys show radical attitudes of the left as well as the right to be miniscule.

Francophone Quebeckers are understandably more favorably inclined than other Canadians, except anglophone supporters of the New Democratic party (NDP), to active provincial government intervention in economic and, especially, culturally related affairs. At the same time they are often politically conservative and economically cautious. There are few Marxist-leaning members of the Quebec National Assembly and there are certainly very few in the senior provincial civil service. The left wing of the PQ parliamentary majority harbors political and economic views less radical than held by those who gained control of the British Labour party in 1980, akin to the thinking of the left-center of the Social Democratic party of the German Federal Republic. Under any scenario for Quebec, including independence, the likelihood of a Castro, Allende, or Sandinista-type of regime is virtually nil.

As for anti–Americanism, diversely worded surveys between the mid–1930s and the mid–1970s indicated that it was generally less prevalent in francophone Quebec than in anglophone Canada.[56] Francophone intellectuals and the university-educated in general are more favorably inclined toward the United States than their anglophone counterparts[57] and certainly more so than their European francophone counterparts. Protected by a different language from more direct U.S. influence, and in need of foreign investment, francophones are less concerned about American cultural and economic intrusion and more favorable to expanded U.S. investment than anglophones, especially those in Ontario.[58] No influential Quebec politician of any party has expressed views on Quebec's neighbor to the south comparable to those of a number of NDP politicians and of economic nationalists in the national Liberal party. On the contrary, many francophone elites consider U.S. investment, trade, and other economic and institutional linkages as desirable counterbalances to anglophone Canadian influences in Quebec.

Moreover, whereas anti–Americanism is more prevalent among younger anglophones, it has no such correlation with age among francophones.[59] Nor are Quebeckers who are sympathetic to the PQ, independence, or sovereignty-association more, or less, anti–American than francophones who vote for the Liberals (PLQ) and favor either less drastic constitutional reform or the federal–provincial status quo. Furthermore, at least in the general francophone public, those with a favorable attitude toward France also entertain on the average a more favorable attitude toward the United States than francophones whose sentiments toward France and the French are more negative.[60] Unlike many nationalist anglophones, particularly in Ontario, Quebec nationalists on the whole regard the United States as an unduly indifferent but nonetheless friendly neighbor.

Some Americans have misgivings with respect to the prospect in Quebec for excessive provincial intervention and dirigisme, nationalization of industry, fiscal laxness, and socialism generally. The PQ government's program to purchase control of the Asbestos Corporation from the General Dynamics Corporation has aroused American apprehensions about unfair treatment of American-owned enterprises. Some American observers are concerned that able university-educated francophones will be attracted to careers in government rather than private enterprise, resulting in an ambiance inhospitable toward business. They regard the PQ government as having little sensitivity to the realities of business and a dynamic free-enterprise economy, and some fear a potential shift away from private enterprise by more socialistic, radical elements in the PQ or to the left of it.

Although there is some truth to some of these perceptions, most are in large measure explained by particular, probably temporary, historical conditions that have affected the francophone majority, conditions that are likely to change in the future for the better from the perspective of American critics. When the Lesage Liberal government took power in 1960, virtually all commerce and industry other than small, low-technology consumer manufacturers with local francophone markets and local retailing and services were controlled by anglophones, operated mainly in English, and employed few francophones in decisionmaking, technical, or other jobs attractive to university-educated people.[61] The more alert and ambitious francophones were priests, doctors, lawyers, professors, politicians, union leaders, journalists, artists, and members of the cultural elite.

Only the provincial government was thought to be able to represent the interests of the francophone majority in the face of anglophone economic power and to alter the rules of the game in order to encourage francophones to develop the self-confidence and talents to participate in the economy in proportion to their numbers. It was natural that the new activist government became the most attractive alternative to the church and the professions for ambitious young francophones who wanted to be where the action is.

It was also understandable that the activist Lesage government took over the private utilities—which had hired very few francophone managers, engineers, accountants, or other talent—and put them under control of a public corporation, relatively free of direct government intervention, in which employment became a mark of achievement for francophone university graduates working primarily in French. However, Lesage's action was not atypical of Canada or Quebec itself. A Liberal government nationalized Montreal utilities in the 1940s. Utilities have been nationalized in all provinces except Alberta and Prince Edward Island, mostly by Tory governments.

As interesting technical and managerial careers in private enterprise have gradually been opened in Quebec to talented francophones who want to work in French, more and more French-speaking students have majored in such fields as engineering, economics, accounting, and business administration and have gone into the private sector. The bright younger relations of able francophones who went into the clergy in the 1940s and early 1950s were going into government out of universities in the 1960s and early 1970s. Since 1977 when the PQ government restricted expansion of employment in the public sector, their counterparts have moved much more frequently into private enterprise.

Thus by 1980 Quebec had one-quarter of the university students in Canada but one-third of all Canadian students in business schools, the vast majority of whom would pursue careers in private business.[62] The number of students of engineering and applied science in Quebec francophone universities approximates the Canadian national average in proportion to population.[63] Francophones are now much more strongly represented among younger private sector managers than among their seniors, particularly in larger companies that a generation ago included few francophone university graduates.[64] Moreover, Quebec francophones on the mass level have been less hostile to big business and more critical of trade unions than anglophone Canadians at all educational levels, including university graduates.[65]

Like Western Europeans, Canadians have traditionally been more favorably disposed toward governmental intervention in their economy than have Americans. Most Canadians want and expect government, including provincial government, to take active roles in promoting economic development. Quebec francophones have been more supportive than Canadian anglophones (except NDP supporters) to redistribution of income and expanded social welfare, but on most other economic issues they have diverged little from the national pattern.[66] The PQ government has extended its role in the economy but not to a degree exceeding that of recent NDP provincial regimes.

Had the PLQ won the 1976 and 1981 elections, it would have given less emphasis to the public sector and more to private enterprise. In this respect the PQ has represented those who voted for it: PQ voters and those in favor of sovereignty–association or independence are more supportive of intervention, redistribution of wealth, controls over foreign investment, the objectives of the labor movement, and mildly social democratic programs than voters for the PLQ and those opposed to independence with or without association.[67]

Nevertheless PQ Finance Minister Jacques Parizeau, though a staunch independentist favoring governmental intervention to achieve economic and social objectives, has been cautious and pragmatic, as have other cabinet members charged with economic portfolios. They envisage dynamic private enterprise as essential to a viable economy and have been frequently criticized by the PQ social democratic minority outside parliament on that account. The appointment of Rodrique Biron, former leader of the economically conservative Union Nationale Party and owner of a successful business, as minister of industry, commerce, and tourism subsequent to his election as a PQ deputy in 1981 reflects that pragmatism. Understandably, provincial policies have accorded priority to encouraging small and medium-sized businesses, where francophone entrepreneurs still prevail.

The PQ government has established a government-owned asbestos company to coordinate research and development, expand local processing and fabrication, stimulate markets threatened by stagnant or declining demand due to health hazards, operate and develop the Bell Asbestos Corporation, which it purchased amicably from British interests in 1980, and eventually take over the Asbestos Corporation and transform it into a prototype for other producers.

Asbestos, however, is a special case, going back at least as far as the prolonged and emotionally charged strike in the Eastern Townships in 1949. Events there aroused public sympathy and Church

support for the workers and prompted successive provincial governments to give serious, albeit quiet, consideration to some form of
intervention in the industry, including takeover of one or more companies. Health considerations are also salient. The Asbestos Corporation is the second largest rather than the largest among the five major (all foreign owned) companies and was selected for takeover in
part because most of its production went to Western Europe and
elsewhere overseas rather than to the United States, in which country
the PQ leadership wanted to minimize negative repercussions.

The critical considerations in the case of asbestos do not apply to
other major foreign owned enterprises. Moreover, the intentions of
the PQ government relative to asbestos were pronounced well in advance, prior to the 1976 campaign. No further overt takeovers of
foreign controlled enterprises have been suggested or, according to
knowledgeable observers, seriously considered by the government.
Nor could the government generate large funds to do so short of
sharp public controversy accompanied by serious disagreement in the
government itself.

The PQ government inherited a congeries of crown corporations
from its predecessors, especially in resource industries so important
in exports to the United States. By 1976, in addition to Quebec
Hydro, important provincial corporations included SIDBEC, a provincial steel company that has usually lost money, SOQUIP for
oil and gas exploration, SOQUEM for other mineral exploration,
SOQUIA to modernize and develop agriculture and food processing,
the Deposit and Investment Fund for pensions and other investments, and the General Investment Society (SGF) to help finance
and encourage private enterprise in the public interest in fields in
which it might not otherwise enter. These last two entities have apparently outgrown their initial functions, however. By virtue of their
significant equity holdings in certain private corporations, Domtar
in particular and perhaps Noranda Mines, they are now seeking board
representation and a management role. Such provincial government
activity may well be for purely economic reasons, but circumstantial
evidence points to a further purpose. Other provinces also engage in
business activity; and federal entities such as the Canada Development Corporation and Petro–Canada are well known for their efforts
to obtain controlling equity positions in private corporations, notably in resources.

Petromont, in the petrochemical industry, is a new joint venture of SGF with Gulf of Canada and Union Carbide—a formula likely to become more widely utilized. The aforementioned enterprises have no special privileges over private companies, pay the same taxes and 20 percent of their earnings as dividends to the Quebec Treasury, and must live by the rules of the marketplace. By 1981 the more significant ones other than SIDBEC were making substantial profits.

In addition to asbestos, the PQ government has become increasingly active in forest products, in which sector it established REX–FOR, a provincial corporation to work jointly with private companies to accelerate research and development, modernization, and marketing. The forest products industry is not only the largest employer in the province and vital to its economy and balance of payments. It is also technologically obsolete and at a competitive disadvantage in the U.S. market, where it competes with the newer forest industry in the Southeast, where trees grow much faster and labor is less unionized.

Quebec's personal income taxes are higher on upper income brackets and less on lower brackets than are those of Ontario and of Canada generally. Quebec is now alone among the provinces to levy higher succession taxes on larger estates. But Quebec's taxes on resource exploitation and corporate profits generally are somewhat lower than those of other industrialized and major resource-producing provinces.[68] The PQ government has been neither more, nor less supportive than its predecessors of Quebec's politically influential but high-cost, obsolete, labor-intensive textile, clothing, leather goods, and furniture industries—none of which can compete except behind high protective barriers but which together account for approximately one-quarter of Quebec's manufacturing jobs.[69]

With respect to international trade and investment, particularly with the United States, the PQ government and any alternative provincial government will seek to expand exports of hydroelectricity and processed raw materials, to obtain a reduction of foreign barriers to its processed raw materials and manufactured goods, and to encourage foreign investment in the province (see final section of this chapter).

Another area of anxiety for Americans has been the foreign-policy preferences of a potentially more autonomous Quebec. This concern should have been alleviated by the postelection shift of the PQ, following its victory at the polls in 1976, from a semineutralist and pacifist stance to one of active support by a potentially sovereign Quebec of NATO, NORAD and other commitments of the present federal government.[70] In foreign policy the Lévesque government has gone beyond its Liberal predecessor in seeking to convince the United States of its desire to establish a mutually fruitful relationship with that country. Many Americans, however, perceive this foreign policy turnabout as tactical, opportunistic, and of low priority for the PQ government.

Quebec political leaders, regardless of party, have never accorded much priority to foreign policy, nor have they thought systematically about Quebec's basic interests in that domain. They have been preoccupied with matters closer to the province, as have been the political elites in other provinces. Moreover, francophones generally have, until recently, left Canada's foreign policy and diplomacy to anglophone elites. Except in respect to the United States, the French-speaking world, and certain international economic issues, the international thinking of the PQ government in 1981 diverged relatively little from that in Ottawa. Outside of these three domains, foreign policy has had little bearing on the priorities of any of Quebec's governments. However, the Ministry of Intergovernmental Affairs, under Claude Morin as deputy minister and later minister, has gained increasing sophistication and realism in international domains pertinent to Quebec.[71]

Survey interviews of the foreign-policy attitudes of individual francophones reveal a narrowing of differences between them and anglophone Canadians on most international issues. Apart from their traditional opposition to conscription for military service abroad, however, francophones are less likely to express opinions on world affairs and manifest less information and less interest than anglophones. They are also less optimistic about the apparent drift of world affairs toward war and the possibilities of doing much about it.[72] Francophones are somewhat more sympathetic to less-developed countries (except for accepting their labor-intensive exports),[73] are somewhat less apt than anglophones to favor the Israelis over the PLO and the Arabs in the Middle East conflict,[74] and are more anti-Soviet and more inclined to consider communism a threat to Canada.[75] Nevertheless, perhaps because of their opposition to conscription, they have been less likely than anglophones to feel that Canada should remain in NATO[76] or should send troops abroad under UN auspices.[77] In general, however, they hold more favorable views of the UN than anglophones.[78]

Finally, Quebec francophones who favor independence, sovereignty-association, or a major devolution of federal powers to the provinces are more cosmopolitan and international in their attitudes and are more supportive of Canadian foreign policy in most fields than those who favor the constitutional status quo. Clearly, foreign policy has not been much at issue between Quebec nationalists and the federal government. Differences have been largely those of emphasis.

Francophone Quebeckers ascribe significantly higher priorities to relations with *francophonie* in general and lower priorities to those with the English-speaking Commonwealth than do their English-speaking compatriots.[79] For example, Quebec's trade with black Africa and the Maghreb was C$0.5 billion, 45 percent of total Canadian trade with these countries in 1978.[80] French-speaking Quebec companies and Quebec subsidiaries of anglophone controlled enterprises have the advantage of providing a broad range of North American products and services in native French.

The anxieties of some Americans that the government of France may exert undue political influence on Quebec's behavior in spheres critical to U.S. interests appear to be unwarranted. Both Quebec and French elites, regardless of partisan persuasion, conceive of Quebec–French relations in primarily cultural terms, as a significant reinforcement of francophone culture to help overcome the geographic isolation of Quebec in an overwhelmingly anglophone North America. Cultural and educational exchanges have thus grown greatly since Premier Lesage initiated a formal cultural accord with President de Gaulle, and modern electronic technology is making transatlantic communications increasingly effective. The Lévesque government has intensified the cultural relations that evolved under four predecessor governments. But the influences of French taste, ideas, perceptions, and points of view—as transmitted by French magazines and books, by Agence France Press, which covers most international news in Quebec francophone newspapers, by French television now available daily, by French theater and films, and by growing personal contacts—are significant only up to a point.

Most French cultural influence must be adapted to an inherently very different North American mentality and experience. Though Quebec francophones feel much more affinity for France and less for

Britain than do other Canadians,[81] francophones in general hold considerably warmer feelings for the United States than for France or any other foreign country.[82] Moreover, francophones in Quebec ascribe much higher priority to relations with the United States than to those with France.[83] Furthermore, these two French-speaking cultures are so different as to result in considerable tension in interpersonal relationships, including, albeit decreasingly, perceived French attitudes of superiority and condescension so irritating to Quebeckers.[84]

Quebec elites are aware that few French elites take Quebec seriously and that meetings of successive Premiers Lesage, Johnson, Bertrand, Bourassa, and Lévesque with their French counterparts, whatever the symbolism and rhetoric, have resulted in growing cooperation primarily in fields related to culture and language.

Franco–Quebec economic relations, though gradually expanding, remain quite limited. Quebec has little French investment. Although trade is increasing, by 1979 Quebec's trade with France ranked only fifth after that with the United States, Britain, the German Federal Republic, and Japan. Whereas the trade balance with the United States has been consistently in Quebec's favor, that with France has been consistently negative for Quebec.[85]

The greater affinity with French culture rather than with that of the United States is understandably much more apparent among intellectual, academic, cultural, and, to a lesser degree, practicing professional elites than in the general Quebec population. Many of the former received their graduate or professional education in France, or, to a lesser extent, in Belgium and Switzerland. Most with classical Quebec secondary and university schooling are familiar with French literature, history, philosophy, and arts. Much of their serious reading and theater are of French origin, and many maintain personal contacts in France. Their tastes are much more influenced by Europe than are those of the Quebec masses. Conversely, their familiarity with American literature, history, politics, and mentality frequently leaves a good deal to be desired. However, these observations apply much less to the growing Quebec business and technological community, whose occupational models and standards, tastes, and styles of life are based much more on those of the United States than of Europe.

OTTAWA'S POLICIES: CONTINUING CONFRONTATION

The concept of Quebec nationalism increasingly endorsed by francophones in that province has not been accepted as a valid basis for serious constitutional negotiations by Trudeau governments in Ottawa. Nor have Quebeckers had much oportunity to exercise their preferences in this regard in federal elections. The opposition parties have alternated between a tentative recognition of Quebec views and a one-Canada concept tinged with antifrancophone overtones. Neither the Progressive Conservatives (PCs) nor the NDP has had much political base in francophone Quebec; neither, since Diefenbaker's success in 1958, has won many seats there; and neither has included francophones in its national party leadership. Their failure to come to grips with the issue is thus politically understandable.

NDP leaders have usually argued for further federal centralization to achieve their social democratic objectives and to limit U.S. economic influence, a platform counter to Quebec's aspirations and interests. The Progressive Conservatives nationally have increasingly represented the economic interests of the anglophone middle class and business community.

Both the PC's and the NDP have at times recognized the concept of two nations and cultures. The PC's mentioned it in their 1968 platform. Without explicitly recognizing duality in their 1979 campaign and in their subsequent brief period in power, the PC government of Joseph Clark adopted a more flexible posture than the previous Liberal government regarding devolution of authority and spheres of action from Ottawa to the provinces generally, in effect projecting a conception of the relative roles of the two levels of Canadian government more acceptable to Quebeckers than that of its predecessor. There are also indications that several of the likely anglophone successors to Trudeau as Liberal party leader would be more flexible in their public stance and perhaps more willing to compromise substantively with the key demands of Quebec nationalism. But for most of the period since 1968 Trudeau's view of Canada concerning Quebec has been the central consideration.

The idea that the cultural and linguistic cleavage of Canada should be geographical in the sense conceived of by Quebec francophones has always been heresy in Ottawa. As French Canadians concentrated their nationalism in Quebec, federal politicians and officials tried to devise ways to make French Canadians feel more at home throughout the country. A geographical cleavage between French and English Canada was felt to be dangerously divisive and essentially corrosive of the Canadian nation. Federal officials argued that it would pave the way for the separation of Quebec from the rest of Canada.

Some able French Canadians are attracted by the idea of sharing power in governing a large country rather than confining their ambitions, energies, and allegiance to Quebec. Pursuing successful careers at the federal level and engrossed in the national scene, they typically underestimate or ignore the intensity and pervasiveness of the Quebec francophone sense of uniqueness and desire for separate status. Perhaps more than many of their anglophone colleagues they have become staunch critics of Quebec nationalists who prefer to remain and work at home. Paramount among them stands Prime Minister Pierre Elliott Trudeau.

The position of Trudeau and his associates on federal–provincial issues is described in some detail in Chapter 7 and will not be repeated here. In respect to the special case of Quebec, Trudeau has consistently repudiated the concept of Quebec nationalism as outlined here. He has declared that a central reason for his going into federal politics in 1965 was to counterbalance Quebec aspirations for expanded powers. He has long been critical of nationalism generally as intrinsically ethnocentric, prejudiced, anticosmopolitan, and dangerous to human understanding and progress. He feels it is both preferable and possible to remain truly francophone in language and tastes while participating fully in the joint Canadian enterprise with others of diverse ethnic and cultural backgrounds. In Trudeau's view there exist a single Canadian identity and way of life, a number of ethnic groups, including French Canadians, and two official languages.

Trudeau has opposed devolution of powers to the provinces, and, especially, special status for Quebec. He has felt strongly that either, but particularly the latter, would result in an ungovernable Canada. Many Quebeckers believe he would prefer a unitary to a federal system of government to deal with the heterogeneity and inherently centrifugal forces and conflicting interests within Canada.

As prime minister, Trudeau has simultaneously pursued the implementation of the Official Languages Act and the consolidation of powers into the federal government. Under the Official Languages Act, large federal sums have been granted to French Canadian communities outside Quebec for educational and other efforts to reinforce the use of the French language. Substantial funds have been devoted to making federal employees bilingual and extending radio and television broadcasting in French over vast areas with only small potential audiences.

The federal government has also attempted systematically to give Canada a truly bilingual image abroad. Ottawa would participate fully in *francophonie*, inviting, as well as Quebec delegates, representatives of Ontario, New Brunswick, and Manitoba to speak for their francophone populations in international meetings. Bicultural diplomacy has become an important part of Canadian foreign policy.

In its deemphasis of the intimate interconnection between language and cultural milieu, federal policy runs counter to the findings of the report of the Royal Commission on Bilingualism and Biculturalism of 1965, to many subsequent analyses, and to the thinking of much of the Quebec francophone elite. A live and healthy French language, as most Quebec elites have been quick to remark, is much more than a set of symbols for relatively superficial communication. It carries with it a way of thinking, a philosophy, a congeries of values, priorities, and emotions, and a social structure with supporting institutions. What is seen in Quebec to be at stake is not the possibility of an individual to obtain services in French at an airport or government office but the evolution of a truly francophone society and the possibility of living in an environment made more congenial by a similarity of language and culture.

Nor does the federal policy take into serious account the asymmetrical nature of the two major languages and related cultures in Canada and North America as a whole. One cannot constructively deal with a giant and a pigmy as though they were equals. Treating French Canadianism as the same throughout Canada is contrary to census trends documenting the fact that outside Quebec the French language is disappearing into the majority language and culture in spite of Ottawa's considerable efforts to prevent that from happening.

It is true that fluency in French in the federal government, particularly in Ottawa, is much more prevalent than a generation ago. The number of native francophones at all levels of the central government has grown considerably. Many anglophone civil servants have undergone intensive immersion programs. Those ambitious to rise in public service or to national roles in nongovernmental agencies are obliged to follow discussions in both languages. Even those who aspire to national leadership in the PC and NDP Parties have become minimally bilingual. Nevertheless, French has become a working language primarily in a minority of offices specially structured to achieve that result; elsewhere English is normal.[86] Bilingualism in a four-to-one ratio in Canada (forty-to-one in North America) is very apt to mean that one language will be the practical working language, the other an idiom into which to translate at great expense for comprehension by the minority.

Although francophones outside Quebec have largely welcomed federal bilingual programs in their areas and have been apprehensive lest sovereignty for Quebec should result in curtailment of bilingual efforts elsewhere, their leaders have generally supported the arguments of Quebec nationalists in their conflicts with federal policies. Thus, no influential francophones outside Quebec and the federal government advocated a "no" vote in the referendum. They have supported René Lévesque's opposition to unilateral patriation with a bill of rights and amendment via referenda that they argue would further relegate the fate of francophones to the anglophone majority.[87]

The Trudeau government, supported by many Canadian anglophones and some federalist francophones, maintains that Quebec has enough constitutional powers now to achieve its legitimate cultural and linguistic objectives and points to what Quebec has already accomplished—Law 101, a growing rapport with other francophone societies, and so forth. Nevertheless, most francophone Quebeckers feel that even these achievements are fragile, unstable, and threatened under the current constitution as applied by a federal government utlimately controlled by growing Canadian anglophone majorities unsympathetic to, or at least according little priority to, basic Quebec objectives. For example, the constitutionality under federal law of Quebec Law 101 and other key provincial statutes seems doubtful and has been challenged in the courts.

Communications, central to the future of francophone culture, are still largely controlled by the federal government. Furthermore, the federal government has demonstrated a propensity increasingly to move into fields regarded by Quebec francophones to be primarily of provincial jurisdiction. Quebec elites have been especially critical of federal use of the power of the purse and of the constitution to press for national unity based on Trudeau's principles, whereas they feel that they lack the authority and the economic means to achieve their predominantly cultural objectives.

Finally, there has gradually developed a consensus in Quebec that the present federal system, at least as it is increasingly applied, feeds animosity between Ottawa and Quebec, produces an ever-growing, increasingly "meddling" federal bureaucracy for the most part un-sympathetic to francophone Quebec's purposes, and results in unnec-essary duplication of effort or in activity at cross purposes.

Francophone Quebeckers are fond of Trudeau, admire his political skills, his charisma, his character and determination, his reputation as an international statesman, his elegance, style, and taste as Quebec's closest approximation to an aristocrat and even his patrician con-descension and flipness. He and his overwhelming majority of Liberal members of Parliament (MPs) elected from Quebec are seen as favor-ite sons who "made it" in the wider English-speaking world. But evi-dence points to the fact that their conception of the role of Quebec in Canada is contrary to the preferences of most Quebec franco-phones who are interested in the problem and are politically active.

This evidence is to be found not only in opinion studies, as cited above, but in the fact that many Quebeckers voting for federal Lib-eral MPs were at the same time supporting the PQ and the notion of independence with or without association.[88] Support for Trudeau and the national Liberal party was a poor predictor of how franco-phones voted in the 1980 referendum. A "no" vote in the refer-endum was not a vote for Trudeau or his policies on the Quebec issue.[89]

All Quebec provincial parties, whether or not in power, have regu-larly opposed Trudeau on the status of Quebec in Canada. Although Premier Bourassa and his Union Nationale predecessors, Bertrand and Johnson, were never as popular among francophones as Trudeau, they received the support of francophone majorities in their several conflicts with Ottawa having constitutional overtones, like Bourassa's decision not to accept the Victoria Charter in 1971 as a basis for patriation of the constitution.[90]

When in 1978 PQ Finance Minister Parizeau rejected a proposed federal sales tax rebate, he received unanimous support in the Que-bec National Assembly, including that of all Liberal deputies. Provin-cial Liberal leader Claude Ryan led his party's campaign for a "no" vote on sovereignty-association on the theme of Quebec national distinctiveness with the slogan "Mon 'non' est Québécois." Since the referendum he and his associates have been highly critical of the Trudeau government's proposals for constitutional change because of the continued emphasis on a single Canadian people and the apparent "ignoring of the aspirations of a large number of Quebec federalists as well as of those who favored sovereignty-association" [my translation]. In July 1980 Ryan cautioned that "the central government should avoid every attitude and initiative that would force the Liberal Party of Quebec to ally itself with the Parti Québécois" [translation],[91] implying that the postreferendum actions of Trudeau and his aides were pushing the PLQ to that political extremity. The policies of the Trudeau government on constitutional repatriation and other issues of concern to francophones were a major cause of the PLQ's defeat in the 1981 election.

In sum, Trudeau's conflicts with most provincial premiers over federal–provincial powers, his unilateral effort to patriate the constitution with amendments via referenda and a bill of rights that would probably invalidate Quebec's Law 101, and his recent energy policies are widely perceived in Quebec as efforts toward further centralization rather than preservation of the federal–provincial status quo. Many Quebeckers, including those who voted against sovereignty-association, feel they were misled by Trudeau's vague promises of constitutional reform during the prereferendum campaign. Should he achieve his principal constitutional objectives before leaving public life, they appear to run sufficiently counter to fundamental Quebec francophone trends and convictions as to seem unlikely to resolve the current federal–provincial conflict.

WHITHER QUEBEC: IMPLICATIONS FOR THE UNITED STATES

Some observers argue that the referendum and other indicators show that Quebec nationalism is on the decline.[92] A few, including some pessimistic francophone nationalists, go so far as to predict the eventual assimilation of Quebec into anglophone North American culture.

A much larger minority, at the opposite pole of opinion, argue that the federal government and anglophone Canada are unlikely to accept sufficient devolution of powers to Quebec in time to halt secession, with or without economic association. They believe that in the light of his history and conception of Canada, Trudeau will never accept the minimal compromise required to head off this eventuality. They believe he is more willing to accommodate the anglophone provinces with a devolution of resource-related economic powers than to concede a corresponding degree of cultural autonomy to Quebec whose nationalism he regards as more threatening to the long-term integrity of the Canadian nation.

They observe that the PQ, although returned to office in 1981 in part because of its pledge that if reelected it would not call another referendum or "snap" election on the independence issue, has not given up independence as its ultimate objective. They maintain—and rightly, it seems—that unless Ottawa makes major concessions of at least the character of those recommended by the Pépin–Robarts task force, a Quebec majority, including many federalists who voted "no" in 1980, will vote for the PQ in 1984 or 1985 on a clear platform of independence or will vote for independence in a referendum subsequent to reelection of the PQ.

Still a third scenario envisaged by some, including some Quebec nationalists, anticipates that Trudeau, acting through the Parliament against the opposition of a majority of provincial governments, will succeed in patriating the constitution in accordance with his controversial amendment process and bill of rights, with the approval of the British House of Commons.[93] While maintaining that he was acting to preserve a viable Canada, Trudeau would continue further centralization. Tensions with the provinces other than Ontario would grow, but through his determination, force of personality, and political skills, Trudeau would for the most part achieve his objectives. He might then accept a "draft" to run in the next election and could conceivably remain in power for as much as a decade longer.

According to this third scenario Trudeau would appeal to left-of-center anglophone nationalism, with the support of the NDP, through such measures as his new energy policy. Economic tensions with the United States would mount, perhaps higher than during the Nixon years. Quebec nationalism would be held at bay, at least until Trudeau left office. Thereafter, a process of federal–provincial negotiation would begin that would ultimately result in the transfer of significant authority to the provinces.

The first scenario—a decline of francophone nationalism and an associated process of francophone assimilation—seems very unlikely.

Also unlikely is scenario 2—the prospect that Quebec would with-draw from confederation if the recent policies of the Trudeau regime continued for a decade with minimal or only cosmetic compromises with Quebec's claim to greater autonomy. Even if Trudeau were to succeed with further centralization of power in the next several years, it is likely that the buildup of centrifugal forces in Quebec and elsewhere, excluding Ontario and perhaps the Maritimes, are such that his achievements would unravel.

In this brief space let us focus on the third scenario, the one that seems the most probable—a significant devolution of powers to the provinces by the year 2000. (As Professor Howard Cody believes, this process has been underway for some years.) Within this scenario varying degrees of devolution and diverse patterns could have rather different effects on long-term American interests. The rationale for this scenario takes account of Canadian trends and opinions outside Quebec.

A majority of people in the West, the Prairies, and Newfoundland believe that their provincial governments are more representative of their interests than the federal government,[94] are manifesting grow-ing discontent with the current federal system, and increasingly favor devolution of resource-related powers to the provinces.[95] In October 1980, for instance, 84 percent of adults west of Ontario agreed that "the West usually gets ignored in national parties because the politi-cal parties depend on Ontario and Quebec for most of their votes"; 60 percent believed that their region had "sufficient resources and industries to survive without the rest of Canada"; 53 percent consid-ered that "in many ways western Canadians have more in common with the western United States than with eastern Canada"; and 28 percent felt that "Western Canadians get so few benefits from being part of Canada that they might as well go it on their own."[96]

A different survey in Alberta about the same time arrived at simi-lar conclusions: 60 percent believed independence would be to their economic benefit or that they would be at least as well off as under the current federal system, and 24 percent favored independence if the Trudeau government persisted with its present policies.[97] As of 1979, Albertans had become almost as prodevolution as Quebeck-ers.[98] As early as 1977–78, 56 percent of corporate leaders and nearly half the leaders in the legal profession and the media in the three westernmost provinces together favored devolution.[99] Thus, economic self-assurance seems to provide an impetus to "going it alone" in the three westernmost provinces, whereas in Quebec concern for the economic consequences of sovereignty-association was a distinct deterrent to a majority "yes" vote in the 1980 referendum.

Turning from the westernmost to the easternmost provinces, Newfoundlanders, particularly their elites and university-educated minorities, have come to think more like western Canadians with respect to their relations with the federal government than have Maritimers and, especially, Ontarians. Newfoundlanders have always felt isolated from central Canada.[100] Newfoundland joined Canada by only a very close vote in 1949 after being rebuffed by the United States. With a per capita income lower than that of any other province, it wants control of offshore oil, as does the federal government. In a survey several weeks after the federal government's announcement of its new energy policy, 69 percent of Newfoundlanders—nearly as high a percentage as in the energy-producing Prairies (72 percent)—opposed the effort of the federal government unilaterally to patriate the constitution, contrasted with but 55 percent opposed in Quebec.[101]

The styles and tactics and, to some degree, the issues pursued by western and Prairie provincial governments in their efforts to achieve greater autonomy will undoubtedly continue to depend on the particular parties, and to a lesser extent, the personalities in power. Should the NDP oust the Social Credit William R. Bennett regime in British Columbia, for example, a David Barrett (or other) NDP government would probably behave, at least in the short run, more in the moderate fashion of its Allan E. Blakeney Saskatchewan counterpart. However, short of significant federal compromises, ultimately at the expense of Ontario, autonomist sentiments in British Columbia are likely to grow, especially among corporate and political elites and, to only a somewhat lesser degree, among those in the media, the professions, and other walks of life. Support by the general public in the western and Prairie provinces would probably follow, with some time lag. The higher incidence of devolutionist sentiment among younger and better educated anglophones in Canada[102] would reinforce that trend.

Ontario, of course, has the most to lose from a devolution of federal authority. The broad support of Trudeau's postreferendum policies by Ontario politicians and other elites represents the views of the politically articulate university-educated, the middle and upper classes, and, to a lesser extent, the general electorate. For example, a majority of Ontarians, more than in any other province and much more than in the West, the Prairies, Quebec, and Newfoundland, have a positive view of Canada and the federal government, believe themselves fairly treated by that government, consider the federal government more important to their personal lives and interests than their provincial government, favor either the federal–provincial status quo or still stronger federal powers vis-à-vis those of the provinces, and oppose devolution.[103] Ontarians, like Quebeckers, support relatively high tariffs against imports of less-expensive manufactured goods from abroad, which barriers are opposed by majorities of those with opinions west of Ontario and in the Maritimes and Newfoundland.

The Maritimes, not including Newfoundland, are caught between the conflicting economic interests and demands of the other provinces. Their dependence of federal equalization payments provided from taxes on the richer provinces moderates their quarrel with central Canada regarding high-cost, protected manufactured goods. However, expansion of their fish exports, as they profit from the new 200–mile fishing limit, and of their timber, gypsum, electricity, and a few other natural resources would tend to align their interests with those of the resource-intensive provinces. Should major oil deposits be found in or offshore Nova Scotia, which seems quite possible, the effect relations between Nova Scotia and Ottawa would be considerable. The Canadian government has seldom won in its past confrontations with provinces over control of natural resources, and henceforth the potential coalition of parallel provincial interests is likely to be both more widespread and profound.

As of mid-1981, much of the collaboration of Quebec, western, Prairie, and Newfoundland governments in opposing the federal-provincial policies of the Trudeau government has been a matter of ad hoc convenience. Their parallel provincial interests are criss-crossed by divergencies of an economic nature and by cultural, political, and historical differences. As noted earlier, Quebec's labor-intensive sector has protectionist interests parallel to those of Ontario's branch-plant economy, in opposition to the freer trade interests of most of the rest of the country. All of the provinces east of Saskatchewan want the oil and gas of those further west at minimal cost as well as a maximum share of the profits therefrom.

Westerners dislike the economic and political influences of Quebec and Ontario. Western, Prairie, and Newfoundland inhabitants have little sympathy with Quebec's cultural and linguistic objectives. Nevertheless, the recognition on the part of Quebec and the resource-intensive provinces of a community of interests vis-à-vis Ottawa and Ontario will probably grow beyond the considerable degree of collaboration as of mid-1981. Whereas Quebec's objectives are primarily cultural, its demands for devolution of economic powers to achieve its cultural purposes do not generally conflict with the economic objectives of these other provinces. The Quebec government's active support of Alberta's claim to provincial control of energy pricing and of the three westernmost provinces' opposition to a federal export tax on gas and the new federal energy policy are probably only the beginning of a growing coalition of these provinces.

Should Trudeau remain in office, the process of federal accommodation with Quebec and the other devolutionist provinces would probably be delayed, perhaps leading to an escalation of federal-provincial tensions. But an anglophone Liberal prime minister might be considerably more flexible. Similarly, a Progressive Conservative government, in recent decades more pro-private enterprise, less "dirigiste," and less centralist than the federal Liberals under Trudeau, might negotiate a mutually acceptable compromise. Such negotiations could continue for a half-decade or more. By this wearing process the negotiators could conceivably "muddle through" to a prudent agreement, particularly if the breakup of Canada seemed the alternative. Although a definitive arrangement would seem unlikely, a federal structure might evolve that would diminish the heat of federal-provincial confrontations and provide a framework for dealing more effectively with the basic issues over the next generation or so.

Majority anglophone opposition to de jure special status for Quebec[104] could perhaps be finessed by an approach recommended by the Pépin-Robarts task force whereby powers sufficient to satisfy a majority of Quebeckers were available to all provinces but in fact were utilized chiefly by Quebec. Most Quebeckers would accept whatever devolution of economic powers satisfied the other major resource-producing provinces. Quebec would probably deem it tactically wise for the anglophone provinces to take the lead, with Quebec's support as a quid pro quo for their support of Quebec's cultural demands.

If federal powers under such a federal-provincial arrangement included continued aid to less affluent regions and sufficient revenues to the central government to finance such aid, the Maritimes might well decide to go along. Alternatively, perhaps a coalition of richer provinces—Alberta, British Columbia, Ontario (and, should their resources develop as they hope, eventually Saskatchewan and a petroleum-affluent Newfoundland)—might agree to continue to support the Maritimes with subsidies that would decrease as the latter developed their resource, light industry, tourism and other economic bases. If cooler heads in Alberta, British Columbia, and Saskatchewan went along, so would Manitoba, perhaps with the honey of a lesser, but likewise declining, subsidy than the still poorer Maritimes received.

Independentist Quebec leaders, including a number of intellectuals and trade unionists, would object to limited devolution among the Pépin–Robarts' model and would continue for a time to campaign against such a sell out, but their potential support would come from a rather small, albeit articulate, Quebec minority. This scenario assumes that the other provinces whose economies would benefit from lower barriers to imports of manufactured goods would not press hard in that sphere, at least not during the negotiations. Such pressure would activate the opposition of Quebec's soft-goods producers, the relevant trade unions, and the large minority of the electorate whose family incomes depend on such labor-intensive industries. Ontario would resist such change. However, if the prairies, western, and Atlantic provinces did not threaten its manufacturing sectors with loss of tariff protection, thereby encouraging alliance with soft-goods sectors in Quebec, Ontario would effectively be isolated in the federal–provincial negotiations.

The long-run implications for the United States of such a federal–provincial accommodation would depend in considerable measure on the details of the new arrangement. Insofar as it provided a framework for gradual resolution of the Canadian duality-of-cultures issue, it would be a major gain for Canada and thereby a gain for the United States. Able Canadians of both linguistic groups could refocus their energies from that congeries of problems to coping more effectively with the many others that, due to this diversion, have in recent years received less thoughtful attention than they deserve. Such an arrangement, if it remained stable, might permit the anglophone cultural and economic nationalist minority to devote more energies to anti–Americanism, but that eventuality is problematical and much less injurious to American interests than a divisive escalation of conflict between Quebec and the rest of Canada.

American companies with plants in Canada based on national rather than provincial markets would have reason to be concerned lest such devolution result in increased provincial barriers to the movement of goods, and, to a lesser degree, of services and labor. Many Canadian corporations would be even more vulnerable to such developments, which could perhaps be minimized through tradeoffs agreed to in the course of federal–provincial negotiations. Some provinces, less likely Quebec than those that elect NDP governments, would undoubtedly become considerably more "étatiste" in regard to their economies than others; for example, Saskatchewan under Premier Blakeney. Wider provincial differences in economic policies, particularly in respect to natural resources, would probably develop than exist under the current federal system.

But, on the whole, in such an economic environment American and other foreign business interests should have greater, rather than less, bargaining power than at present. They would be freer to negotiate mutually beneficial arrangements with partners in individual provinces. Relevant decisionmaking on the Canadian side should be simpler and quicker, involving fewer bureaucrats at fewer levels. The attitudes of individual provinces have often been more hospitable to American business than those of Ottawa,[105] their interests more directly linked, and their officials more accessible and less encumbered with considerations of national consistency, national standards, or national priorities.

Quebec, for example, would see little advantage in continuing to sell electricity at a significantly lower price to Ontario and New Brunswick than to New York, New England, New Jersey, and Pennsylvania, its iron ore to Hamilton for less than to U.S. steel mills, or its copper, zinc, aluminum and other metals to Ontario fabricators at prices below those offered by their European and American counterparts. It would resist the powers of FIRA and the National Energy Board to intervene in provincial decisions.

Electricity exports would become Quebec's strongest suit in its relations with the United States. It could seek to bargain hydropower exports in exchange not only for capital with which to expand generating capacity and transmission systems but also for reductions of U.S. tariff and nontariff barriers on processed and semifabricated aluminum, copper, zinc, iron ore, asbestos, and timber products. The United States would remain the chief source of foreign capital and principal trading partner of Quebec and of most Canadian provinces. Indeed, Quebec's economic relations with the United States, in particular with the energy-deficient U.S. Northeast, would probably intensify, whereas there might be some corresponding reduction in

Quebec's economic interdependence with Ontario. Most Quebeckers would welcome such a development.

Alberta, Saskatchewan, and British Columbia, like Quebec, might well seek to negotiate U.S. access to their energy resources—oil, gas, tar sands, and perhaps uranium—in exchange for U.S. capital and technology to develop the production of petrochemicals, along with a reduction in the U.S. tariffs on such products. Should Quebec join forces with these provinces in their negotiations with U.S. entities, protectionist groups in the United States might well lose out to those eager for Canadian energy. If Quebec brought New Brunswick into the provincial power coalition, and if it should reach a compromise with Newfoundland on electric power transmission from Churchill Falls, thereby drawing Premier Peckford of Newfoundland or a successor into constructive negotiations with American interests, the joint provincial leverage could be even greater vis-à-vis the United States. A somewhat fragmented Canada might well reknit itself together according to new economic patterns.

One such new pattern would probably appear in a reduced protection of Canadian domestic industry. In the long run, expanded provincial economic autonomy in resource-related domains would probably lead to greater leverage by the West, Prairies, and Atlantic provinces in their arguments with Quebec and Ontario regarding reduction of Canadian barriers on manufactured goods. Unless, in the interim, the resource-rich provinces developed protected industries on a large scale, their combined bargaining power would probably result in greater liberalization of trade barriers than under the current federal system. Such freer trade would redound to U.S. interests, especially those in competition with many Ontario and Quebec manufacturers that enjoy a protected Canadawide market.[106]

Under this scenario of greater provincial autonomy, the least threatening one for both Canada and the United States, federal, state, and local governments in the United States as well as American private institutions and individuals would have to deal with individual provinces much more extensively than is now the practice. Some powers of coordination and negotiation of conflicting interprovincial economic arrangements across the U.S. border would probably remain with Ottawa, but more bilateral negotiation would take place with individual provinces and coalitions of provinces, the composition of which would depend on the issue. The results might not be in the narrow interests of certain protectionist groups in either country, but the net results could well be in the economic interest of not only particular U.S. regions but also the United States as a whole.

Whether from the standpoint of U.S. worldwide political and strategic interests such devolution of economic and cultural powers to the Canadian provinces would represent a net gain, loss, or a neutral effect would depend on what powers Ottawa succeeded in keeping. While control over resource-related policy, and, to some extent, trade and investment generally, would shift toward the provinces, to be viable, a central government would need to remain in control of monetary policy. So far, neither the PQ government in Quebec nor any other provincial government has argued otherwise.[107] Furthermore, it seems unlikely that Quebec or the other provinces seeking devolution of authority would question Canada's international commitments and the retention of centralized power of decision in such fields of interest to the United States as Canadian participation in NORAD, NATO, in the OECD, and in the United Nations and its agencies, particularly the IMF and the World Bank.

The two critical aspects, from the standpoint of American interests, are likely to be (1) the quality of Canadian decisionmaking with respect to the growing network of international issues that are intimately linked with economic phenomena and (2) the ability of the central government to command sufficient resources to finance viable foreign policies, including aid to developing countries and a significant defense force. It is already the case that the provisions of recent years for federal consultation with the provinces already render it cumbersome for Canada to evolve clear foreign policies. Further devolution of authority could result in less coherent Canadian responses to foreign-policy problems. A constitutional compromise that would satisfy the aspirations of the provinces and at the same time reserve to Ottawa both the essential foreign-policy decisionmaking and the financial wherewithal effectively to implement such decisions could be difficult to achieve.

SOME SUGGESTIONS FOR AMERICANS

The foregoing speculation as to the future course of Canadian federation, Quebec's role in particular, and the implications for the United States points to the need for guidance for Americans in this complex situation. The basic stance of the United States government should not be other than it has been: deal correctly with the Canadian federal government; keep an ear to the ground in Quebec and in the other provinces through U.S. consulates and other representatives; do nothing that could be construed as supporting one faction, argument, alternative solution or another; and encourage Canadians to work out their difficult problems among themselves. U.S. officialdom and Congress must maintain truly neutral positions in the highly controversial and volatile federal–provincial struggle wherein long-term U.S. interests are not clearly on one side or another.

Because it goes against the instincts of most Americans to contemplate the kind of linguistic–cultural autonomy that most Quebeckers favor, there is a tendency to be influenced on the side of "Canadian unity" as defined by anglophone Canadians and federal government officials. The sovereignty-association arguments pressed by Quebec cabinet ministers during their numerous prereferendum visits to the United States should have been viewed here as but one alternative, long-range solution to the problem of Canada's cultural duality, an alternative favored by some but not necessarily a majority of Quebeckers. But the Quebec visitors' perspectives were generally received with polite disbelief and disapproval, although probably no more one-sided than the obverse perspective of Ottawa and Toronto by which many Americans appear to be influenced. It would seem to be in the U.S. national interest for responsible Americans to develop an awareness of and respect for Canadian francophone opinion, particularly as the leaders of that province become increasingly open to the rest of the world.

Greater American sensitivity and sophistication will be essential if those in official or private capacity are to avoid actions and utterances likely to alienate Quebec opinionmakers and weaken the more moderate and constructive leaders whose political survival will depend on their success in achieving the basic francophone objectives short of secession. Unwarranted American anxieties about the potential influence of anti–American leftist francophone minorities, about a possible shift of provincial policies sharply toward dirigisme and the takeover of private enterprise, and about the supposed incompetence of francophones to run a primarily private-sector economy could become self-fulfilling prophecies.

Most Quebec elites, from independentists through federalists, are open to American efforts to establish a better interchange and rapport. They are disturbed by the lack of American interest in their concerns and by the American tendency to adopt Canadian anglophone and federalist perceptions, for they know that the success of any feasible solution for Quebec will depend in large measure on a mutually satisfactory relationship of Quebec with the United States.

There will be problems for Americans in developing a rapport with francophone Quebec apart from those of language and related cultural differences. For example, there will probably be some asymmetry between the relevant actors in the relationship. Those most influential in Quebec have been the more literate professionals, educators, and intellectuals, many of them somewhat suspicious of business people; whereas the Americans most interested in Quebec are likely to be businesspeople and financial experts. Americans will find it valuable to communicate beyond the circle of the Montreal francophone businesspeople associated with American and Canadian anglophone controlled corporations whose views may represent the thinking of only a minority of those who will ultimately decide Quebec's future.

The development of American contacts with francophone Canadians comparable to those with anglophone Canadians must take place in a variety of spheres, encompassing political elites in the major provincial parties; intellectuals in universities, the media, and cultural life; civil servants; the practicing professions; and leaders in public and private economic institutions. A pool of American talent fluent in French, knowledgeable about the complexities of Quebec, and in touch with a broad spectrum of its diverse elites should be developed not only in universities and research institutions but also in the major areas of practical American involvement with Quebec.

In widening their contacts north of the border, Americans must take pains not to create the impression that they are choosing sides in federal–provincial disputes involving Quebec or other dissident provinces. At the same time they must expect to encounter complaints and ruffled feelings on the part of Canadian federalists and anglophones in response to even the most prudent efforts to establish greater American rapport, especially with francophone Quebec.

Still more delicate and difficult will be the task of communicating to the appropriate federal and provincial leaders the legitimate interests and concerns of the United States and its citizens if and when federal–provincial negotiations for a wider sharing of federal powers do take place. As noted earlier, some federal–provincial arrangements would be in the American interest; others would not. Some would serve the interests of particular American groups but not the overall U.S. interest. Even the most tactful and perceptive efforts to communicate critical American concerns will undoubtedly irritate certain Canadians and be regarded as undue interference by one Canadian interest or another.

Until then, it behooves Americans to remedy the present deficiency in their relations with the Quebec francophone community. Continuing American ignorance and indifference could heighten the francophone sense of isolation and thereby contribute to forces that would alienate Quebec from the rest of North America and ultimately bring about the dismemberment of Canada.

NOTES TO CHAPTER 8

1. See, for example, Yvan Allaire and Roger E. Miller, *Canadian Business Response to the Legislation on Francization in the Workplace* (Montreal: C.D. Howe Research Institute, 1980), p. 8.
2. September 20, 1964. Quoted by Claude Morin, *Le Combat Québécois* (Montreal: Boreal Express, 1973), p. 68. See also by the same author, *Quebec versus Ottawa* (Toronto: University of Toronto Press, 1976).
3. *A New Canadian Federation.* Constitutional Committee of the Quebec Liberal Party, Montreal, 1980, p. 13.
4. "The chief protagonists (of the Canadian crisis), whether they are entirely conscious of it or not, are French-speaking Quebec and English-speaking Canada. And it seems to us to be no longer the traditional conflict between a majority and a minority. It is rather a conflict between two majorities: that which is a majority in all Canada, and that which is a majority in the entity of Quebec. That is to say, French-speaking Quebec acted for a long time as though at least it had accepted the idea of being merely a privileged 'ethnic minority.' Today, the kind of opinion we met so often in the province regards Quebec practically as an autonomous society, and expects her to be recognized as such. This attitude goes back to a fundamental expectation for French Canada, that is, to be an equal partner with English-speaking Canada . . ." *A Preliminary Report of the Royal Commission on Bilingualism and Biculturalism* (Ottawa: Queen's Printer, 1965), pp. 133 ff.
5. See the Report of the Task Force on Canadian Unity, Ottawa, Queen's Printer, 1979.
6. Sociologist Marcel Rioux, "Bill 101: A Positive Anglophone Point of View," *Canadian Review of Sociology and Anthropology*, 15 (no. 2, 1978):143, noted that the name "French Canadian" has been used less and less since the beginning of the 1960s by Québécois in designating

themselves, that it has been reserved in recent years to describe non-Quebec francophones. Bernard Blishen, "Perceptions of National Identity," ibid., p. 132, documents this impression with results in a national attitude survey.

7. The ratio of anglophones of British extraction in Quebec has been declining for over a century; only anglicization of immigrants who spoke neither French nor English has prevented the francophone proportion from growing faster (Richard J. Joy, *Languages in Conflict* (Toronto: McClelland and Stewart, 1972), pp. 41, 59, and 91–109, and Hubert Guindon, "Modernization of Quebec and the Legitimacy of the Canadian State," *Canadian Review of Sociology and Anthropology*, 15 (no. 2, 1978): 242.)

8. Despite Canadian political rhetoric contrasting Canada's multiethnic policies with the U.S. melting-pot ones, the rates of assimilation into anglophone culture and loss of native ethnic language in the second and third generations after immigration have not differed greatly in most of anglophone Canada from those in the United States. See Howard Palmer, "Mosaic versus Melting Pot: Immigration and Ethnicity in Canada and the United States," *International Journal*, 21 (no. 3, 1976): 488–528.

In the early 1970s nearly 50 percent of the children of one or more francophone parents in provinces other than Quebec, New Brunswick, and Ontario could no longer speak and understand French. Daniel LaTouche, "Quebec and the North American Subsystem: One Possible Scenario," *International Organization*, 28 (no. 4, 1974): 942. For confirming statistics on growing rates of assimilation outside Quebec and Acadian New Brunswick, see Charles Castonguay, "La Position des Minorités francophones," *Le Devoir*, October 25, 1980, and Castonguay, "Exogamie et Anglicisation chez les Minorités canadiennes français," *Canadian Review of Sociology and Anthropology* 16 (no. 1, 1979): 21–31. See also Sheila McLeod Arnopoulos and Dominique Clift, *The English Fact in Quebec* (Montreal: McGill Queen's University Press, 1980), p. 231, and Guindon, "Modernization of Quebec," pp. 233–239.

9. André de Leyssac, "Le Scandale du français universitaire hors Québec," *Le Devoir*, September 30, 1980, noted that the figure in 1980 alone would approximate C$250 million.

10. In 1980, 43 percent of the population of New Brunswick and 7 percent of that of Ontario was francophone (*Le Devoir*, October 21, 1980). Richard J. Joy, *Canada's Official Language Minorities*, Accent Quebec Series (Montreal: C.D. Howe Research Institute, 1978), p. 1, found that only in the heavily French-speaking areas of northern New Brunswick and along the Quebec–Ontario border do the two languages coexist outside Quebec. Moreover, 80 percent of Canada's bilingual citizens are of francophone rather than anglophone or immigrant backgrounds (James Laxer and Robert Laxer, *The Liberal Idea of Canada: Pierre E. Trudeau and the Question of Canada's Survival* (Toronto: James Lorimer, 1977), p. 182). And

60 percent of all these bilingual Canadians live in northern New Brunswick, eastern Ontario, and western Quebec (Joy, ibid., p. 5). Outside Quebec itself, only 45 percent of all Canadians of French descent use French regularly at home (Kenneth McRoberts, "Bill 22 and Language Policy in Canada," *Queens Quarterly* 83 (no. 3, 1976): 464–477). Even in New Brunswick near the Quebec border, the longevity of French is in serious question (Robert M. Gill, "Bilingualism in New Brunswick and the Future of Acadie," *American Review of Canadian Studies* 10 (no. 2): 61.

11. Castonguay, "La Position des Minorités francophones," and study by Rejean Lachapelle and Jacques Henripin, reported in *Le Devoir*, August 2, 1980.

12. Ibid. and Michel Amyot et al., "La Situation démographique au Québec," *Le Devoir*, May 16, 1980. In 1980 at least 97 percent of Haitians in Canada were in Quebec (report of Julien Harvey, S.J., to the Quebec Ministry of Immigration, reported in *Le Devoir*, September 8, 1980). Half of all Lebanese-born Canadians and over half of Arabs from the francophone Maghreb and of European francophones in the country were likewise there. In 1978 Haitians and French were respectively the first and second most numerous national groups among immigrants settling in Quebec. The next year, Vietnamese were the most, French the second most, and Haitians the third most numerous (*Québec Hebdo*, 2 (no. 16, April 28, 1980). Since the "quiet revolution," growing numbers of francophones from elsewhere in Canada have likewise migrated to Quebec, many of them strong nationalists and supporters of the PQ. Conversely, immigrants from anglophone countries of birth have declined every year since 1974, from 12,032 that year to 3,844 in 1978 (Jacques Couture, "Les Politiques Québécoises et le Projet de la Charte fédérale," *Le Devoir*, November 3, 1980). Francophone Quebeckers have understandably been more opposed to anglophone immigration to Canada than have their anglophone compatriots.

13. Lise Bissonnette, "La Loi 101 en Bonne Voie," *Le Devoir*, December 6, 1979, noted that by 1978, the year after enactment of Law 101, the proportion of children of immigrants whose native language was neither French nor English in Quebec French schools had jumped to 52 percent from only 25 percent two years previously. Such children constituted 74 percent of children in English nursery schools just before that bill was legislated, but only 48 percent a year later, while children of francophone parents in English nursery schools dropped from 2.4 percent to 0.6 percent in the same period. (*Québec Hebdo* 2 (no. 29, August 4, 1980).

14. See, for example, Arnopoulos and Clift, *The English Fact in Quebec*.

15. See, for example, the analysis by Michel Roy, *Le Devoir*, September 30, 1980, and by then PLQ deputy Solange Chaput–Rolland, a member of the task force, in *Le Devoir*, October 28, 1980.

16. Michael D. Ornstein and H. Michael Stevenson, "Cracks in the Mosaic: Elite and Public Opinion on the Future of Canada," unpublished paper,

Quality of Life Project, Institute for Behavioral Research, York University, Downsview, Ontario, 1979, pp. 26–28.

17. For comparative distribution of these attitudes by demographic groups, see Blishen, "Perceptions of National Identity," pp. 129–132; Harold D. Clarke et al., *Political Choice In Canada*, (Toronto: McGraw-Hill Ryerson, 1979); Alan Kornberg, Harold D. Clarke, and Lawrence LeDuc, "Some Correlates of Regime Support in Canada," *British Journal of Political Science*, 8 (no. 2, 1978):211; Ornstein, Stevenson, and Williams, "Public Opinion and the Canadian Political Crisis," pp. 173–181; Ornstein and Stevenson, "Cracks in the Mosaic," pp. 23 ff; and Maurice Pinard and Richard Hamilton, "The Parti Québècois Comes to Power: An Analysis of the 1976 Quebec Election," *Canadian Journal of Political Science*, 9 (no. 4, 1976), and "The Bases of Parti Québécois Support in Recent Quebec Elections," ibid., 9 (no. 1, 1976).

18. CBC survey reported in Joel Smith and David K. Jackson, "Restructuring the Canadian State: Prospects for Three Political Scenarios," unpublished paper, Duke University, 1980, Table 2.

19. CBC survey of March 1979. For similar findings of other surveys, see Jon H. Pammett et al., "Political Support and Voting Behavior in the Quebec Referendum," unpublished paper prepared for Duke University Conference on Political Support, November 21–22, 1980, p. 13; Michael D. Ornstein, H. Michael Stevenson, and A. Paul M. Williams, "Region, Class, and Political Culture in Quebec," *Canadian Journal of Political Science* 13 (no. 2, 1980):253; and Ornstein and Stevenson, "Cracks in the Mosaic," p. 17. In the latter reported survey of 1977, substantially more than half of Quebec francophones favored redistribution of powers in favor of provincial governments and only one-tenth favored increased powers in Ottawa. In the May 1980 survey reported by Pammett et al., 57 percent favored renewed federalism, and 52 percent a special status for Quebec. Diversely worded surveys since 1965 have documented gradually increasing majorities among francophones expressing opinions in favor of independence, greater autonomy, and/or a special status for Quebec. Maurice Pinard, "La Dualité des Loyautés et des Options constitutionelles des Québécois francophones," in "Le Nationalisme québécois à la Croisée des Chemins," *Choix*, 7 (1975): pp. 75–80.)

20. Survey sponsored by the Quebec Ministry of Intergovernmental Affairs.

21. Reported in *Le Devoir*, October 16, 1980.

22. CBC survey of March 1979.

23. *Le Devoir*, April 6, 1981.

24. Ronald D. Lambert and James E. Curtis, "Dissatisfaction and Non-Confidence in Canadian Social Institutions," *Canadian Review of Sociology and Anthropology*, 16 (no. 1, 1979):52, Table 1. In 1974 francophone Quebeckers contrasted with other regional populations were least apt to have written to their member of Parliament or to believe he or she would

read the letter from them or do anything about any problem they might raise (Kornberg, Clarke, and LeDuc, "Some Correlates of Regime Support in Canada," p. 203). However, the proportion of non-Ontario anglophones with little confidence in the federal Parliament representing their interests has probably increased significantly since 1974.

25. Harold D. Clarke et al., *Political Choice in Canada*, pp. 71–77.
26. Survey reported in *Le Devoir*, October 16, 1980.
27. Smith and Jackson, "Restructuring the Canadian State," footnote 18 and Table 7.
28. Ibid., p. 38, and Clarke et al., *Political Choice in Canada*, p. 254.
29. Pinard, "La Dualité des Loyautés et les Options constitutionelles des Québécois francophones," 84; Maurice Pinard and Richard Hamilton, "The Bases of Parti Québécois Support in Recent Quebec Elections," pp. 3–26, and "The Parti Québécois Comes to Power," p. 743; Michael D. Ornstein, H. Michael Stevenson, and A. Paul M. Williams, "Public Opinion and Canadian Political Crisis," *Canadian Review of Sociology and Anthropology* 15 (no. 2, 1978): 159; and Radio Canada Survey of March 1980.
30. SOREC/CBC survey of March 1977.
31. Radio Canada survey of March 1980, reported on p. 12 of Pammett et al., "Quebec Referendum," p. 12.
32. Ornstein, Stevenson, and Williams, "Public Opinion and the Canadian Political Crisis," pp. 162–67.
33. Ornstein and Stevenson, "Cracks in the Mosaic," pp. 20–26.
34. Ornstein, Stevenson, and Williams, "Public Opinion and the Canadian Political Crisis," pp. 162–63.
35. *Quebec Hebdo*, April 20, 1981.
36. In 1974, only 16 percent of francophones had negative opinions of the bilingual program, many of them because they felt the federal government should do more in that domain. Almost three-fifths of francophones supported the program (Clarke et al., *Political Choice in Canada*, p. 254). See also Ornstein, Stevenson, and Williams, "Public Opinion and the Canadian Political Crisis," p. 165.
37. *Le Devoir*, October 22, 1980, and Ornstein, Stevenson, and Williams, "Public Opinion and the Canadian Political Crisis," p. 168.
38. Smith and Jackson, "Restructuring the Canadian State," p. 32. In 1974 nonfrancophones in Quebec felt more favorably toward Canada and less favorably toward their province than the populations of the other provinces (Clarke et al., *Political Choice in Quebec*, p. 74).
39. Pammett et al., "Quebec Referendum," p. 18, and a CBC survey of March 1979. The latter found that 70 percent of nonfrancophone Quebeckers opposed increasing provincial powers by constitutional change and only 21 percent favored such. The corresponding figures in the other nine provinces were 64 percent versus 27 percent.

54. See Stein, "The Politics of Multi-Ethnicity in Quebec," p. 22; Arnopoulos and Clift, *The English Fact in Quebec*, pp. 191–202; and Lise Bissonnette, "Un Nationalisme en Perte de Culture," *Le Devoir*, September 30, 1980.

55. The proportions of the francophone population who are critical of "left-wingers" and of "right-wingers" approximate those of anglophone Canadians (Curtis and Lambert, "Educational Status and Reactions to Heterogeneity," pp. 194 and Table II).

56. John H. Sigler and Dennis Goresky, "Public Opinion on United States–Canadian Relations," *International Organization*, 28 (no. 4, Autumn 1974): 650–651, 656, and 658–667; J. Alex Murray and Lawrence LeDuc, "Public Opinion and Foreign-Policy Options for Canada," *Public Opinion Quarterly*, 40 (no. 4, 1976): 492; J. Alex Murray and Mary C. Gerace, "Canadian Attitudes toward the U.S. Presence," *Public Opinion Quarterly*, 36 (no. 3, 1972): 388–397; J. Alex Murray and Lawrence LeDuc, "A Class Sectional Analysis of Canadian Public Attitudes toward U.S. Equity Investment in Canada," Toronto: Ontario Economic Council, paper 2–75, June 1975; LeDuc and Murray, "Public Attitudes toward Foreign Policy Issues: Some Recent Trends," *International Perspectives*, May–June 1976, pp. 38–40; Terrence A. Keenleyside, Lawrence LeDuc, and J. Alex Murray, "Public Opinions and Canada–United States Economic Relations," *Behind the Headlines*, 35 (no. 4, 1976); David K. Jackson, "Anti-Americanism among French Québécois, Young and Old," unpublished paper, Duke University, presented at 42nd Annual Meeting of the Southern Sociological Society, April 4–7, 1979, pp. 27 ff; Carl J. Cuneo, "The Social Basis of Political Continentalism in Canada," *Canadian Review of Sociology and Anthropology*, 13 (no. 1, 1976): 63, and "Education, Language, and Multidimensional Continentalism," *Canadian Journal of Political Science*, 7 (no. 3, September 1974): Table I, as well as *Social Class, Language, and the National Question in Canada*, unpublished Ph.D. dissertation, University of Waterloo, 1973, pp. ii, 31, 81–83, 99, 139, 185, 221, 259, and 361–366; H.F. Angus, *Canada and Her Great Neighbor: Sociological Surveys of Opinions and Attitudes in Canada Concerning the United States* (Toronto: Ryerson, 1938); William P. Irvine, "Recruitment to Nationalism: New Politics or Normal Politics?" *Canadian Journal of Political Science*, 5 (no. 4, 1972): 503–520; Smith and Jackson, "Restructuring the Canadian State," Table I; Mildred Schwartz, *Public Opinion and Canadian Identity* (Los Angeles: University of California Press, 1967), p. 71; and LaTouche, "Quebec and the North American Subsystem," p. 939.

57. Jackson, "Anti-Americanism among French Québécois," p. 12; and Gérard Gaudet, "Forces Underlying the Evolution of Natural Resource Policies in Quebec," in Carl E. Beigie and Alfred O. Hero, Jr., *Natural Resources in U.S.-Canadian Relations*, vol. 1 (Boulder, Colo.: Westview Press, 1980) p. 148.

40. One statistical analysis concluded that the "no" vote among n‹ phones was virtually unanimous (Pierre Droully, "Les Nonfran‹ et le Referendum," *Le Devoir*, September 18, 1980).

41. Ornstein, Stevenson, and Williams, "Public Opinion and Canadian Crisis," pp. 162–63.

42. Pinard and Hamilton, "The Parti Québécois Comes to Power," p. 7‹

43. Even before the election of a PQ majority, in 1976, 33 percent of phones and 19 percent of other nonfrancophones who had gra‹ from high school five years before had left the province (study ci Arnopoulos and Clift, *The English Fact in Quebec*, p. 91). Undou‹ the figures in 1981 for those five years out of universities are much h‹ especially for anglophones.

44. Charles E. Curtis and Ronald D. Lambert, "Educational Status and F tions to Heterogeneity," *Canadian Review of Sociology and Anthro ogy*, 13 (no. 2, 1976): 194.

45. Ornstein, Stevenson, and Williams, "Region, Class and Political Cultuʀ pp. 258–260.

46. For particularly perceptive analysis of Quebec nonfrancophones, ‹ Arnopoulos and Clift, *The English Fact in Quebec*, and Michael B. Stei "The Politics of Multi-Ethnicity in Quebec: Majority–Minority Grou Consciousness in Transition," unpublished paper for Columbia Universit conference, "Multi-Ethnic Politics: The Canadian Experience," April 4 1980.

47. Only some 20,000–30,000 of approximately 310,000 Canadian Jews have spoken French on arrival. Most of those have been of North African background and have settled in Greater Montreal, where Jews total around 115,000. Most Jews are first or second generation Canadians. But a 1978 study of Montreal Jews found 75 percent spoke English with their spouses, ten times as many as spoke French (W. Gunther Plaut, "From Monkton to Squamish," *Moment*, 6 (no. 1, December 1980): 33–48).

48. Curtis and Lambert, "Educational Status and Reactions to Heterogeneity," p. 94. Werner Cohn, "English and French Canadian Public Opinion on Jews and Israel: Some Poll Data," *Canadian Ethnic Studies*, 10 (no. 2, 1979): 31–47, found francophones more negatively inclined toward Jews in four out of five questions between 1967 and 1975. However, francophone–anglophone differences, though consistent, were relatively small.

49. Curtis and Lambert, ibid., p. 197.

50. Ornstein, Stevenson, and Williams, "Public Opinion and Canadian Political Crisis," pp. 173–178 and 205.

51. Plaut, "From Monkton to Squamish," pp. 33–34, 44, and 45.

52. Ibid., p. 34.

53. E.g., ibid., pp. 33 ff.

58. Gaudet, ibid., p. 248; Curtis and Lambert, "Educational Status and Reactions to Heterogeneity," p. 194; Jackson, Tables I and II; Keenleyside, LeDuc, and Murray, "Public Opinions and Canada," Tables 2, 3, 5, and 6; and J. Alex Murray and Lawrence LeDuc, "Attitudes of Canadians toward Foreign Policy and Trade Issues," Windsor, Ontario Institute of Canadian–American Studies, University of Windsor, 1980, pp. 2, 9, and 11.

59. Jackson, "Anti-Americanism among French Québécois," p. 29.

60. Ibid., pp. 40–41, and Table III, and Jane Jenson et al., "1979 Panel Study," unpublished paper, University of Windsor, 1980. However, in the author's experience, Quebec intellectuals identified with the PQ, Quebec independence, social democratic ideology, and/or European French intellectual values do tend to be less favorably inclined toward the United States than their counterparts of federalist, PLQ, more generally conservative, and less pro–French orientations.

61. E.g., Allaire and Miller, *Canadian Business Response to the Legislation on Francization in the Workplace*, pp. 9–15.

62. Ibid., p. 22, and *Quebec Update* 3 (no. 30, August 4, 1980).

63. *Quebec Update* 3 (no. 36, September 15, 1980).

64. Allaire and Miller, *Canadian Business Response to the Legislation on Francization in the Workplace*, pp. 17–22.

65. Curtis and Lambert, "Educational Status and Reactions to Heterogeneity," p. 194 and Table II.

66. Ornstein, Stevenson, and Williams, "Public Opinion and Canadian Political Crisis," p. 260.

67. Ornstein and Stevenson, "Cracks in the Mosaic," pp. 23–31.

68. Gaudet, "Evolution of Natural Resource Policies in Quebec," p. 261; *Challenges for Quebec: A Statement on Economic Policy* (Quebec: Editeur Officiel de Québec, 1979), p. 84; and Judith Maxwell and Gerard Bélanger, *Impôts et Dépenses au Québec et en Ontario: Une Comparaison* (Montreal: C.D. Howe Research Institute, 1978), pp. 17–21 and 28–31. Corporate employers argue that higher personal income and estate taxes provide a serious deterrent to attracting able managers and technical personnel to Quebec. Such comparative negative effects are however quite limited on francophones due to their disinclination to leave their French-speaking culture.

69. R.B. Byers and David Leyton–Brown, "The Strategic and Economic Implications for the United States of a Sovereign Quebec," *Canadian Public Policy*, 6 (no. 2, 1980): 338.

70. See Byers and Leyton–Brown, ibid., pp. 328–329, for a chronology and analysis of the steps in this policy shift.

71. For this evolution, see Louis Beaudoin, "Origines et Développement du Rôle internationale du Gouvernement de Québec," in Paul Painchaud (ed.), *Le Canada et le Québec sur la Scène internationale* (Montréal: Centre

Québécois des Relations Internationales and Presse de l'Université de Québec, 1977), pp. 441–470.

72. Saul J. Frankel, *Study of Source Documents Dealing with Differences in Political Attitudes between French and English Canadians: Political Orientation and Ethnicity in a Bicultural Society* (Ottawa: Royal Commission on Bilingualism and Biculturalism, 1968), p. 78; CIPO 348, July 1971; and CIPO 379, August 1975.

73. CIPO 371, December 1974, and survey of Goldfarb Consultants of July 1979. The latter found that Quebec francophones ascribed higher priority than anglophone Canadians to aid the less developed countries, to Canadian support for human rights there, and to relations with Mexico and to some extent with Latin America in general.

74. Cohn, "English and French Canadian Public Opinion on Jews and Israel," pp. 38–39.

75. In 1975, 52 percent of francophones versus 45 percent of anglophones thought "communism" either a "very serious" or a "fairly serious threat" (CIPO 370).

76. CIPO 332, 1968.

77. Schwartz, *Public Opinion and Canadian Identity*, p. 71, and CIPO 362, October 1973.

78. CIPO 351, May 1972, and CIPO 406, November 1977; also CIPO 362, November 1973.

79. Kinley, p. 15. However, Premier Lévesque and his minister of intergovernmental affairs, Claude Morin, on several occasions while in office made favorable remarks about the Commonwealth and implied that an independent Quebec might remain associated with it.

80. *Québec Hebdo* 2 (no. 21, June 2, 1980).

81. Kinley, pp. 22–23, and Jackson, "Anti–Americanism among French Québécois," p. 32.

82. Jackson, ibid., p. 42.

83. Daniel La Touche, "Le Québec et l'Amérique du Nord," *Choix*, 7 (1975): 126, cites a 1973 survey wherein 65 percent ascribed first priority to Quebec's relations with the United States versus only 20 percent to those with France. La Touche became a key official aide to Premier Lévesque in 1978.

84. See Philippe Meyer, *Québec* (Paris: Seuil, 1980), pp. 12–19, for a perceptive and even-handed French analysis of these divergent traditions, stereotypes, and attitudes of these two peoples regarding one another and their impacts on relations between the two.

85. Paul Morisset, "Le Bilan des Echanges franco-québécois," *Le Devoir*, October 4, 1980.

86. During the initial half-decade after the B and B recommendations, francophones among professional and executive personnel in the federal civil service and in crown corporations rose only from 13 percent in 1966 to 14.4 percent in 1971. Moreover, disproportionately large numbers of

francophones in the federal bureaucracy have been from bilingual backgrounds outside Quebec (Guindon, "Modernization of Quebec," p. 232).
For more recent analysis, see the testimony of the federal Commissioner
on Official Languages before the Joint Parliamentary Committee on Official Languages, summarized in *Le Devoir*, November 3, 1980; André Pré-
fontaine, "La Réforme Progresse Lentement," *Le Devoir*, November 5,
1980; and Marcel Adam, "L'Anémie d'Ottawa en Matière linguistique,"
La Press, April 25, 1981, in *Le Devoir*, November 17, 1980.

87. E.g., statement of the Société des Acadiens du Nouveau–Brunswick in
Le Devoir, November 17, 1980.

88. Clarke, "Partisanship and the Parti Québécois," pp. 30–31 and 36.

89. Pammett et al., "Quebec Referendum," pp. 26–29.

90. Asked in 1970 with which government they are generally in accord when
those in Ottawa and Quebec are in conflict, 40 percent of Quebec francophones replied the Quebec one, only 15 percent the federal one. In 1969,
47 percent replied that the Quebec government is the more important to
them, 41 percent the federal government. In 1965, 36 percent felt the
Quebec government defended their interests better than did the federal
government, only 9 percent the reverse (cited in Pinard, "La Dualité des
Loyautés et des Options constitutionelles des Québécois francophones,"
p. 67).

91. Quoted in *Le Devoir*, July 7, 1980.

92. Dominique Clift, *Le Déclin du Nationalisme au Québec* (Montréal: Libre
Expression, 1981).

93. The Supreme Court of Canada ruled on a suit brought by certain of the
provinces challenging the authority of the federal government unilaterally
to proceed with the proposed constitutional measures. Ottawa was found
to be empowered to proceed after consultation with the provinces.

94. Clarke et al., *Political Choice in Canada*, pp. 77–80.

95. Ornstein and Stevenson, "Cracks in the Mosaic," p. 18, and Pammett
et al., "Quebec Referendum," p. 18.

96. Survey for Canada West Foundation, October 1980.

97. Survey cited in *Le Devoir*, November 25, 1980.

98. Smith and Jackson, "Restructuring the Canadian State," Table III.

99. Ornstein and Stevenson, "Cracks in the Mosaic," p. 18.

100. Newfoundlers, like francophone Quebeckers, are less identified with the
federal government than with their provincial government and are less satisfied with their treatment by Ottawa than any other provincial group,
including Quebeckers and Albertans (Ornstein, Stevenson, and Williams,
"Region, Class, and Political Cultures in Canada," pp. 250–253, and
Ornstein and Stevenson, "Cracks in the Mosaic," p. 18). Only in Newfoundland did a larger majority than in Quebec feel in 1974 more warmly
toward their province than toward Canada (Clarke et al., *Political Choice
in Canada*, p. 70).

101. CIPO poll of late November, 1980.
102. Smith and Jackson, "Restructuring the Canadian State," p. 64. Based on rather persuasive evidence, these authors argue that most of the current anglophone university-educated generation less than age thirty-five will by and large maintain their prodevolution views as they grow older and become more influential.
103. Clarke et al., *Political Choice in Canada*, p. 80; Smith and Jackson, "Restructuring the Canadian State," pp. 43, 48, 58–60, and Table III; Ornstein, Stevenson, and Williams, "Region, Class, and Political Cultures in Canada," p. 253; and CBC survey of March 1979.
104. For example, in 1977 only 19 percent of anglophones outside of Quebec approved of the requirement of Law 101 that French become the language of work in medium and larger enterprises in Quebec. Only one-third of anglophones favored redistribution of powers in favor of the provinces— about the same proportion who preferred expanded centralization (Ornstein and Stevenson, "Cracks in the Mosaic," p. 18, and Ornstein, Stevenson, and Williams, "Public Opinion and Canadian Political Crisis," p. 203). While in 1975 francophone Quebec majorities favored "major" concessions by the federal government to satisfy Quebec's demands, majorities of nonfrancophones outside Quebec favored either no or only "minor" concessions (Clarke et al., *Political Choice in Canada*, p. 165). However, constructive interest and support for concessions have been significantly higher among younger and better educated anglophones and particularly among elites not associated with the federal government (Michael D. Ornstein, H. Michael Stevenson, and A. Paul M. Williams, "The State of Mind: Public Perceptions of the Future Canada," in R. B. Byers and Robert W. Reford, *Canada Challenged: The Validity of Confederation* (Toronto: Canadian Institute of International Affairs, 1979), pp. 98–101).
105. See, for example, Harald von Riekhoff, John H. Sigler, and Brian W. Tomlin, *Canada–U.S. Relations* (Montreal: C. D. Howe Research Institute, and Washington, D.C.: National Planning Association, 1979), p. 50.
106. *Quebec Update*, 3 (no. 35, September 8, 1980).
107. However, many Quebecker independentists argued prior to the referendum that the PQ government made a mistake in not including a separate currency and monetary policy in its sovereignty–association proposal.

A NOTE ON FISHERIES

A survey of Canadian–U.S. relations which does not include some discussion of fisheries problems would strike many readers as inadequate. The subject is a major issue between the two governments. Nevertheless, it does not fit easily into any category treated in the preceding chapters. Hence this note.[1]

Ever since the United States obtained its independence from Britain there have been contentious questions about fishing off the northeast coast, involving first the British government and later the Canadian. Countless agreements have been reached. Some have been ratified and adopted; some have not. Some have expired; some remain. During the first six decades of U.S. independence the U.S. border with Canada in the Northeast was uncertain and in dispute. It was finally settled by the Webster Ashburton Treaty of 1842, which decided what was the St. Croix River and where was its main channel, settled offshore islands (except one) on Canada, and recognized boundary lines out to a 3-mile limit. For generations U.S. and Canadian fishermen plied their trade in each others' waters, and both made free use of the Georges Bank, which was regarded as open sea.

In recent decades the respective U.S. and Canadian authorities have felt impelled to respond to issues raised by the competing nature of their commercial fishing industries and by the recent shared concern over the conservation of resources and over protecting them from the voracious appetites of third-country fishermen, notably from Eastern Europe.

The current problems between Canada and the United States in regard to East Coast fisheries arise from the decisions of the two governments to extend their fishing zones to 200 miles, as against the very limited 12 miles previously claimed. Canada's claim to a 200–mile fisheries conservation zone was at first strongly resisted by the United States in principle; but later, faute de mieux, the United States found itself claiming the same thing. The Canadian claim had not been considered too much of a practical obstacle because Canada had not seen fit to interfere with "customary" U.S. fishing in the newly claimed 200–mile zone. But with the assertion of U.S. claims of a similar nature, and with world competition for Georges Bank fish rising ever higher, the need for some kind of agreed regime was only too obvious.

The negotiation of such an international agreement is made difficult by institutional and sociological factors. Canada regulates fishing for conservation reasons, either by federal fiat or provincial regulation or by an agreed system of self-regulation. There are quotas for different types of fish; there are seasons when fishermen must stay in harbor; and there are sizes of sealife that must not be taken out of the water. The New England fisherman is an entrepreneurial spirit who dislikes any form of government regulation. Nevertheless, international agreement on conservation of fisheries, or on division of waters or catch in areas that have always been the high seas, requires quotas, limits, and seasons, or other forms of regulation. It also requires full and accurate reporting of catches, or it is meaningless. The New England fisherman will eventually recognize such regulation as necessary for the purpose of limiting the catch of the Russians or others from another hemisphere. As for the Canadian fisherman, his view is that Canadians and the Americans should be free to compete in all the Northeastern waters.

Any agreement reached by the U.S. and Canadian governments is bound to be regarded with suspicion by the fisherman on both sides, and this was the case with the agreement negotiated with great effort in 1979. The Canadian negotiators had apparently done a better job than the Americans of carrying their constituents with them in the negotiating process. And when the process of treaty ratification got underway in the United States the fishing interests saw to it that it hit serious snags of a highly political nature, sometimes on issues unrelated to the region or to fish. Dismay is too light a word for the Canadian reaction at all levels, despite a long and rich experience with the American treaty process. According to highly articulate Canadian official spokesmen, the issue was one of the hottest and could not be resolved too soon.

The failure of the treaty to be ratified is bound to be related to the type of agreement that was reached. It was recognized that the boundary issue (Where is the boundary of the 200–mile fishery conservation zone off the continental shelf?) was inextricably tangled with the fishery issue (Who could catch how much of what in the waters comprehended?). The device selected by the negotiators for settling the boundary issue was a very simple one—to hand the problem to someone else, namely a chamber of the International Court of Justice (ICJ).

The Canadian view is that the line marking the boundary should be equidistant between the coastlines but can take account of special circumstances. The U.S. view is that the boundary should be drawn according to equitable principles that take into account the shape of the coastline and the build-up by tidal action of such coastal areas as Cape Cod. Thus there are three lines on the map of the Gulf of Maine. The U.S. line would give the United States the entire Georges Bank; one Canadian line would give Canada about one-third of it; and the latest Canadian line, with which the United States does not agree, would split Georges Bank half and half, roughly. The conclusion of this matter by an impartial tribunal will make a great deal of difference in the net result of the proposed fisheries arrangement, because the concept of the parallel fishery agreement is to have joint management of the resource in the area, with proceeds divided approximately according to the area controlled by the respective nation.

In addition to deciding that the ICJ should determine where the boundary lay, the treaty proceeded to divide fishing areas into blocks within which the catch of specific types of fish would be apportioned according to particular formulas. It also agreed to the creation of a joint Canadian–U.S. Fisheries Commission to establish the total take for conservation purposes, meanwhile binding fishermen of both countries to detailed reporting and compliance with regulations.

It is not surprising that American fishing interests, confronted as they are with higher costs for boats, fuel, gear, and labor, and with more depleted nearby resources, should object. And given the election-year politics of 1980, it was not surprising that the U.S. Senate stalled.

President Reagan took a look at the matter before he went to Ottawa in March 1981 and decided that the fisheries treaty had no chance of ratification. He also noted that there had been no criticism of the device of asking the ICJ to settle the boundary issue, so he proposed that the treaties be decoupled. The Senate approved the boundary treaty on April 29, 1981, and the United States awaits indication from Canada that it is ready to proceed with ratification. The president undertook to instruct the coast guard to forbear enforcing U.S. regulations against Canadian vessels in certain areas claimed by Canada, and he asked the New England Regional Fishery Management Council to prepare a plan for protection of scallop resources in the area in response to charges that the absence of a treaty would result in drastic reduction of scallops through over-fishing.

These measures were prudent and reasonable and give evidence of U.S. intent to resolve the basic problem through negotiation. Whether they are so seen in Canada depends on how well the U.S. situation is understood and on the interests of the beholder. Certainly Canadian fishermen, bound as they are by regulation and reporting requirements, will find their patience wearing a bit thin; but it should be clear to all that agreement on fisheries management, no matter how good the principles, will not be forthcoming so long as the boundary line is not fixed.

Meanwhile there have been a couple of important fishery and boundary problems on the West Coast, primarily related to albacore tuna and salmon. The albacore tuna is a highly migratory fish that now and then enters the 200-mile fisheries conservation zone claimed by Canada on the West Coast. The United States does not accept the assertion that coastal states have a right to control highly migratory species. The problem has been how to reconcile this difference in principle with the needs of the tuna fleets of both countries. This has been done in a treaty approved by the U.S. Senate on July 20, 1981, which is ready for ratification by the two countries whenever the Canadians are ready. The treaty is a pragmatic settlement that permits Canadian tuna fishermen to land their albacore catch in certain U.S. ports for sale commercially, where they will get better prices than at home, in exchange for the opportunity for American tuna fishermen to use certain Canadian ports, where they can buy fuel more cheaply than at home. Meanwhile both Americans and Canadians are free to catch tuna anywhere. Both fishery industries approved this transaction, which seems to be a triumph of sense over principle.

Salmon are different because of their unusual reproductive habits. On the West Coast there is concern on the part of Americans and Canadians that fishermen might intercept salmon enroute to spawning rivers or young salmon on their way back to sea. Both countries have it in mind to protect salmon fisheries and will continue to negotiate to this end although delayed by the need for endless technical data on the habits of the salmon population.

Off the East Coast, the problem is quite different. There the intercepting fishermen are primarily from Europe, catching salmon enroute from Canadian or American rivers to Greenland or vice versa. A similar problem arises off the Faroe Islands, and the only answer must be an international convention among the European Community countries, Iceland, Sweden, Norway, and the Faroes, together with Canada and the United States. Obviously Canada and the United States share certain objectives about the salmon caught off Greenland, although they apparently differ on the methods any multilateral control structure should use. An international convention is not a major bilateral problem but is of vital importance for the survival of East Coast salmon and for the salmon sport fishermen, a rather vocal international fraternity.

The policy implications of the foregoing are as follows:

1. The boundary issue affecting the waters off New England and Canada is now subject to an ICJ decision if Canada agrees. The quicker it comes within the court's purview the better.

2. Depending on the solution to the boundary issue, the fishery management problem of the Georges Bank and the Gulf of Maine should be carefully examined and some form of agreement reached through intensive negotiation. This issue will fester if not dealt with in a constructive and positive spirit.

3. When the U.S. negotiates with Canada with a view to concluding a treaty, the executive branch should be extremely careful to make sure of support by the Senate, so that Canadians are not confounded by rejection of something they thought was agreed.

4. By the same token, the United States should make sure that Canada is carrying with it in a negotiation the relevant provincial authorities, so that there is not a recurrence of what happened in the case of the Columbia River agreement.

5. Until an East Coast fisheries agreement is reached, the United States and Canada should keep each other informed fully of their respective regulations and statistics, with a view to maximizing basic conservation of fish resources.

NOTE

1. The best short account of the Canadian–U.S. fisheries problem is Erik B. Wang, "Canada–United States Fisheries and Maritime Boundary Negotiations: Diplomacy in Deep Water," published by the Canadian Institute of International Affairs, Toronto, April 1981. See also various releases by the U.S. Senate foreign relations committee and the U.S. Department of State.

INDEX

319